Praise for "The Death of Fred Astaire"

"Leslie Lawrence's essays are sympathetic and patiently observed; she ably demonstrates that hard choices call for careful and humane decisions."

— John Irving

"*The Death of Fred Astaire* assembles a realistic and venturesome portrait of the author—as writer, teacher, mother, grieving partner, perennial seeker—while capturing the complicated texture of the post-1960s decades of American life. Lawrence's reach is wide, her narrative skills highly honed, and her tone is resonant with a sense of truth being told."

— Sven Birkerts, author of *Changing the Subject: Art and Attention in the Internet Age*

"*The Death of Fred Astaire* is warm, wry, and rich in detail. A lovely read!"

— Kate Clinton, comedian

"In this stirring collection, Lawrence boldly plumbs her many lives—as lesbian mother, writer, widow, teacher, student, border-crosser. Each is rich beyond description. *The Death of Fred Astaire* is a marvelous book. Read it and rejoice through your tears!"

— Hilda Raz, coauthor of *What Becomes You*

"This lively and eclectic collection of personal essays will appeal to a wide range of readers, educating some about an era of American cultural history and for others providing material for an associational romp through their own memories. Additionally, *The Death of Fred Astaire* will provide useful material for courses in education, nonfiction writing, cultural studies, and women's studies."

— Pamela Annas, University of Massachusetts Boston

"*The Death of Fred Astaire* is a smart, thought-provoking collection. Leslie Lawrence is at once a wise, companionable guide, as well as an empathetic narrator who points out and identifies with our collective yearnings and desires, our foibles and idiosyncrasies— which are, after all, the central human qualities that link each of us to one another."

— Michael Steinberg, author of *Still Pitching: A Memoir*

The Death of Fred Astaire

The Death of Fred Astaire

And Other Essays from a Life outside the Lines

LESLIE LAWRENCE

excelsior editions

State University of New York Press
Albany, New York

Cover photo courtesy of Queer Tango Paris

Published by State University of New York Press, Albany

For information, contact State University of New York Press, Albany, NY
www.sunypress.edu

Production, Diane Ganeles
Marketing, Michael Campochiaro

Library of Congress Cataloging-in-Publication Data

Names: Lawrence, Leslie, 1950– author.
Title: The death of Fred Astaire : and other essays from a life outside the
    lines / Leslie Lawrence.
Description: Albany : Excelsior Editions/State University of New York Press,
    [2016] | Includes bibliographical references.
Identifiers: LCCN 2015030782 | ISBN 9781438461045 (pbk. : alk. paper) | ISBN
    9781438461052 (e-book)
Subjects: LCSH: Lawrence, Leslie, 1950– | Lawrence, Leslie, 1950—Family. |
    Lawrence, Leslie, 1950—Travel. | Women—United States—Biography. |
    Mothers—United States—Biography. | Lesbians—United States—Biography. |
    Families—United States.
Classification: LCC CT275.L271556 A3 2016 | DDC 306.76/63092—dc23
LC record available at http://lccn.loc.gov/2015030782

10 9 8 7 6 5 4 3 2

For my mother, Frieda Lawrence
and in memory of
my father, David Lawrence, 1922–2015
and
Sandra Kanter, 1944–2004

Contents

IV

Acknowledgments

I have so many people to thank.

My parents whose love and respect gave me the courage to be myself and whose generosity gave me the means to become a writer.

My son Samuel Kanter Lawrence: A better man than I could have hoped for, more joy than I could have imagined.

Sandra Kanter: She fell for the writer in me before she fell for me, and she let me pay less than my share. She fell for Sam the moment she saw him and was the best co-mother a woman could have.

Neal Harrington: Loyal and terrific Dad. I knew what I was doing when I asked him; he knew what he was doing when he said Yes. And Sarah Hamilton, honorary stepmom, appreciative reader, and friend.

Ronnie Leavitt, my always loving, supportive sister who welcomes anyone and everyone, my intrepid traveling buddy, too.

Robin Becker, who lived through just about all of this with me—and held my hand throughout. On hugging terms with *her* dry cleaner, she taught me to find meaning in every interaction. Friend and writing pal for life.

Barbara Greenberg, my most trusted reader and best teacher. Her allegiance to both beauty and truth has been my guide. When I fall short, the fault is my own.

Jennifer Rose, my phenomenal in-house copy editor and expert on all manner of book design and production. She welcomed every panicked call and never said no.

Merrill Kaitz, generous and sensitive editor and friend. His enthusiasm for my work and our shared reverence for literature renewed my faith when it was faltering.

Steve Craine, expert, lifesaving proofreader.

Miriam Goodman. Championing the artist in everyone, she turned the mowing into a nourishing community of co-creators.

Frankie and Harvey Tolman, for sharing the mowing with all of us.

Patricia Papernow, wise and loving healer.

For their computer savvy and patient, last-minute help with graphics: Holly Broussard and Mario Davila.

And to so many fellow writers and readers and dear friends along the way, including Kathleen Aguero, Brad Crenshaw, Roy and Serena Crystal, Kendall Dudley, Patricia Eakins, Jyl Felman, Jai Footsoar, Patricia Garcia-Rios, Barbara Goodstein, Deborah Gorlin, Jeanne Heuving, Richard Hoffman, Beth Horning, Geri Kahn, Judith Kahn, Joan Lane, Jeff Laurie, Susan Levene, Suzanne Jill Levine, Deb Navas, Andee Rubin, Dee Shapiro, Rachel Skvirsky, Shane Snowden, Pat Sollner, Leslie Ullman, Kathleen Vetter, and Judith Winters.

Gigi Kaye and all the hard-working people at the American Fondouk in Fez, Morocco.

The Fenway Community Health Center for providing support for lesbians whose partners have cancer, and to Liz Coolidge for facilitating our group with extraordinary grace.

The women in my Rosh Chodesh group and the members of Temple Shir Tikvah, who have demonstrated the central role community plays in Judaism.

The Boston-area dance community that brought me back to life.

Michele Karlsberg, for her practical wisdom delivered with spirit.

And finally, my thanks to all the marvelous people at SUNY Press who worked on my book—James Peltz, Diane Ganeles, Michael Campochiaro, Rafael Chaiken, Dana Foote, Sue Morreale, and Elise Brauckmann—it's been a pleasure.

Grateful acknowledgment to the editors of the publications where versions of these essays originally appeared.

"The Death of Fred Astaire," *The Colorado Review* (Winter 1993)
    Daily Fare (University of Georgia Press) 1993
    Against the Current (Prentiss Hall) 1998
"Becoming Jennie," under the title "My Grandmother, Myself," *Forward* (April 16, 1999)
"King for a Day," *The Oberlin Alumni Magazine* (Spring 1997)
"Fits and Starts," *The Massachusetts Review* (Spring 1997)
"Karl Will Bring a Picnic," *Solstice* (Spring 2013)
"Dogs and Children," *Witness* (1999)
    Life Studies, seventh edition (Bedford Books), under the title "Propelled by Love" (2001)
"Andee's 50th and the Way We Live Now," *Soundings East* (Spring 2015)
"Why I Never Miss a Yard Sale," *Redbook* (May 1996)
"The Third Hottest Pepper in Honduras," under the title "Hamlet in the Hood," *Solstice* (Fall/Winter 2011)
"On the Mowing," *Fourth Genre* (Spring 2003)
    Five Years of Fourth Genre (2006)
"Enough Tupperware," *Oberlin Alumni Magazine* (Winter 2000)

"My June Wedding," *Fusion* (2005)
"What Can You Do!," *Prairie Schooner* (Winter 2007)
"At the Donkey Hotel," *Solstice* (Summer/Fall 2014)

I

The Death of Fred Astaire

When I was a child I accepted without question that I would one day be a mother. In my twenties I told all my boyfriends that I would someday want children. At thirty I told Robin, my first woman lover, that even though I loved her, had never felt more in love, never been happier in my life, I knew we wouldn't last more than a few months because I wanted to get married and have children. Two years later when Robin and I broke up, I began searching in earnest for a man to start a family with. That's when I found Sandy—a sturdy, vital, grown-up woman with a full-throated laugh, a tenured job at a local university, computer know-how, inspiring political commitments, and great cheekbones. A woman who wasn't an artist but who loved good literature and theater, opera and running, and, quite possibly, me.

I gave myself over to the pleasures of new romance. Not until almost a year later, the summer I was thirty-three, did I realize that my desire for children had changed from being a rather abstract assumption about some future I could not seem to catch up with to a yearning I could taste. This panicked me. Sandy had bought a house in Cambridge that I had helped pick out, and we were planning to live together in the fall. This arrangement was not likely to lead to anyone's pregnancy.

I had heard of lesbians raising children together, children conceived when their mothers were with men. I had heard of lesbians adopting children and even of conceiving them through artificial insemination. I felt sure these options were for other people: committed lesbians, women who not only loved women but thought it better to love women, women who had great anger or bitterness about aspects of their own childhoods and thought raising children with another woman would result in better children, a better world. I was none of these women.

Though none of my relationships with men had lasted more than a couple of years, I considered them as happy and healthy as most I had seen. I had loved some of these men and was still attracted to men. I loved dancing with them—fast, slow, old style, new. I liked watching them play basketball, fiddle with car engines, dress wounds, argue in court. I had enjoyed wearing my boyfriends' shirts—they made me feel thin and sexy—and nothing turned me on more than the sight of a man holding an infant in the crook of his arm or throwing a baby into the air.

Certainly, I considered myself a feminist. I recognized ways in which I had compromised myself in my relationships with men. I had discovered that when I was with women I felt more fully myself and more deeply loved. Still, I had never been entirely comfortable with phrases like "overthrowing the patriarchy," probably because in many ways that patriarchy had treated me well. I remembered my childhood as happy, had only minor complaints about the way my parents raised me, and perhaps most significant of all, I was a daddy's girl—a fact apparently so obvious that even though I never had much of a voice, in a camp musical revue I was chosen to sing "My Heart Belongs to Daddy."

I was Daddy's little helper, trotting behind him with the rake, the caulking gun, the monkey wrench. He taught me to ride a two-wheeler, to keep my head throughout a geometry proof. His loves were my loves—rousing music, veal parmigiana, the first forsythia. His values were my values—naturalness, honesty, persistence, daring, and, especially, family. In my early twenties I began to discover all I admired in my mother: her graciousness, generosity, intuitive feminism, intelligence, love of art and literature—in short, her depth of feeling and understanding. Up until then it was my father I held on high and aimed to please. So the thought that my little girl (for, of course, I would have a little me) might not have a father at all, and certainly not in the same way I had mine—this was nothing I was ready to imagine.

As a child of the sixties, I did not want to replicate my parents' lives, but my idea of doing things differently went no further than marrying a man with long hair, maybe an earring, most likely a non-Jew with a meager income; of doing it not in a temple or country club but on some mountaintop, *sans* ice sculptures, *avec* wildflowers. It was preferring chamber music to symphonies, sending my children to Quaker camps, never consulting an interior decorator. It did not include, as the title of a book I eventually read on the subject put it, *Having a Baby Without a Man*.

Perhaps if my mother had once been a nightclub singer (in sequins!), or my sister had eloped, or my father taken bribes—if anyone in my immediate family had just the tiniest secret or blemish. Or if I was used to being left out or taunted. But we were Jews who lived among Jews, and my experience with feeling different went no further than having been briefly forced to wear shoes with protruding metal plates designed to correct my pigeon toes. Accustomed as I was to approval, when I was in my first lesbian relationship, I boldly told nearly everyone I knew. But I also had dreams about being corralled and branded, I lived in dread of so much as a raised eyebrow, I daily chose to look as straight—no, straighter!—than I always had. When I knew, really knew, I wanted a baby, I thought: this having-a-baby-without-a-man idea might be fine for lots of people but not for me.

This was 1984, just two years after the Sperm Bank of California became the first to provide services for lesbians, a year before Rock Hudson announced he had AIDS, five years before the appearance of *Heather Has Two Mommies*—the first children's book to depict a lesbian couple parenting. I knew of only one lesbian who'd had a child "without a man." Lois had grown up across the street from me. I hadn't seen her in years.

So why didn't I just tell Sandy I couldn't move in with her?

Love didn't come easily to me. When it had come with others—a few men, and then Robin—I eventually ran scared. Of course I was older now, and Sandy older still. She had stature in the world, something I associated with men. She had integrity. She also had a groundedness that calmed me, but a lightness of spirit too. She loved my writing and gave me plenty of space. We spent long hours side by side in her sunny attic doing our separate things. I was touched by her tender heart, by the hurting places inside her. I felt sure I could heal them. The qualities in me that drove my exes crazy just made her laugh affectionately. Who knows, I thought. Maybe, because I had climbed mountains, run a 10K, ventured into dark lesbian bars, I might someday be courageous enough for a life that, at present, felt beyond me. Worth mentioning, too: When I first met Sandy and casually asked if she wanted children, she didn't hesitate before saying, "Yes."

Me? I wanted a baby soon, but not quite yet, so when a friend pointed out, "Just because you move in with someone doesn't mean you can't move out!"—even though this seemed like just the sort of thinking that traded pain in the near future for agony later on, I found myself repeating the line like a mantra, even quoting it to friends:

Just because . . . doesn't mean . . .

No doubt the line was not far from my mind that late August morning while I was scouring my summer sublet before heading back to Cambridge. *My Fair Lady* was playing on the radio, and although I had long ago decided show music was too lowbrow for sophisticated me, I was enjoying singing along: "I Could Have Daaanced All Night," "Would-n't It Be Lov-er-ly." I was belting it out until somewhere in the middle of "The Rain in Spain," when I dropped the sponge and burst into tears. A minute or so later, dry-eyed again, I wondered: What was *that* all about?

The song was a happy one, not about anything that particularly hit home, but back to my scrubbing, it came to me: how we sang at the tops of our lungs, my Daddy and I—mimicking Rex's haughty Britishness, howling along with Julie's triumphant *Spaaains* and *plaaains*. My throat tightening again, I thought, not without some amusement: well, maybe I'm sad because it looks like I'm *not* going to marry my father, after all. Nor even a man like him. Nor any man at all.

A year or so later, after Sandy and I moved in together, a friend asked, "If she were a man would you marry her?"

I barely hesitated before saying, "Yes!"

Not that things were perfect. I was beginning to realize that Sandy's wounds went deeper than I thought—and my talents as healer were flimsier. Still, we were fierce advocates for each other. Together we'd created a beautiful home (with, come to think of it, much help from "our architect," the yuppie's interior decorator). More often than not, that home was filled with laughter and sweetness. One friend who'd spent a weekend with us commented on the balance, the grace she saw in our lives. I was touched; I felt it, too. And Corky, her dog whom I had come to love . . . Since I'd appeared on the scene, he was healthier, happier, better behaved, and—most important—wild about both of us.

And so, when I saw a notice about a discussion at the women's center on lesbian parenting, off I went—alone, for although Sandy was interested in raising children with me, she feared that coming out, or being found out, would jeopardize her job prospects. She'd moved up in the academic ladder and had her eye on being a college president someday. Furthermore, unlike me with my appetite for hashing things out in groups, she preferred to make her decisions in private.

I had expected the discussion to be geared to lesbians considering parenting, and I had assumed that, like many feminist events, it would be an upbeat, cheerleading sort of thing. What it turned out to be was a support group for women already *doing it*, women who clearly needed support. The children being discussed—well, one teenage daughter was so intent on proving her heterosexuality that, according to her mother, she had become a "slut." Another daughter's best friend's parents had prohibited their daughter from visiting. A son avoided the problem by never inviting his friends home. One woman's ex-husband was suing for custody. All the women looked exhausted. They all had money problems.

Still, I focused on how much I liked these women, how impressed I was by their strength, integrity, and resiliency. In all cases, their children, born while one of the women was *with* a man, had expectations of normality and a relatively recent relationship to the co-parent. And none of them appeared to have the class privilege I had. This was something I knew I was supposed to feel guilty about; still, I couldn't help thinking: Perhaps I, with my sense of entitlement, not to mention my actual entitlement, will be spared some of these women's difficulties.

That same winter I attended a local health clinic's introductory meeting on "artificial insemination," as it was called then, before they changed it to "alternative insemination" because "really, there's nothing artificial about it." I can't remember how I first heard about this meeting, but I was told to call the clinic and, without mentioning my purpose, ask for a certain person. Only then was I told the time and place. I was shocked by all the secrecy. It had never occurred to me that what I was contemplating was risky in any realm other than the social or emotional. I still don't know what law I was breaking or what the clinic feared—loss of funding, bad press, chastisement from the archdiocese?—but as I entered the specified building and located the basement stairs, I felt like a novice member of some underground cadre meeting to plan their next bombing. And I guess, in a way, I was.

It was a small gathering including a straight, single woman in her late thirties, three lesbian couples, and the two presenters, a nurse and a lawyer. The nurse spoke first:

The sperm was flown in from California. Someone met it at the airport with dry ice. It was crucial the client get to the clinic within a few hours. Of course all of this had to be carefully coordinated with one's cycle. Each insemination cost fifty dollars, usually one did two or three a cycle, and, on the average, pregnancy was achieved after about six months, but sometimes it took years. One's chances of a healthy pregnancy and baby were no better or worse with "A.I." The bank screened its donors carefully, but there were no guarantees—though their donors were not paid, which meant they were more likely to answer the questionnaire honestly. One received some basic information, including donor's height and weight, race and religion, hair and eye coloring, occupation, special talents. There were two possible arrangements—one in which the father would stay forever unknown, though you could get certain medical info, another in which the father could become known when the child reached eighteen.

Then both nurse and lawyer fielded our questions:

Yes, it was possible your child could be the half-sibling of someone else's child and never know it, and, if the two fell in (heterosexual) love and reproduced, their offspring would be at greater risk for abnormalities. Yes, although they were very cautious in their labeling, names were never used and a mix-up wasn't impossible—you could end up with a baby who was not the one you ordered. Yes, it was possible in the case of donors who never intended to identify themselves that the child could have a medical condition that necessitated genetic information beyond the basics on record, and that info would now be difficult if not impossible to obtain. And no, she didn't know if there were Xeroxes of the records or what would happen if there was a fire in the building that housed them.

These were answers to questions I would never have thought to ask. What I thought to ask but didn't was, what do I tell my child when she asks who her father is? What do I say when she is older and wants to know who I thought I was that I could deprive her of a father? And will we—the child and I—spend the rest of our lives (or a mere eighteen years) walking down the street, into the supermarket, onto the airplane, searching the eyes of every man for some telltale sign that they belonged to her father?

Such questions told me that neither the eighteen-year wait nor the life of eternal ignorance were the right routes for me. And artificial insemination, the actual process of racing to the clinic and climbing upon a cold metal table—well, there was nothing inherently horrible about it, unless a person once had rather different images of conception. Which is all to say that although I dutifully took notes (for I could no longer assume what was out of the question now would remain that way), when I got home I began the list in the back of my little black journal. It included former lovers, men I had dated once or twice, old friends, husbands of friends, friends of friends, someone I once shared an office with, my handsome car mechanic . . . I remember trying to maintain a brainstorming mentality, but I see now I must have censored from the start. Absent, for example, is the name of my one gay male friend (the HIV test wasn't out yet) and a straight man I came close to marrying, not because I felt this would be too sticky but because of his sister's colitis, his brother's asthma, his father's blood pressure. I remember thinking that if I had married him, none of this would have prevented me from wanting his child. I also remember realizing that if Sandy and I could procreate and I was applying the same strict standards to her family history, she would not have passed the test. Still, I told myself it was entirely appropriate I should apply different standards to a donor than a husband or mate, and when the word "eugenics" grazed my mind, I swallowed the bad taste it left.

Shortly after I entered the first round of names, I received a formal-looking envelope from someone on the list, an old college friend who had, for one night, been my lover. Though I had been sure this man wasn't for me (too intense, too wounded, too many drugs), when I saw the wedding invitation, I couldn't not, at least for a moment, think that *I* could have, *should* have been the one to marry him. More lingering was the realization that his marriage would make it less likely—no, just about impossible—that he would want to father a child with me. It seemed to mock the whole plan, exposing its full ridiculousness, its inevitable failure. I declined the invitation, never even sent a present. The longer I looked at my list, the clearer it became that really, there were hardly any genuine possibilities. Certainly, not the husbands of friends, especially not the one whose wife had just had a hysterectomy—and to think I had once viewed that as an auspicious sign! Not the ones I barely knew, or the one who had horrible teeth, or the one who would insist on the kid going to his alma mater. Not the one who might interpret a missing button or dirty face as a sign of bad mothering. Or the one who, once he had his "own" children, would forget our kid's birthday. Or the one who was probably still in love with me. Or the one who worked in a lab with blood. Or the ones who might not be absolutely, unequivocally okay on the lesbian issue.

That didn't leave many options, but in the spring of '85, after endless difficult discussions with Sandy, who was at least as scared as I about embarking on such an uncharted route, I wrote Neal (one of the old friends—straight, single, childless, first on the list) and asked if he'd consider fathering my child. He promptly replied with an antique postcard, a photo of an elegantly dressed man and woman in a rowboat, its title something like "Lifelong Friendship." Neal's own words were brief. *Very flattered, very nervous, very interested.*

How perfect! I thought. The photo, its title, his message. For a few minutes at least, this no longer seemed like such a crazy idea.

That summer, I was further spurred on when I visited Lois and her family—that is, her lesbian partner, her partner's teenaged son from when she was married, and the now four-year-old daughter whom Lois had conceived and was raising with her partner. I'm not sure what I expected, but I remember feeling relieved that the child looked normal, even pretty, and was adored by her older "brother," who struck me as an unusually thoughtful and articulate sixteen-year-old. What I most remember was how at bedtime the daughter climbed into Lois's partner's lap and clung happily to her, in no way displaying surprise, confusion, or distress over the womanly breasts and smooth cheeks.

Neal and I started talking on the phone a lot. He told me he wanted to be a father, and it was looking less and less likely he'd become one in conventional circumstances. For a long time he'd had no serious girlfriends. Women claimed they preferred un-macho men, he explained, but when it came right down to it, that wasn't true. Now, finally, he was in a serious relationship, but the woman already had two nearly grown children. I told him I wanted the child ("our" child?) to know its father and see him regularly; nevertheless, Sandy would be the other primary parent, and if anything should happen to me, she would become the legal guardian. I told him to think about it. In a subsequent call, he said he'd been thinking—and talking to friends. Most were supportive. The one who wasn't hadn't swayed him. He was still interested.

Though normally a sucker for rarefied cafes that served arugula and chèvre, when, about a year later, my parents were visiting from New

York, I suggested a large, noisy deli I hoped would make them feel at home (despite the small portions and inferior rye bread). They'd already endured three blows: I was involved with a woman, after her a second one, then that one and I moved in together. Even so, telling them my latest plan wasn't going to be easy. It would slam the door on any lingering hope that this was all just a phase. More important, it would slam that same door on me. Preparing for this moment in therapy, I often cried. I certainly didn't want to cry now—nor did I want to sound overly casual about the potential problems. In my previous comings out to my parents I struggled with similar conflicts, and, while proud to have shielded them from the depth of my pain and uncertainty, I also longed for them to know the real me.

In any case, they took the news calmly. The Bloody Marys I suggested probably helped. Also, my mother wasn't entirely surprised—she knew I'd visited Lois, and that had started her wondering. Quickly getting into the spirit of the thing, they surprised me by arguing in favor of an unknown donor. I figured they, of all people, would share my desire for a live and involved father, that link to heterosexuality who could provide at least a whiff of normality. But they were more concerned about the possibility of "complications." And they were not alone. Sandy had mixed feelings on the issue. My sister, her husband, and several friends with firsthand knowledge of disastrous situations involving a known father felt as my parents did. Nevertheless, I proceeded with my plans, albeit rather slowly, in part because I had my own anxieties but also because I had gotten a new teaching position and didn't think it wise to have a baby—with or without a man—my first year on the job.

About a year after our lunch at the deli and shortly after a weekend family party celebrating my father's sixty-fifth, I phoned my parents to discuss the latest baby news. I mention the celebration because we'd all gotten along well over the weekend, and my parents had been particularly warm to Sandy who, for the first time, felt fully accepted into our family. Also, the poem I'd written for my father had been a big success. After my recitation, as my father walked toward me with open arms, oblivious to everyone else in the room including his beloved brother Karl who had traveled so far to be there, I could see that even after I had betrayed him (for that's how I thought of it—he'd given me his all so that I might become the perfect wife for a man a lot like himself), even now when it was becoming less and less likely that I'd ever come around—I was still his best girl, the apple of his eye.

I approached the phone call with optimism—I would view my parents as allies. After some chitchat, I asked for their opinions on some weighty legal and medical matters. Things seemed to be going well until my mother got off the phone to take another call and my father said, "Look, we've been dealing with this and will continue to, but I want you to know what a great disappointment it is."

"Disappointment": a relatively mild word, said in a mild tone, yet, I couldn't bear it. I grunted a good-bye and hung up.

A few minutes later the phone rang—my mother wanting to make sure I was all right. As we continued to talk, she recalled that Mother's Day when I was six or seven and we went out for lunch at Tavern on the Green. Did I remember? Yes, I remembered—unless I was just remembering because she'd mentioned this not too long ago, shortly after I'd sent her a book that included a section on lesbian daughters coming out to their mothers, a section she said she found very moving. I remembered the lushness of Central Park, the horse-drawn carriages, the tables with linen cloths and pastel flowers, the ladies in their spring dresses, men in their dark suits, the roving violinists. And yes, I remembered, more or less, what my mother most remembered: how I sat in my party dress, elbows on knees, absolutely transfixed by the couples dancing. As my mother now spoke of this again, she choked up and I wondered exactly what was getting to her so. Surely not my unladylike position hinting at future lesbianism—I'd always been on the girlish side. More likely it was that she could not find the thread connecting that child to the woman I'd become—or even if she could, it pained her that I was never going to be a part of those handsome couples that had so entranced me.

Later that night I watched *Eyes on the Prize* on TV. There were the proud parents of Andrew Goodman, the white college student murdered by the Klan for his activism. There was Medgar Evers's wife just after her husband was killed by a white supremacist. And Fannie Lou Hamer, a poor uneducated woman speaking out so passionately. All that hope, dignity, and courage—it moved me so, tonight especially because it was my disappointed father who had taught me about Rosa Parks and *Brown v. the Board of Ed.*, and had told me, again and again, how important it is to stand up for what you believe.

The next morning, crossing the river in the car my father handed down to me, I heard Yehudi Menuhin playing Brahms's Violin Concerto, one of my father's favorites. Turning onto Storrow Drive, I shifted into fourth, and hearing the rising curlicue of strings my eyes stung at the memory of that music filling the house of my childhood—the order, the sunlight, the faith in the future.

Neal and I met in a Mexican restaurant. After a round of margaritas, I asked him: If you do marry and have other children, will you still visit "my," "our" child? If the child isn't normal, will you love it anyway? If, for any reason, I decide I want an abortion, will you protest?

He gave all the correct answers. He even offered financial help, but I told him I'd heard that might lead the courts to grant him more rights than I wanted to grant. I emphasized that Sandy would be the other primary parent.

He asked me: "What are you worried about—too much involvement or not enough?"

My answer: "Both."

Over the next few months, Neal and I, and Sandy and I, had countless separate conversations. At one point, the three of us had dinner. I would have preferred more three-way meetings, but Sandy, though craving a child, was apprehensive about this arrangement and preferred to do her negotiating with me.

The contract Neal and I eventually signed gave him visitation rights and the right to be apprised of the child's development—nothing else. It specified that if I should die the child would go to Sandy. It also stated that "certain clauses stated herein may not be enforceable in a court of law," nevertheless, "the parties choose to enter into this Agreement and clarify their intent . . ."

That summer Fred Astaire died. I heard the news on the radio and was surprised by the depth of my grief. Sure, I enjoyed the guy's skill and grace and sprightliness—but he was of my parents' generation, certainly no heartthrob of mine. (Too skinny! Too pale!) So why this lumpy throat, these tears on their way.

"The end of an era!" The announcer declared. "Of style! Of dancing cheek to cheek!"

Ah, so that was it! Not the soloist hoofing with his cane, but Fred *together* with Ginger, gliding through their ballroom numbers—he in his top hat and tails, she in that swirly chiffon; he knowing his steps, she knowing hers. I was really going to do this thing: *Have a baby without a man*, and, apparently, I wasn't done mourning yet.

Farewell Fred, I cried—not really, but that was the feeling. *Good-bye Steve, Jim, John, the Other Steve, Alben, Gary, Seth* . . . Surely the end of an era warranted a good cry, and I allowed myself a few hearty sobs. *Good-bye to all the world smiling at what a fine figure we cut.*

And hello . . . ? Hello to what? Making it up as we go along?

In October of '87, I went to the Gay Rights March on Washington with Robin. When Robin and I were lovers, I would not have been up for such an event. Now that I was with Sandy, she wasn't game. I knew that if I *did* have a child, it would be easier to pass as straight. At the same time it would become even more important that I—and Sandy, too—be out and proud of who we were. Walking through a city overtaken by gay people, doing my habitual accounting of ways I was and was not like other gay people, I couldn't help noticing what seemed like a particularly high proportion of people of both genders in red glasses. *I* wore red glasses and I loved my red glasses, had always felt they were "me." So maybe that's what clinched it—all those red glasses. I was glad to be there, I identified, I belonged. I felt that way even at the mass gay "wedding," a lengthy, hodgepodge ceremony full of Christian and pantheistic rhetoric, liberation politics, flowers, and kitsch, where all the weirdest had gathered—the fattest, skinniest, hairiest, smoothest, queens, bulldykes, down and outest—even there I felt at home, felt as if this was the right, the logical place for me to be, given everything I was—an outspoken New York Jew, a graduate of progressive Oberlin, my card-carrying ACLU father's daughter, my mother's daughter, too. I wished Sandy were there with me so we could marry, but since she wasn't, I married Robin—for old time's sake and ongoing friendship. We didn't have a ring but we kissed; we threw rice.

A journal entry from late August '88: "Last night I checked my mucous—stretchy. Neal called to say we're on for Saturday. Last session with shrink helped me decide on A.I. as opposed to intercourse. It's more important for Sandy to be there and feel part of this from the beginning. I picture us making love beforehand, and then me crying, for a change. But I can also imagine feeling happy, close, excited. And Labor Day weekend—how auspicious!"

What actually happened: It poured on our way to Vermont, but just as we drove up to Neal's funky farmhouse, the sun peeked out. On the oak kitchen table sat a vase of pink and violet wild flowers. Neal appeared with a bottle of champagne and three crystal glasses. We toasted to I don't remember what. Soon after, Neal disappeared into his room and Sandy and I sat out back with Corky. In ten minutes, maybe fifteen (it was beginning to seem like Neal might be running into difficulties), he walked out the back door and stuck up his thumb. We cheered. Sandy and I (and Corky) headed into his cool, damp bedroom with its brass bed, white comforter, tree-graced window. Neal had left his offering in a glass on the night table. I had my syringes. Never dexterous, I fumbled through the procedure. And then, we waited the requisite twenty minutes, urging the miracle to occur.

It didn't.

Not that time. Nor the next couple. But one Thursday afternoon in November (Veterans Day!) I drove up by myself feeling something in the air. Neal wasn't home yet when I arrived, and I'd had such a heady trip I took out my notebook and began writing:

I will call you A. And tell you how it was—the ride up to Vermont for your conception. Late fall, still filled with ambivalence, I imagined turning around—but midway my mood changed. The mountains? The music on the radio? The way men in passing cars looked at me with approval and I couldn't help feeling pleased? I imagined I was going to see my lover to make a baby, you. Then remembering it wasn't like that, I imagined how, years from now, I would describe the night you were conceived. I never asked my parents about my conception, but if you *want to know whether you were born of love, you were. That's what I'm trying to say. Tonight I loved my life—the darkening sky, the journey, the freedom. I stopped for gas. Self-service was crowded so I splurged. I stopped to buy wine for later, coffee for now. It started to drizzle. I felt a fleeting pain near my right hip—a little egg dropping from my ovary? I touched my breast—not swollen yet. I threw my quarters into the basket and one fell. I wanted to tell you all these little things, stories with no point except that I was here, caressing it all—the ordinary, the strange, the way it was and wasn't what I'd always wanted. Your mother—she almost missed her exit, got teary-eyed with Dvorak. And then the news: "One quarter of the N.Y. prisoners have AIDS. Texas will be the site for the $4.4 billion atom-smasher. Bush, elected two days ago, is working to smooth out his transition to the White House." No, the world isn't going the way I'd like. Even my life—not the way I imagined. Harder. But I headed north off the highway. It got dark and began to rain. At Route 107, I made a sharp right, and Anabel's Colonial Inn was all lit up, and somehow that was enough—sublime. And you . . .*

I realize now I've been thinking of you as a boy.

Two dogs are curled up beside me now in front of the woodstove. I just got off the phone with Sandy. She felt close by. You are on your way.

This is not, of course, the end of the story. That boy—we named him Sam (a regular, everyday name to offset all the rest)—is growing fast, and there's much that could be said about how it has been and how our family puts us both on the margins of conventional society and, at the same time, smack in the middle of it. In a recent fantasy I imagined a Mother's Day a few years from now. We go to Tavern on the Green and Sam, in his Sunday best, sits, enchanted, watching his two Moms dance.

But who am I kidding? I'm not that brave. And even if it became perfectly acceptable for two women to slow-dance at Tavern on the Green—it's not just the dance that holds such sway. It's the tension between the dress and the suit, the smooth and the rough, the swinger and the one swung.

Or so I thought. Now I'm not sure.

A few weeks ago I went to a performance of ballroom dancers. To my surprise, I found all that cheek-to-cheek stuff rather dull and bloodless. At first I decided this was probably because the men were all gay. Then I read in the program that most of the couples were married—to each other! So I thought, well, maybe *that's* why it's so desexualized. Then the tangos began: first women tangoing with women, then men tangoing with men, eventually, the usual. But when the curtain fell, even the straight woman I was with agreed that the same-sex couples were the most fun to watch. The odd thing was, nothing seemed odd about them. There was no cross-dressing; the women all wore black sheaths and high heels, the men tight, black suits; no partner seemed to lead the other; and yet—how they sizzled!

So who knows?

Here in our cabin in the country, we have time and air and mountains. Sometimes we put on Sam's red plastic Sony cassette player and dance in the kitchen—Sandy, Sam, and I, all together or in some combination or Sam alone—and then I catch Sandy's eye and we smile and I think: I'm not missing anything, this is the whole thing.

◆

Becoming Jennie

One good bra. The first item on a list of things my grandmother apparently wanted to pack. I found it—the list, not the bra—in her top dresser drawer a week after she died. I was twenty-nine; she had been eighty-six. "Brassiere" was the word I expected from my grandmother, a woman whose speech and dress were formal and painstaking, whose breasts were a force to be reckoned with. But "good" surprised me even more—for weren't all my grandmother's bras "good"? All her silverware was gleaming, her sheets bleached and starched; not a letter was missing from her well-used Scrabble game. That she, like me, might have had her share of shabby, yellowed, stretched-out bras . . . Well, suddenly I felt a new kinship, a new sadness, too. Who *was* this woman? Now I'd never know.

Many women have told me that they felt more of a connection to their grandmothers than their mothers, but this was never true for me. To me, Grandma Jennie—my mother's mother and the only grandparent I knew at all—was hidden beneath long dark dresses and a few uncontestable rules dictating behavior becoming a lady, these taught to me by my mother who learned them from Jennie. *Always cross your legs. Wear white gloves to synagogue. If your grandmother serves you three mushy vegetables for lunch, eat them all without a fuss.* Not that Jennie was ever harsh or unkind, not that she didn't indulge me with sweets and embroidered hankies and write me real letters when I went away to summer camp. It was just that even though she was in her fifties when I was born, even though she, like me, was born in New York, to me she was always old-fashioned, old-world, plain old *old*—no one I aspired to be. Second-wave feminism was percolating when I was a teen. By the time I graduated from college my consciousness was raised a notch or two. Still, like the I-can-do-anything coeds I teach, I became cavalier about my right to wear pants, dance (barefoot and braless!) in a city park, speak my mind, write my life, love women as well as men, dismiss my grandmother. Yet since that good-bra-find, I have discovered other artifacts and heard tidbits suggesting that my grandmother was not the woman I thought her to be—or certainly not only that.

About a decade after she died, in a box filled with my old report cards and compositions, I found a hefty booklet, typed and securely stapled. *Mrs. Jennie Diamond* it said on the inside cover, the script distinguished only by its regularity. And printed on the title page: *Notes on the Art of Conversation and Effective Public Speaking . . . as Taught in Adult Education Courses.* I thumbed through the Dos: *Be alert, Be a good listener, Be interested in others, Be interesting.* Nothing to argue with there.

As for the list of acceptable topics of conversation—*Current Events, Commerce, Finance, Business, Sports, Music, Art, Ideas*—they were fine as far as they went. Maybe it was the Don'ts that so set me against the author, Dr. Jesse (male spelling) Grumette:

Don't talk about your political views unless you are specifically asked about them.

Don't discuss art, literature, music, or any subject unless you know enough about the subject to speak with authority.

Don't rave about your children, except to a doting grandparent or intimate friend who has children of her own.

No doubt Grumette was only trying to spare people the embarrassment of ill-considered opinions and tedious blathering—but he was effectively silencing much of the population. Brisket, bloodstains, temper tantrums—not to mention good old gossip beneath which lay all the great themes—love, longing, fury, revenge, despair—these were absent from his list of permissible subjects. Yet what else were mothers and housewives authorities on? I resented his view of conversation as a means to social acceptance, rather than a way of soliciting, conveying, or clarifying an incipient thought, a tender feeling; not as a way of making a genuine connection. And I don't mean the strategic variety, "networking," but the kind that leads to nothing more than fellowship. I thought of my child's, my students', my own clumsy efforts at self-expression—of how deeply buried the gold would have remained if we'd not received a sympathetic nod signaling permission to stammer and grope. Might the booklet explain why telephoning my grandmother was one of my earliest lessons in doing what I did not want to do? The "conversations" were always a bore, perhaps because Jennie had mastered her version of *Don't ask, don't tell.* No wonder that my predominant image of my grandmother had long been that of a small mouth moving up and down like a ventriloquist's dummy, the rest of her face without expression.

I tossed the booklet back into the box. I understood that *I* wouldn't have been privy to my grandmother's most nuanced thoughts or intimate feelings, but in my imagining, even when lunching with a friend at Schrafft's (date-nut bread and cream cheese—my mom and I also loved this), Mrs. Jennie Diamond was made bland by the decrees of Dr. Grumette.

I retrieved the booklet.

That signature—it was not entirely without distinction. The loopy capital J sported a tail extending to the right, a flourish that underlined the n-n of Jennie; and beneath the i-a of Diamond lay another small but emphatic line. In light of Grumette's dicta pushing self-effacement, this *Here-I-am!* declaration went straight to my heart.

Over the years I've pumped my mother for more family history. "There's not much to say," my mom claims when I ask about her own life. (Maybe some Grumettisms seeped in?) About *her* mother, she's more forthcoming.

An excellent homemaker, Jennie was—a real *balabusta*. But also, especially after my grandfather died, an avid traveler and culture bug, always going to museums and concerts, always taking courses. She was president of Hadassah. Once my mom got to stay home from school to listen to a speech she gave on the radio.

Ah! So *that*, I thought, is why she took Grumette's course—less for the conversation part than the public speaking! She hadn't been so confined after all—she'd even made her small mark on the world. Now instead of seeing a wooden-jawed puppet on someone's knee, I could picture her behind a bulky microphone in a campy, old-fashioned radio studio.

"What did she talk about?" I asked.

"Who knows!" my mother said. "It was a lifetime ago. But I remember how proud we were."

Later I learned that my mother had had her own finds—a little notebook in which Jennie recorded all the books she read. Also, other lists—these of unfamiliar words she'd found in those books. My mother's most revelatory find: a form, half-completed, requesting Jennie's high school transcript, a prerequisite for applying to college.

"Nothing ever came of it," my mother said with a sigh. "I think my father didn't approve. He was old world, protective—came over all alone at fourteen. Maybe he was just trying to keep her safe." She shrugged. "Maybe he was afraid it would create a chasm between them—he never finished high school, you know."

I didn't know. I had never thought to wonder. "But I don't want you to think badly of him," my mother added. "He was a wonderful man. Kind, considerate. Every day until the day he died he treated her like a new bride."

My mom graduated from college and a master's program, too. She was an instinctive feminist, and also a well-read one. But a daddy's girl like me, she said that bride line without irony—and I didn't have the heart to call her on it.

"Oh my," my mother said, studying a photo of herself, "I look just like my mother!" We were midway through an annual family reunion in Maine. Pre–digital camera days, I'd just returned from town with photos I'd taken earlier in the week. We were sitting in one of those double wooden porch swings overlooking the lake. I had to agree there was quite a resemblance—those creases extending down from the corners of her mouth, and, beneath her double chin, an arched hollow the shape of a palace door. With people increasingly telling me how much I looked like *my* mother, I knew it was just a matter of time before I became Jennie—became, as Francine du Plessix Gray has deemed it, a woman in "The Third Age," whose "means of attention-getting" depended not on appearance but on "presence, authority, and voice."

"Are you sure you don't remember what she said on the radio?"

"For all I know it could have just been a fundraising thing."

"Still," I said.

She nodded. We swung. The chains made a melancholy whine, and the setting sun made the lake glitter.

"I'll never forget that night," my mom began, "maybe a year before she died. She couldn't go out on her own anymore, and once on the phone she told me she was alone so much she was afraid she'd forget how to talk. Still, we had to twist her arm to let us come pick her up so she could spend the weekends with us. She was so worried about being a bother. And then most of the time, she'd keep to herself so as not to interfere. But one summer night after dinner, we sat at the kitchen table and she just started talking." My mom took a swallow the way she does when she's feeling more than she wants to. "She talked and talked and poured out her heart."

"What did she say?" I asked. Who cared, really, about the Hadassah speech. Here was the gold I wanted.

But my mom said she couldn't remember, "unless, maybe, *that's* when she said she was so lonely?" With a sigh and a shrug my mother signaled she was finished. Our swinging had flagged and now we resumed it.

For the first time "poured" struck me as onomatopoetic—the lingering vowels suggesting just how much came out, how good it must have felt; but also how bad—all those years of holding so much back. That's what I think made my mother sad. And I had to wonder how long she would wait before she poured out her heart to me. (*There's not much to say!*)

As for liberated, free-spirited me, who has always liked exposing the naked emperor, liked speaking to groups in classrooms and synagogues, some fullness in my chest made me wonder whether I'm really so different. Whether any of us are—the way, even with intimates, we hold back, so worried we are of seeming a whiner, self-centered, pathetic, a bother.

(*I didn't* like *being treated like a new bride.*)

(*I wanted to go to college. To have educated opinions, smart new friends.*)

Whatever it was, it's some solace to imagine that once in her life at least, in magnificent defiance of Dr. Grumette, Jennie Diamond poured out her unbecoming heart.

———————◆———————

King for a Day

I was teaching at a small women's college in New England—a nice place but with too many bake sales. Faculty dressed like bankers, communicated via polite memos. A few brave students had green hair or no hair or tongues studded with jewels, but, by and large, daring, eccentricity, or even the usual collegiate mischievousness were absent. So imagine my surprise when Beverly stopped me in the hall to tell me Faculty Development was sponsoring a Cross-Dressing Workshop!

Immediately, I volunteered.

Not that cross-dressing had been a longstanding interest, but I had recently gone to a well-publicized art exhibit on the subject. In fact, I had seen a video there about just such a woman-to-man workshop, and while initially I assumed this wasn't for me, I became intrigued when the women claimed the experience gave them more confidence and clout in the workplace. I could use some more of those, I thought. My non–tenure track job was scheduled to end soon and I had been feeling beaten down, even wimpy.

"Don't you want to think it over?" my colleague asked.

"Nope. Put me down as a definite."

Within a few weeks my voice mail started getting more interesting. One day it was Laura telling me to start thinking about the man I planned to become; a few days later, Betsy, reminding me about shoes and underwear and a penis, too. Then, Betsy again: Forget the penis, she and Laura would take care of that—as well as the ace bandages for breast binding. She went on about the construction of the penises and, not yet in the know about the school's fancy phone system, I marveled at the patience and presence of mind she must have had to send such a message *twelve* times.

The day of the workshop we gathered in the "Special Functions Room." I'd always found that name to be a mouthful, but now I found it oddly appropriate. We drew the shades. Then, nervous and giggly, we disrobed, bound our breasts, discussed the proper way to position our disappointing penises (cotton batting wrapped in gauze!), donned the male duds we had each brought for ourselves, looked in the mirror, and saw—ourselves, women dressed as men.

That was before Bobby, the makeup man, had his way with us. One by one, we submitted to his gels, pencils, powders, and whiskers and left the chair transformed. Christine became Christopher, an Oxford Don with slicked-back hair, pert mustache, wire-rim glasses, and an effete, imperious manner. Though we'd not yet received any instructions, Christine instinctively knew that as a man she should abandon that telltale female trait: the smile—*the aren't I cute/nice/comforting, the confide in me, like me, love me, but don't goose me* smile. Deena, who'd bought her suit and shoes at the Salvation Army, became Carlos, a Mafioso in construction. I, in my own button-fly jeans, sixties Frye boots, and clunky leather belt, as well as my father's shirt and my neighbor's tie and khaki jacket . . . became . . . Well, I had thought I would want to be a "new man," sensitive, expressive, searching, modest; but the moment I glared at my unsmiling, mustached mug with its five-o'clock shadow, I knew I had to be . . . Mighty Man: crude, virile, self-assured, smug, and successful in all the ways *I* wasn't. Jeff Sykes was the name that came to my lips. Immediately he came into focus. Handsome, of course; bisexual; a rising sculptor with a tenured position at a nearby college more prestigious than my own. I started shaking hands with the others who'd been made over. These included a nerdy science teacher, a strong silent cowboy, a swishy international art trader, a bandanna-clad forest ranger—each to her/his fantasy.

Finally we were ready for formal training:

When walking, lumber; lean slightly forward and exaggerate the weight shift. When dancing, move only from the waist down and stick to the step you learned in ninth grade.

When picking up a drink, do so decisively, with your whole hand.

When entering a room, don't check things out from the doorway, but charge in like you own the space.

Most difficult, when talking, don't say much, don't end a sentence in a questioning tone, look slightly to the side of the person you're talking to. If things get tense, just imagine your own eyes are set way back in the rear of your skull so as to create a feeling of distance—and safety.

After practicing each skill separately, we were set loose to improvise at a "party."

"Hey, Sykes, how's it going?"

"Not bad. Not bad at all. Sold everything at the opening. Five galleries called last week."

Such shameless boasting was fun, as was strutting around, slapping the other guys on the back, making bold remarks I would normally censor or at least regret. How much more energy I had now that I wasn't worrying so much about everyone's feelings. And how relaxing it was flopping down into a chair rather than remaining perched, ready for flight. I liked reaching into the bowl of beer nuts, for once not retreating—too fattening!—but digging in deep with my whole fist, again and again. I loved wondering who Jeff—and Leslie—were attracted to, and what that revealed about him/her/them. The permutations were endless and confirmed my belief that sexual attraction is as difficult to grasp as a spunky trout. Friends say I read as comfortably female—I've certainly always *felt* female—so I was surprised by how easily I could transform myself, by how quickly the new me felt nearly as genuine as the old: a good lesson in the power of appearance; a good opportunity to question whether our gendered behavior is as "natural" as most of us assume.

Leaving the college grounds, I was grateful it was already dark and, ironically, Halloween. The plan was to regroup, still in drag, at a Thai restaurant. Though I like to think of myself as someone uninterested in public opinion, I was seriously not happy about the prospect of being perceived as a gender outlaw. As for passing as an ordinary man—I wasn't keen on that either. Even so, in the relative privacy of my car I remained Jeff, shifting gears more forcefully, changing lanes with more bravado. And out on the street again, the grand promenade of students that is Commonwealth Avenue, as I debated about how much to withdraw from the ATM, I rejected my habitual $60 in favor of the more manly $80. Being a man had a lot to recommend itself.

But as I strode toward the restaurant, anticipating dinner with a bunch of men, my pleasure in the role ended. I didn't want to talk stocks or conquests or even galleries and dealers; I wanted to talk . . . girl talk. To lean in close, stare intently, confess all, nod sympathetically, gossip brilliantly. In short, I wanted myself—and Laura, Betsy, Christine, and Deena.

Entering the restaurant, we resisted smiling—which wasn't easy. (It's one thing to be cold and imperious with one's friends, quite another to be that way with hard-working Thai waitpersons.) But once we matter-of-factly gave our orders, we—except for Bobby the makeup man who, rumor had it, was actually a woman, or had been until recently—slid easily back into our female selves, smiling big, passing around tastes, "processing" our day.

To my surprise, several had not enjoyed the experience as much as I. They didn't want to be like men, or they wanted it too much, or they feared they were already too manly, or . . . or . . . Some were unable to explain the resistance they felt. We all steered clear of the attraction issue.

Halfway through my pad thai, I asked Betsy, a psychologist, if she thought my son Sam, four then, would be upset if I arrived home looking like this.

"Remove the mustache," she advised. So I did, peeling it off right then and there, then wondering what to do with the wad of little hairs. (My pocket? Under my plate?) "Just toss 'em under the table," Lisa suggested. "That's what a man would do." We all laughed. I tossed, then went to the men's room. Fortunately it was a single—no one to spy my feet pointing the wrong way, to share my surprise when the penis lodged in my underwear fell to the ground. I washed off the mustache glue and the five-o'clock shadow, and, looking into the mirror, saw myself again—smiling. Did I say I don't give much weight to public opinion? What a lie! Confronting that smile in the mirror, I realized that I never, or almost never, exit a public restroom without first checking out that smile—making sure that the face I present as I walk out the door is the right face, my prettiest, the one that will make others like me. This, I felt sure, was not something Jeff Sykes did. Maybe he looked in the mirror, but the face he fashioned was surely less eager to please, more self-possessed.

Driving home, I reverted to my old, languid shifting. When I arrived, Sam just shrugged off my outfit and was disappointed that the mustache was gone. He wanted one himself—not pencil but real hairs—and I regretted not putting the wad in my pocket.

The next day, I felt a bit jet-lagged—not so much tired as shaky and disoriented. But as with my reentry after other exotic sojourns, I was surprised by how quickly I readjusted to my old culture. By lunchtime, barely a tic from Jeff Sykes remained. I was walking, talking, smiling, and thinking like the old me—only now I had the unsettling knowledge that without much effort, it could be otherwise.

As for the other participants, no big changes as far as I know, but I did notice that one day a normally mousy participant wore a bright red blouse, and another wore jeans to a faculty meeting. Christine, whose reassuring smile is back, insists her professional life would be far easier if she were Chris. As for Jane—she seemed so much more at home as a man that I thought she might just *become* Kevin, but she returned as Jane, wary as ever.

All this was months ago. I still enjoy passing around the pictures; everyone is interested, some envious. The man who cuts my hair (and spends part of each week as a woman) asked the most right-on question. "Was it fun?"

Lately, I've noticed my attire sends mixed messages. I wear pearls with jeans, clunky boots with granny skirts. I've taken to buying more expensive footwear—shoes do really make the woman. I don't long to be a man. But I'm not so quick to assume that a quality I lack but admire in others, men or women, is beyond my reach.

When I went for my annual conference with the dean, I tried to smile less. It didn't hurt; it didn't help. My contract is still scheduled to end. I can't claim to have gained clout, but I do like to think that ever since that day, I have felt a little less depressed, even a little—well—*cockier.* But if that's true, it probably has less to do with having been a man for a day than with my shored-up faith that, as Sam's annoying T-shirt says, *I can be anything!* Tinker, tailor, soldier, nurse, midwife, astronaut. Well—probably not any of those; still, it's a good feeling to have when you're a writer looking for an academic job in Boston.

———◆———

Fits and Starts

Notes on (Yet) Another Writer's Beginnings

SPLIT ROCK, POCONO MTS., LAKE HARMONY, PA.

The fifties: winter in the Poconos. We are eating dinner in a large, knotty pine dining hall, my family and another family, the place noisy with clattering, laughter, and conversation—ours perhaps about the wind suddenly shifting, whipping our ice boat, puck-speed, across the frozen lake. What luck not to have crashed into another boat! What a miracle the boom, swinging around so hard and fast, didn't knock off someone's . . . Or maybe we are exulting over our hike up Split Rock, when a crash of dishes suddenly silences all. At the head of a distant table. a woman emits a high-pitched, fluttery sound. A crowd surrounds her, blocking our view; men in white coats march in and carry the woman out.

For a moment, not a sound. Then my father whispers, "An epileptic fit," as much a question as an answer. Others nod or shrug, look left and right. Someone lifts a fork, someone else reaches for the butter; soon, the full symphony and we continue our vacation.

The early sixties: my mother, father, sister, and I are at home eating dinner. "She wants to go to the earlier show," my father says to my sister and me. Or, "She thinks we need a new dining room table." It could have been anything on that order; I don't remember the subject, only the explosion of sound as my mother slams her fist on the table, shrieking so loud that my own throat feels scraped and raw: "*She?*" Her fist comes down again. "*Who*"—the Lazy Susan wobbles, the dishes rattle, her eyes tear, her head quivers—"*Who is* She?"

I stare at the wallpaper's onion pattern. It seems to pulsate, a visual echo. Finally my father ventures, "What are you getting so hysterical about?" My mother doesn't answer. None of us dares look at each other, but we seem to have reached consensus: *A complete fit over nothing.*

The nineties: I'm sitting in Al's Lunch in Cambridge, Massachusetts, with four women who meet there weekly to do timed, free-writing exercises usually inspired by a line from a book. "No fury like women's fury," someone suggests today. Within seconds we are all scribbling—*furiously*, and although my first thought is of Fury, the magnificent, untamable horse on the TV of my childhood, by the second line, I'm on to two women fighting in a parking lot, and how it wasn't until my first lesbian relationship that I could fight like that, "daring to do the totally unlovable," uttering "a sound I hadn't known I could find," kicking the tire on her car, wrenching my leg, bruising my foot, hurling, of all things, a tea bag at a subsequent woman lover. Then suddenly there's my mother's fist slamming the table, and in the same sentence: the woman who had the fit at Split Rock Lodge, "foaming at the mouth like the dogs my father doctored . . ."

Reading my entry aloud, as we do after the ten minutes are up, I'm surprised to find those images linked. It must have been then that I started remembering more.

My parents and I were driving from Philadelphia back to Queens. It was the late seventies. We had been visiting my sister, her husband, and their new baby. While we were there, my father told me how disappointed he was that my boyfriend had decided not to go to medical school. I, myself, was not pleased by this decision, but I didn't like hearing about my father's displeasure. After a while of private seething, I told my father that I wished he'd keep his disappointment to himself. That was the end of that until something on the ride home set me off and I found myself crying in the back seat about my sister having the perfect husband (a doctor!), the perfect baby, the perfect house and job, and I wasn't going to ever have anything because obviously anything less than perfect wasn't good enough!

Having gotten this out, I sobbed some more, until my father, in a tone more bewildered than cruel, said, "I didn't know you were such an infant."

Crying harder, I had to wonder if he was right.

"But David!" my mother exclaimed. "These are important issues. She's entitled to have strong feelings about them."

With no words to thank my mother for hers, I cringed—not at the memory of her fist on the table or her deafening scream, but at how I had betrayed her—and myself—by allying myself with my reasonable, even-tempered father.

And half a dozen years before the incident in the car: A new friend complained to our brilliant professor that he only accepted a male style of discourse.

Is there any other? I thought. I'd been in a consciousness-raising group; I'd stayed up half the night with this same friend talking about men and sex and the amazing Theodore Roethke—yet somehow when I thought of "women's style of discourse," all I could imagine was screaming and crying and I couldn't believe she'd be advocating that. For *that*, I had as much respect as the eminent professor—and my father—did.

A woman standing on a wooden floor gives birth to a baby whose head is completely severed from the body. The head rolls around on this hard, shiny floor as if it were a bowling ball and then, seemingly by chance, the two parts meet and join like beads of mercury.

I dreamed and recorded this a few years after my friend complained to our professor. Though the dream ends well, what stayed with me was not that miraculous wedding of parts but the horrifying rolling of the severed head. It launched my career as a client in therapy. After just two sessions, my Jungian therapist explained it all: "You are trying to detach yourself from your mother, to form your own image of womanhood."

So did she foam at the mouth? Not my furious mother at the Lazy Susan but the woman who had the fit at Split Rock Lodge? An outdated book I got from the library says that can happen in seizures, but that woman was half a dining room away. Surely, if I recalled a little dribble, I was just filling in the picture I'd conjured.

Like the dogs my father doctored.

Maybe the one who ravaged my father's hand? (A Doberman, as I recall—probably not actually rabid except in my imagination. In high school I had a teacher who protested each time someone said "mad" when they meant "angry." Until then, the two had always meant the same thing to me.) I remember watching TV in the basement, something special—*Peter Pan*, I want to say, but perhaps that's only because I'm connecting my father's imperiled hand to Captain Hook's hook. My father's hand was wrapped with layers and layers of white adhesive. The long TV program afforded the opportunity for a good soak. I remember the thick sound and my father's wincing as he tore off the layers, each taking some of his hair with it. I remember his last brave tug exposing the bloodied, shredded hand. My horror at seeing what madness wrought. My awe at how calm and contained my father was.

And did she really die—the woman at Split Rock Lodge? I remember some whispering to that effect—which would explain the incident's staying power. But death seems unlikely, perhaps something I imagined because she never reappeared.

Finally, what of those men in white coats? I thought of them as doctors akin to my father—saviors? disposers of corpses?—but there were four of them at least, and what would that lodge be doing with all those doctors? They must have been waiters.

I remember the woman as having short, dark hair, as *I* did in those days, but as grown women generally did not. I remember her sitting at the head of her long table. In pants. I think of her as unmarried. And now, just for a moment, I wonder if she was a lesbian! Not impossible, but probably that occurs to me because with all the fear and shame surrounding epilepsy in those days, I'm piling on the ways she was marginal, someone who didn't "fit."

Epilepsy, I've recently learned, is from the Greek for "taking hold." It's been known as the "demon disease," as well as the "sacred disease." Among the rumored sufferers are Julius Caesar and Napoleon, Saint Paul and Joan of Arc. Also Van Gogh, Flaubert, and Dostoyevsky. One symptom of temporal lobe epilepsy is hypergraphia, or excessive writing, especially of poetry and journals. Yesterday in a sauna, skimming *The Practice of Poetry*, I startled at the words "convulsive beauty"—a phrase from André Breton who, in his surrealist manifesto, championed a kind of unbeautiful beauty experienced in the body. His buddies, the surrealist painters, liked depicting hysterical women.

Was it fear of being called hysterical (or "infantile," sick, grotesque) that kept my emotions in check with men? Was it that same fear that kept me from braving a writing course until the second semester of my senior year in college, after I'd already been accepted to a graduate program in teaching? Once in the middle of a fight, my boyfriend said, "You're cute when you're mad." I didn't much like that either.

In her essay "Split at the Root," Adrienne Rich explores the notions about Jews that she inherited from her Jewish father. She writes: "We—my sister, mother, and I—were constantly urged to speak quietly in public, to dress without ostentation, to repress all vividness or spontaneity. . . . I suppose my mother, pure gentile though she was, could be seen as acting 'common' or 'Jewish' if she laughed too loudly or spoke aggressively." When Rich went off to Radcliffe, she was warned not to allow herself to be confused with the "raw, 'pushy' Jews of New York, or the 'loud hysterical' refugees from Eastern Europe."

Once during a conversation in which I was trying to communicate my dissatisfaction over some aspect of our relationship, my lover, a man from an old Boston family, called me a Jewish Princess. What he meant was not that I wore the clothes and jewelry, but that I had high (too high?) expectations about the way I wanted to be treated. A Jew, recipient of my father's used BMW, I couldn't find the words to defend myself, but for the first time I saw how that label was not just a Christian's weapon against Jews but was, along with "infantile" and "hysterical," a man's weapon against women.

In Munch's *The Scream*, wavy, concentric lines emanate from the open mouth of a figure standing at the distant end of a long, vanishing street. A genderless child, a friend insists, but to my self-centered eyes: a girl. When we were twelve, my friend Barbara and I admired this picture. We could hear the scream, feel the pulsating air. At the same time, we weren't certain a sound was actually uttered, for there was the sense that no one in the world of the picture could hear it; certainly no one responded. Also, we understood this wasn't a moment in the girl's life; it *was* her life—and would be our life, too, if we didn't do something about it. Write? Paint? Dance? None of this was said, but we were both dabblers then, and the fact that we "understood" Munch's *Scream*, and even knew that his name didn't rhyme with lunch, added to our credentials as potential artists.

In another Munch picture called *Puberty*, a naked, sunken-chested girl sits on the side of the bed. I once read this was a child Munch knew, a relative maybe who was sick and later died, but to me, she was always just a girl like me who was only now learning that to be a girl meant to be viewed, examined, doctored by a man who, no matter how kind and grandfatherly, would see her as the woman she was becoming and leave her awash in shame.

Barbara and I liked this picture, too. Meanwhile, in her basement we'd sing our favorite songs: "I Feel Pretty" and "I Enjoy Being a Girl."

And we did. We were pretty, popular, in the in-crowd. And terrified of being anything other. Which made being an artist a risky venture.

The heterosexual relationship I had at twenty-nine was the most passionate I had had to date—more secrets revealed, more tears and raging fights, more and better lovemaking. When it ended, I felt shaken but also more optimistic about men than I had since college. Perhaps the trend would have continued if my next lover had been a man, but she wasn't—and with her, Robin, there was even more closeness, more tears and raging fights, more and better lovemaking—and it seemed that all this had more than a little to do with her gender.

The adult woman's regressive return to her mother? Freud said something like this about lesbianism. And I can't entirely dismiss this view—can only wonder why they aren't just as guilty, those straight men who find themselves feeling safer, more trusting, more expressive with the women they love? Perhaps this return isn't such a bad idea, as long as both partners get to play child—which I suspect is less likely in heterosexual relationships where so often the woman's experience has made her wary of men's responses to her passionate outbursts.

Watching my three-year-old son's fits of temper and transparent manipulations, I'm reminded of how much of adult behavior is an elaborately disguised, cleaned-up version of fears, rages, and longings not unlike his. Of course aging doesn't guarantee maturity, so perhaps that "regressive return" can be viewed more neutrally as a simple going back to a place we've never really left, a return that, like many returns, breeds insight and healing.

Dreams from when I had my first lesbian relationship point to that:

I've been making love to R and I think I better wash up before I kiss my mother. In the bathroom mirror I see huge blackheads in clusters on my face. (I call them blackheads but they look more like stitches with crisscross threads.) They're horrifying at first but quickly I realize they've been there a long time, waiting under the surface, and now that they've become more visible, they're easier to remove. Sure enough, as I scrub, slowly but firmly, these old blemishes? wounds? fall away.

Or: There's a huge body of water. A young woman jumps in. There is air (sky) way down on the other side of the water so instead of coming up to breathe, you have to go clear through to the other side.

In waking life, in addition to flinging tea bags and kicking tires, once I struck her. Not hard. Also, I wept profusely, often for reasons I had trouble explaining, reasons that might not have held up in male court. We fought in restaurants, on street corners—turning heads with our shameless volume, our venom, our eye-stinging, vibrating ire. Once I flung myself against a wall, then collapsed on the floor and cried in her arms—sensing this was what I was after all along.

In another dream, which speaks to the nurturing I was now freely giving and getting:

We're seated at a table for a meal in a restaurant. . . . I don't remember feeling naked, but suddenly I'm squeezing my right nipple into my soup bowl and out comes chicken soup! None of this is surprising to me. Apparently, it happens all the time. Still, I find it amusing, and delightfully convenient.

When my first woman left me for another woman, I cried for weeks—in every room in my house, on the streets, in the supermarket, throughout a dance class, in the middle of a class I was teaching. I called friends at five in the morning, I slept at their houses, sometimes in their beds because I felt—yes, like a motherless child—bereft, amputated, frightened. Late one night, after days of crying, I found myself adrift in a silence more terrifying than all my grotesque, anguished sounds, and I feared I might be going mad. I fantasized calling the emergency room (it seemed that once I entered the world of lesbian love, I was often hearing about emotional crises that necessitated such calls), but then I envisioned the men in white coats with their hypodermic needles. I saw myself flailing and screaming, in that moment wanting my pain even more than my lover, wanting the proof that I could love like that—madly, the proof that I had at last left the world of my father. I knew what they were thinking—the righteous, well-meaning men in white coats (the very ones I was supposed to marry): "This is what happens to people with unnatural passions!" And to put the hysterical woman out of her misery they pricked her with the needle and carried her out.

Years before I had dreamed of being injected—again to sedate me—with a thick white fluid which, upon waking, I knew to be sperm.

At five I had my tonsils out. They wheeled me away on the gurney, cupped a foul-smelling screen over my face, made me count backward. I thought I would never wake. When I did, I was in a large room with many children. My throat on fire, I cried, "Mommy, I want my mommy," while an older boy a few beds away kept calling me a baby and telling me that if I didn't shut up he would give me an injection. I understood this to mean an injection to put me to sleep. To the daughter of a veterinarian, this means just one thing.

Among my friends, my ambivalence about living as a lesbian is legendary—and by now, boring. Along with the joys of lesbianism, I've suffered from LBD (lesbian bed death), a consequence perhaps of too much maternalism, too much coziness, a frightening merging of identities. And while lesbianism has deepened my sense of my own femaleness, it has also left me missing another kind of womanly feeling, the kind I used to have in the presence of some men. "But *I* want to be the cute one," I once protested in (lesbian) couples therapy. "Can't you both be cute?" the therapist asked. My instinctive reaction was "No." One night late, reading an Updike story, "The Burglar Alarm," I was moved to quote this passage in my journal: "At night when we come in late, the boy of the house asleep or away (I in my tuxedo and you in your great-grandmother's matched pearls, your wide-shouldered party dress with the low-slung belt, your silver sandals . . .)" Next to this I wrote with an earnestness that now embarrasses me: "I long to be half of that kind of twosome where each can be exciting and vivid in their difference from each other . . ."

And yet at around this same time, when a friend casually asked me if I felt more myself with women, I paused only briefly before uttering a confident *yes*.

Childbirth is one of the few occasions when a woman is allowed to be unseemly. Allowed to be "out of control," I was tempted to say, but that seems like the wrong term for behavior so magnificently functional. Still, some women have told me that's how they felt, "out of control," as if they were "possessed" (seized) by another force, as if they were "splitting apart." They said it was frightening but at the same time thrilling to see their body acting so powerfully without any directions from them.

They were talking specifically about "transition," the stage just before the baby's head emerges. Having ultimately delivered by C-section, I missed that part, but I did experience twenty-eight hours of induced labor and four hours of pushing, during which all unearthly sounds, and grotesque positions, and varieties of excretions were encouraged by the women around me. While I was totally absorbed in my task, my pain, my exhaustion, I retained a shred of surprise at the irony that suddenly now everything was allowed, every behavior deemed fitting.

I find it "fitting" that this "fit" word should contain some seemingly opposing meanings. *Fit* as in "fitting, suitable, or apt," derives from Scandinavian words meaning "to bind into skeins, to knit." And there's also an archaic meaning of *fit*: "part of a poem" or "strain of music." As for *fit*, as in "seizure" (taken hold, possessed), "attack of illness," or "sudden outburst"—*that might* have something to do with the way wool in a skein twists and contorts, or it might hearken back to Middle English in which *fit* meant "struggle." So I'm wondering: could *fit*, as in "suitable," be the successful weaving of strands that in *fit*, as in "seizure," are struggling against each other or against whatever outside force or structure is trying to possess or contain them?

Is it sometimes fitting to have a fit? Is there something inside us that, along with wanting to be ourselves, resists being only and forever beautifully woven together? Something that tires of being harmonious, whole, one; that propels us to splinter, snap, crack, break, be seized, possessed, beside ourselves?

The rock that gave the lodge its name was split by a glacier. Or so implies the guidebook, which also tells me the lodge is still there, a popular honeymoon spot. As I remember it, that rock is more like a large boulder, a mini-mountain, a few stories high. Somewhere in my parents' basement is a tin box filled with black and white photos. Among them are a few of our family scaling that rock.

I can picture the one of my sister and me, our fur-lined hoods surrounding our chubby cheeks and wide grins. I see her on one side of the crack, maybe a foot wide, and me on the other, our hands reaching across, joining, clasping. I recall how excited we all were to be there. And now I wonder if there's not something in all of us that loves a crack, in this case, one that was evidence of some cataclysmic event of unimaginable proportions. Nice to see the outcome without suffering through the upheaval. The split connects us to a time long gone. It reveals a mystery.

Or perhaps it's not the crack, the split, the chasm, gully, or gorge we love so much as the activity it invites—the crossing over. Or the opportunity to explore, get lost, take time out.

Last Saturday, my son fell against the ornate iron door of our coal stove and "split his head open." Well into writing this essay when it happened, that's how I imagined someone phrasing it, though "gashed his forehead" was more like it. In any case, when it happened, Sam cried, long alarming silences between sobs, but by the time we were in the car on the way to the emergency room, he was chatting merrily. After a pause, he said, "I'm happy, now, Mom."

They teach them that in day care these days. At three he is already more conscious of his feelings and articulate about them than I was at twenty. "I'm lonely," "I'm shy," "I'm angry," "scared," "happy" . . . It seemed like an odd comment at a time like this, but I thought I knew what he meant. After great pain and fear, a simple sense of well-being can feel like great joy.

That mood—and a yogurt and the TV—sustained us through our long wait. When finally we were ushered in, I immediately saw that since his last doctor's visit, just about a month ago, Sam had become a new person, or maybe I should say he'd become "a person." He answered the doctor's questions himself, listened to his description of what was to come, and agreed to the proffered deal: "If it hurts too much, just tell me and I'll stop."

Lying on the table under the lights, his hand in mine, he barely flinched as the doctor injected the numbing agent, once, twice, three times.

"He's a lot better than most of my adult patients," the doctor said. "You're making my day," said the nurse.

After establishing numbness, the doctor then went in for the first half of the stitch. Sam winced. "It hurts," he said.

I thought I could see the doctor weighing the pain of injecting more numbing agent against the pain of the stitch or two remaining to be done. "I'm going to have to do that once more," he said, reentering.

"It hurts," Sam said. His face contorted, turned red.

"Almost over," the doctor said continuing. Sam moaned a little but did not cry out, jerk away, or swat. There he lay, perfectly still, fat tears rolling sideways off his cheeks.

There was no denying how proud I felt—though I did have to ask myself: Had I created a little macho man too repressed or inhibited to cry? Would I have felt as proud if he'd been a girl? If I, emulating my often-bitten father, had not been a rather stoical child myself? I could only answer these questions with this hope: What I had seen in Sam was not macho repression or inhibition, it was the arrival of a self—confident, trusting, integrated.

Home again, Sam showed off his stitches to Sandy, his other Mom. Then we phoned Grandma and Grandpa so he could tell them of his exciting adventure. Meanwhile, I sat back thinking, *I'm happy now (Mom)*. After years of shit, vomit, and drool, of separation anxiety, of uncontainable, jaw-quivering fury, and stare-inducing fits on department store and restaurant floors—the arrival of this self-possession was indeed a marvelous occasion. We need this, too, I thought—composure, equanimity—not exclusively but also. A place to return to. A self to tell us where we've been.

And discipline, of course. We need that, too.

And skill.

"Leslie," said Barbara Greenberg, my favorite writing teacher, "with the technical control you have now, you can afford to be a little crazier in your writing."

Control and abandon—the best bedfellows. This vote of confidence and gentle push from Barbara enabled me to close my eyes and jump.

Ever since I learned the word, I have always been interested in the interstices. While the word as we use it refers to a place, "small or narrow, between things or parts," the Latin *intersistere* means "to pause, make a break." I find that a convenient, pleasing example of how language can poetically merge time and place, and I wonder if it explains why instinct told me there was some connection between the seizure I witnessed and the split rock nearby.

My interest in writing arose from the desire to slow down time and explore what is fleeting. I've always been interested in moments that pierce the skin of the day and allow us to glimpse underneath. I've always been greedy for more than my one little life—and so the drive to invent, recollect, and reinvent. But I was a girl—a small cute Jewish one raised before the second wave of feminism; a girl who embraced that "male style of discourse" for fear of being dismissed as flighty, irrational, or unseemly; and I can see now how my journey to become a writer is bound up with my search for a version of womanhood I could live with.

I'm searching still.

All writers know writing is erotic, not only because this most cerebral art draws strength and music from the body, but because it allows you to be yourself—and not yourself—mother, child, demon, lover, "other" of any sort; it demands you voyage out, and usually it delivers you back—to a self that's familiar but larger, humbler, emptier, fuller.

(I'm happy now, Mom.)

———◆———

Karl Will Bring a Picnic

A week or two into my son's first summer at overnight camp, I got a call from my Uncle Karl. Before his "hello" was out I knew who it was. Most of us linger over the "o"; Karl pounces on the "hell" and hangs out there. Rich, emphatic, musical, his voice—like the voice of his youngest brother, my father—never fails to knock the wind out of my anxieties. That day it contained its usual robust reassurance but also a hint of something else. Triumph, I guessed.

And sure enough, "Old Alice finally consented" to let him pay "Sam'l" a visit at camp. Twelve-thirty this Saturday. Karl will bring a picnic. "Sandwiches with bread still warm from the oven. Fresh raspberries. And a bag of GM cookies, of course."

"Sounds great," I said, wondering just how many calls it had taken before "Old Alice" (the camp director half his age) gave in. No matter. Sam will be pleased. He loves his Uncle Karl—not to mention the ginger molasses cookies he always brings.

"Now, Leslie—" Karl said. Names mean a lot to him and he never passes up the chance to utter one, often, as with Sam'l, with his own Karlish spin.

"Yes, Kar'l?"

I would like to believe I said this with a vaudevillian lilt—almost every utterance from Karl puts one in the mood for a little old soft shoe. Truth is, I'm still the eager-to-please niece and just beginning to riff with him as I might with a peer. That some should find this odd—I'm close to fifty—came as a surprise to me. Such is Karl's position in the family pantheon.

"What do you think, Leslie? Roast beef? Or turkey?"

"Either," I said, knowing how the man frowns upon fussy eaters. "But—" I wavered, fearing now that indifferent eaters might be even lower on his list. "Maybe turkey is better."

"Turkey it will be," Karl said. "Now, for the eggs—I could make deviled," he said. "Or do you think he would prefer egg salad?"

I pictured Karl in one of his trademark outfits—khaki slacks, checked shirt, do-it-yourself bowtie—standing, short and paunchy, near his tiny telephone table next to the stairs, reading glasses low on his nose, eyebrows fanning in diverse directions; eyes narrowing as he envisions first deviled, then salad. Which would most please his grandnephew?

The second boy of four born to Ida and Harold Lipsky—she a homemaker, he a junior high vice principal and insurance sales-man—Karl was always intent on bringing joy. My father remembers him at twelve or thirteen, walking proudly down their Brooklyn street, carrying a pot of red tulips for their mother's birthday. Karl was the favorite of the aunts and uncles, my father tells me, and probably of his parents, too. My father says this without resentment. He adores Karl—as do the other two brothers who are all exceptionally devoted to celebrating each other and the Lipsky name—notwithstanding the fact that the two youngest, concerned about how anti-Semitism might affect their businesses, changed theirs to Lawrence.

My earliest memories of Karl are indistinguishable from my memories of his big old barn-red house at the bottom of a steep dirt drive in western Massachusetts. Karl and his wife Jen bought the abandoned house before I was born. By the time I got to see the place, the seven chimneys were in working order, the resident bats mostly gone, the two older kids tearing through the woods, and the giant Lazy Susan on the dining room table had been spun several thousand times. Because my sister and I lived in Queens and spent our summers at overnight camp, most of our visits to Karl's were in fall or winter. I say "Karl's," maybe because he is the blood connection, or because this was the patriarchal fifties and sixties, or simply because it was Karl who came out to greet us; Karl and his sons, Seth and Jed, who dug up some old skis with cranky bindings and lace-up boots and gave us our first lesson on the hill in front of the house. It was Karl who would boost us onto Duster—he owned many horses over the decades, every one of them a "Duster"; Karl who orchestrated autumn hay rides and jingly midnight sleigh rides; Karl who pulled out a kazoo at every occasion that might call for one, and just as many that didn't. *Yes, we have no bananas! Come on, boys, and get your beans.* How could I not adore this man who gave me so many of my memories of song and speed and flight?

Even if he sometimes gets carried away, as with this picnic, and especially this egg business.

Skip the eggs, I was tempted to say. *A sandwich, fruit, and cookies are more than enough.* But I knew better. When Karl, living so close to the camp, put us up the night before delivery day, I made the mistake of telling him what the kid on the camp video said: That Kinderland had only one drawback: the fried eggs, which were "runny and nasty." *This* meant that the next day when Karl came with us to drop Sam off, he raised the pesky egg question, first with Sam's counselor, then with a bunkmate, and, as we were leaving, with the camp secretary, who was just stepping out of her office to go to the bathroom.

"Matthew . . ." "Zach . . ." "Bonnie. Can I ask you a personal question?"

Bonnie's pleasant expression slid into one of mild alarm.

"It's about the fried eggs here . . . ," Karl explained.

For the picnic I suggested hard-boiled. That settled, Karl asked if I recalled a good place for a picnic.

Now I, too, am someone who puts a great deal of thought into finding the perfect picnic spot, but here I was starting to really worry. Sam's just a kid. He can't be expected to appreciate all the effort and deliberation going into this picnic. Sure, he'll enjoy it, for six or seven minutes, but then it will be time for Frisbee or free swim or just plain *schmoozing*, Sam's favorite time, which Kinderland—a camp dedicated to preserving Yiddish culture and the history and ideals of the old Left—has penned into its daily schedule. Karl was setting himself up for disappointment.

"Down by the lake?" I ventured.

After the call, I wished I'd told Karl that he need not make a special trip for homemade bread, that the berries don't have to be "just-picked." Then again: *If it's not worth making a big effort, it's not worth doing at all.* Surely that was Karl's credo. I couldn't suggest he not sweat the picnic because sweating-it is what Karl does best.

And what, by the way, he expects others to do also—as when he called me in Cambridge and asked me to find, and deliver, a Christmas cactus to his friend who was in a hospital near me. And not just any Christmas cactus, mind you, but one in between red and pink, yet slightly closer to pink, and not completely closed, nor fully in bloom, but just on the verge.

"Friendship," Karl told me once when we were out for dinner after a day of skiing. "That's what I value most in life. Friendship, nature, and music."

I was surprised. Before this I might have said Karl's extravagant efforts were driven entirely by instinct. Or compulsion. Perhaps some overactivity in the part of the brain devoted to taste—in food and flowers and—stemware. But during that dinner, alone with him for perhaps the first time, I saw his reflective streak.

Also, I was surprised Karl didn't put "family" in his trinity. Or did he think of his family as friends—never obligatory or merely tolerated but always chosen and relished? That's how he'd made me feel, especially when I was no longer living with my parents and he would invite me to go skiing or to visit him and Marianne with friends. (Jen had died when I was fourteen, and Marianne was the beautiful, cosmopolitan Swedish designer he subsequently married.)

It was during these visits to their house in my twenties, when seeing the place through the eyes of my friends, that I began to realize just how remarkable it was: the structure itself with its eighteenth-century floor boards and huge stone fireplaces, Karl's extensive collections of just about everything—antique spoons and sabers, top hats and fur hats, strops and clocks, marmalades and mustards and candied gingers—and the grounds! He and Marianne had created magnificent gardens, a ring for the horses, trails through the woods. I had never thought of my uncle as rich. I thought of him as a man who bought a house filled with bats. A man whose business selling Americana began in an unheated garage. I often overheard talk of money problems. Yet viewing the house through my friends' eyes, I could see it was an estate. As for the man himself, *he*, my friends informed me, was even more of a character than I'd led them to expect. And while most enjoyed both place and man, one found the amount of stuff in the house suffocating; another was not charmed when Karl woke her early by blowing reveille out of an old bugle. I shouldn't have been surprised that not everyone was as enchanted as I was, but I was surprised. And like many of the once-bedazzled, I became devoted to searching for the hidden smudges and nicks in the shiny gifts bestowed upon me. I began to consider their costs.

A cousin and I had a few heart-to-hearts in which we scrutinized our beloved uncle through our newly raised feminist consciousness. How controlling he could be! How hard it was to get beneath all the natty outfits and showmanship! Maybe there really was no "beneath." Maybe, after all these years, the style had become the man. We wondered whether we were ever really ourselves with Karl, or whether he knew those selves, given that listening wasn't his strong suit and so many "conversations" revolved around such-and-such Pinot Noir or so-and-so's stock of Roquefort. We amused ourselves by trying to characterize a Typical Lipsky Experience, as lived by Karl or his sons, or the rest of us when under their influence—which just might be always. Often it involved a meal at a castle or, better, upon an ice floe; maybe front-row seats at the opera next to a king, or a death-defying ride down the Nile or across the Sahara with a touch of cholera thrown in. Son Jed was the athlete and daredevil, Seth the brilliant political journalist (who reputedly more than once interviewed a world leader while bombs exploded overhead). Somehow his daughter Jill's experiences in the gift business never became part of the family folklore. It seemed clear that typical Lipskyesque qualities were those associated with men—brawny shoulders that could paddle rushing rivers, quick wits that could give clever toasts at large parties. Yes, it was hard for us girls—only moderately athletic and "overly" emotional, more inclined to grope for our words and choke up when we said them—to find our place within the Lipsky Legacy. Hard for us to find a man who might live up to the ideal. (I, for one, instead of choosing men who had that ruddy, muscular, can-do glamour, gravitated toward the skinny, sallow poets or Marxists, and, eventually, toward women.)

These conversations with my cousin were a guilty pleasure. Liberating—yes, but disloyal, ungrateful. True, too hearty a dose of *joie de vivre* can leave one with a queasy feeling, but better our family parties in spectacular settings with too much good food and always some rollicking adventure for the kids (all sporting the identical "cargo vests" Karl ordered from L.L.Bean) than no parties at all, no exuberance or sense of camaraderie.

As for Karl himself, every time I'd settle comfortably into some critique that brought the myth down to man-size, I'd remember a counterexample or witness something new that would surprise, disarm, enthrall me all over again.

True, he got pretty worked up at the sight of my spatula pressing firmly down on the pancakes ("They're supposed to be fluffy!" How did I miss that?), but when my borrowed station wagon backed into his beloved Subaru, he stayed perfectly calm, was actually rather gallant about it.

And sure, he's obsessed with the best—copper pots, cuts of veal—but when he met me for lunch at the college where I worked, he was as enthusiastic about the bowl of cafeteria chili with plastic-wrapped oyster crackers as he would have been over a signature dish at one of Michelin's five-fork picks.

Most touching to me was that icy night early in my pregnancy. Karl, always chivalrous, was opening his car door for me. "Don't forget your seatbelt," he said, nodding toward my barely showing belly. "Precious cargo there," he added.

How happy those words made me. I had been nervous about how my extended family would react to my unorthodox pregnancy, to the child who would be raised by two women—and here Karl was bestowing his blessings.

Which brings me back to Sam, and that picnic.

"Guess what?" Karl said, calling me a day or two after the scheduled event. (Sam didn't show? He forgot to say thank-you?) "I arrived at 12:30 on the dot with a beautiful basket. Sam was there at the appointed spot but—it's the darnedest thing—"

(His handshake was limp. His eyes skittish? Karl has high expectations of kids.)

"He'd already eaten!"

I paused to take in the gravity of this.

"Did he know you were coming?"

"Yes, but apparently nobody bothered to tell him I was bringing lunch!"

I tried to summon up some of his outrage, but irritation was the best I could do. Camp was a busy place. "What a shame!" I said. "Was he able to eat *anything*?"

"Well, yes, a little," Karl admitted "A few raspberries, a bite of turkey and hard-boiled egg—mind you, not runny."

This sounded just about right for a ten-year-old, fed or not.

"But how can you enjoy eating when you've already eaten!" Karl said, dismally. "You know what I mean?"

I did, I did. But I was more interested in whether Sam seemed happy at camp.

"Oh, sure," Karl eventually told me. "He seemed fine."

"It's all about creating memories," Karl declared. This was about a year before the Kinderland picnic. He was staying with us in Cambridge while Marianne was having surgery in Boston. We'd been talking about a camping trip he'd recently taken with his grandchildren— the trip in which he staged some Native American ritual, complete with feathers and shakers—but I knew he meant more than that. He meant just about everything he does. "About creating connections," he added, thinking perhaps about those cargo vests that in truth never got worn simultaneously as he'd envisioned, or about any of the countless ways he continually expands his personal, unvirtual world wide web so that there's barely a place on earth where he doesn't know someone who wants to put him up in the finest style they are able. "About those Ginger Molasses cookies," he volunteered with a let's-not-be-naïve-about-this grin: "I've gotten a lot of mileage out of them. Just last month, when I was over in Amsterdam, I was put up by Jan Heuvingnott, whom I'd once sent cookies to, and in the morning, he took me to meet Van So and So, his uncle, the maker of Delft china."

"Jed," Karl tells me, maybe the second or third night of that same Cambridge visit, "he's trying to convince me to try out the new 'shaped' skis. He says they make it easier to turn. But you know, Leslie," and I'm thinking, "I do. I know." My father has the same constitutional aversion to taking the easier route. "I don't want to get lazy," Karl says.

I laugh. We're talking downhill skiing here, which most people give up by the time they're sixty or seventy. At eighty-five, Karl "doesn't want to get lazy"!

It's easy to forget how old Karl is. True, there's not much hair on his head and quite a bit sprouting from his ears, but when he visits our summer cabin, he sleeps like a boy scout on a mat on the floor. He thinks nothing of driving three hours to lunch with a friend, and he's always phenomenally punctual. That's why when it was twenty minutes past his ETA on that same visit to Cambridge, I began to worry—but only as I might about anyone traveling on a frigid night to a place he hasn't recently been.

Soon the phone rang. "A man who claims to be your uncle arrived at my doorstep," said an unfamiliar voice. "He's acting a little confused."

Only then did I remember that old is old. *Stroke?* I was thinking as I rushed over. The call was from just down the street. *Garden-variety senility?*

Karl's Subaru was in the neighbor's driveway, and there was Karl in his woolen worker's cap, perfectly alert and chipper—though slightly abashed as he explained he'd misplaced my address.

Later over dinner when I mentioned the neighbor's remark about him seeming confused, Karl was mystified at first. His eyes narrowed.

"Unless . . . ," he said, on the verge of a grin. "Hmmm. I noticed through his window, a pair of rather large boots in the hallway, so when he came to the door, I said, 'I see someone here has big feet.' "

"That might explain it," I said. Karl nodded, as if it just might.

I'm never sure how conscious Karl is of his eccentricities. In another story later that night, he told me about meeting someone who eventually became a good friend. "At first the guy wasn't sure what to make of me," Karl said. Then by way of explanation, he added, "I guess I had kind of a 'getup' in those days."

"In *those* days?" I said, and for a moment he actually looked bewildered. "Karl!" I nodded toward his suspenders, his knickers, the graceful curve of his watch chain, "You *still* have a 'getup'! In fact," I ventured, riding the wave of my own boldness, "you might say your whole life is one big 'getup'!"

There was a nanosecond of silence and then we chuckled—both of us a little tentatively.

Did he wonder later, just what I had meant? I know I did. Pleased with myself for taking that leap that seemed to put us on more equal footing, I was also worried that perhaps I'd offended. Still, the more I thought about it, the more the term seemed to embody what is most remarkable about Karl: not just his joyful attention to what goes on his body, his walls, and especially his table, and not just his tendency to bring an element of theater into everything he does, but his exhausting, effortful way of being himself—his ceaseless, miraculous "*get up* and go."

The reward is in proportion to the exertion, it says somewhere in the Talmud. The Lipsky household in Brooklyn had atheism in its water, but perhaps this maxim somehow seeped in. Karl knows that fun is what you make yourself; otherwise it's entertainment. *Poor Sam'l*, I sometimes think, glancing at him in front of the TV or computer screen. Good thing he has Karl to show him the real thing.

These days, Sam is thinking of changing his last name from Lawrence to Lipsky. When I ask him why, he doesn't mention Karl but says he wants a Jewish name. I wonder if this has anything to do with Ringelblum, the man for whom Sam's cabin at Kinderland was named. Ringelblum? My research told me he was initially an historian of Polish Jews during the Middle Ages. Later, confined to the Warsaw Ghetto during the Nazi occupation, he gathered a team of people who collected documents from their imperiled world—official documents and decrees, as well as everyday objects—diaries, school reports, poetry.

"They buried stuff in milk cartons" Sam told me. "Some were found. Others are still missing."

(Eventually, Sam will go to my alma mater and major in history.)

What gets passed on? What left behind? This is what I've been thinking about lately.

About six months after the picnic, and again a few months later, I conducted a test: "Tell me, Sam. What do you remember about that picnic?"

The first time I asked, he said, "I'd already eaten, but I still ate an egg and raspberries, and Karl brought cookies for the bunk."

The second time, he said more or less the same thing, but then added something about a "really neat antique picnic basket with old-fashioned plates and a nice tablecloth. Checkered, I think."

Each time, I kicked myself for underestimating Sam, for forgetting where I acquired my own educated eye and appreciative palate, for even considering that in Karl's case, the Talmud might be wrong about the exertion–reward equation.

Recently, when Sam and I were talking about different kinds of genius, he declared Karl "a genius at making people happy."

This April, I got a call from my father saying Karl had had a small heart attack but was already home and doing fine. Immediately, I mailed a card sporting a photo I'd taken in Italy, a close-up of some blazing cherry tomatoes laid out on white paper atop an ancient stone fence. "Get well soon," I wrote. "Picnic season a-coming." I didn't yet know that later tests would show the need for surgery—a triple bypass and aortic valve replacement.

Within a week Karl was in a Boston hospital. When I called him there early one morning, he told me with some despondency that he'd ordered the oatmeal. "It hasn't come yet," he said, "but," and here his voice gained strength, "I'm not even going to *think* about how it's going to taste without the salt. It's all in the attitude."

All in the attitude. That's his mantra. Me? I think it's all in the neurotransmitters, but now, listening to Karl coaching himself on how to endure the tasteless porridge—this, two days before open-heart surgery that kills more than a few who are twenty years his junior—I can't help thinking that attitude just might be the key after all.

Either that, or those underestimated virtues of denial and displacement.

The day of the surgery, I arrive at the hospital while Karl is telling Marianne about yesterday's scrambled eggs. "Positively degrading," he says. "*De-grading!*" he repeats to assure her this is no hyperbole.

Eggs again! Yesterday's breakfast! An odd topic for a time like this, but of course Karl has his priorities.

"When's Sam'l going to camp?" he asks me. It's the same question he asked on the phone yesterday.

"July first," I say.

He nods, looks toward the ceiling, calculating. "Three months," he says. "I should be on my feet by then. I'll be getting the picnic ready."

About a half hour later Marianne and I accompany the gurney down the hall, onto the elevator, and down another long corridor to the swinging double doors that bar us. If Karl is scared, he doesn't show it. I kiss him good-bye.

Precious cargo, I think, amazed by the baby softness of his cheek.

———————◆———————

Dogs and Children

When I first met Corky, I had no use for him. I hated his name, which reminded me of that stocky, whistle-blowing camp counselor I had not known whether to admire or scorn; nor was I crazy about his breed. Cockers were squat, with drippy eyes and droopy lids—and this one was overweight and undertrained, an obsessive humper with a compulsion to follow his mistress everywhere. (It was she who interested me.)

They, Sandy and Corky, were living in a barn, while I and five other women were in a house a few yards away—all of us part of a mini writer's colony on the Cape, the summer of '83. We were all "creative" writers except for Sandy—she was finishing up her dissertation in economics. Short-haired and athletic, Sandy looked a little like that camp counselor, except for the bold hoop earrings and pink chenille bathrobe I spotted from my second-story window when she crossed the yard to use our shower. When she set out on a beer run, Corky made a reckless dash into her hatchback; when they returned, he careened into the kitchen, always sliding just past his bowl, an admirable move in a ballplayer but not in someone approaching a snack.

By the following summer, Sandy and I were a couple and Corky had become tolerable to me. Under my influence he'd lost weight and gained manners. When I rented a place in Vermont, I was not averse to having him full time, even though Sandy would be up only on weekends. A veterinarian's daughter, I didn't have it in me to deny any dog his summer in the country. Still, I wasn't overjoyed. Instead of roaming the woods with the doggier dogs who lived up the road, Corky would sit glumly by my feet as I wrote. I was still daunted by my new computer, and every time I shifted positions, sighed, saved, or, God forbid, printed, he'd explode in anticipation of an outing. Nevertheless, I found myself becoming a dog-mother who couldn't bear not to take him with me everywhere I went. I'd search the Grand

Union lot for the shadiest spot and delight in *his* obvious delight when I returned with my bundles. I took solace in his presence during lonely nights of presidential conventions and summer Olympics. And I dedicated myself to training him—first to eat his biscuits in the kitchen rather than on the living room oriental, then to stay between me and the road's shoulder so that we could run without a leash. These were not easy tasks. No puppy, no genius, Corky had never been properly trained, nor had I ever trained an animal. We got Mac, the Cairn terrier of my childhood, when I was three or four. My father taught him to heel, my mother to "speak." There weren't a zillion training books then, and it didn't occur to me to consult any now. But what should the command be—"Right"? "Inside"? "Shoulder"? What should I do or say when the shoulder disappeared and we had to switch sides? Corky's confused, pleading eyes shamed me. I became disdainful of his desire to please. Sometimes my frustration frightened me: I shouted or nudged him into line with my leg, wondering if these were legitimate tactics, later suspecting I was acting out some other drama. Somehow, he eventually learned. We loved our runs, and the hours of training, showing us the best and worst of each other, seemed to solidify our bond. About halfway into that summer, I noticed I was planning my afternoons with Corky in mind.

In truth, our inclinations were not so dissimilar; nevertheless, there were days I quit work early or went one place rather than another because I knew he would enjoy it more. And when I realized this—that I had become a person capable of making sacrifices, however minor, for a dog who wasn't mine and wasn't the kind of dog I would have chosen—and later when I realized it was no longer a question of putting his desires before mine, because his pleasure had become my own—then I knew I wanted a baby.

I was thirty-three, had been feeling the urge for several years, but had been plagued with doubts, not only over how I could manage having a baby if I lived as a lesbian, but also over whether my desire was merely a romantic notion. I liked doing things I was good at and I didn't know if I'd be good at all that feeding, changing, rocking, toting. I'm the younger of two, close to the youngest of many cousins. I'd rarely babysat. Mac was a birthday gift to my sister—though he did provide some experience.

"I'm doing this because I love you," I said, knowing it was true. I loved Mac's Toto cuteness, his jumpy, waggy greetings, the way he zoomed around the couch when we turned on the vacuum cleaner. I loved stroking his wheat-colored hair, his velvety pink underbelly, maybe even venturing to wobbly balls. We were on the back patio now. He must have run into the neighbor's yard—from there he could run into the street. "This hurts me more than it hurts you," I said as I slapped him on the flank. My hand stung, my eyes too. But was I also taking a little pleasure in reigning over, in knowing better? In being, instead of the child victim to her parents' scoldings: the perpetrator?

I was a freshman in college when I got the call Mac died. How I cried, knowing even then that my grief wasn't only for him but for my childhood, now over. Parents and children, beginnings and endings, love, sex, power, and responsibility—dogs have often been the locus of these great themes for me. Early on, I saw puppies come out of their cloudy sacs, watched my father slice open a dog on our kitchen table; and, for some reason I can't remember, my parents and I once drove to a New Year's Eve party with a dead dog in the trunk of our car.

The relationship I formed with Corky that first summer was unlike any I'd had with a dog—or anyone. I had full responsibility, his complete devotion and obedience. Wherever I went, he went, and this, especially, thrilled me. Now I no longer needed men for protection.

A woman with a dog could go places a woman alone—or even two women—could not go. So maybe a woman with a dog could live alone? Or with another woman? Maybe two women and a dog could live together and raise a child?

I'm not saying Corky was the clincher—but he did play a role.

My plan for my seventh month of pregnancy was to spend it in my beloved rented cabin in New Hampshire. This was in '89, seven years after I had met Corky and Sandy. As in previous years, Corky was to be my daily companion, Sandy my weekend one, but because I had some social event on the way up, we decided Cork would drive up later with Sandy.

It was a different kind of drive without him there squashed among my stuff in the back seat. I would glance back, a reflex, surprised not to see his beautiful muzzle on the armrest, his eyes open, bored. I missed his steadfast company, even in its most silent, stationary variety. With him, a "solo" trip never felt lonely—it felt airy and grand. And when we turned at the fire station in Dublin to climb the winding road to Harrisville, he would always rise, circle in his spot, then hang his head out the window, sniffing in whatever let him know we were near: water, I suspect, muddy, fishy. Seeing him like that—his mouth open and relaxed so he looked as if he were laughing—my own excitement would rise.

Once we arrived, he would dash to the back porch where we kept his food the year before, then stick to my heels as I unloaded the car, his whole rear half wiggling. When that task was complete, we'd walk down the mowing (the acres of downward sloping meadow in front of the cabin), and he'd run ahead just so far, disappearing in the tall grass so that I could only see him when he leaped, which he did, every few seconds, looking his most graceful then, his most doggishly gorgeous. From there, we'd head down the road toward the lake. Midway, at the brook, he'd clamber down for a drink, and when we got to our beach and I dove in, he would sit like a statue guarding my backpack while I swam. I liked to swim far from shore, but I'd glance back often in search of the bright blue of the pack, the burnished red of his perfect form. My beacon, my home plate, my pal.

Not that it was so bad, arriving without him. "Different," I reported to Sandy on the phone that night. "More intense in a way, with nothing to keep me from my thoughts, moods, rhythms. Interesting for a day or two, but I couldn't bear it much longer."

The next morning Sandy called early. "He's blind," she said. "He was fine last night but woke up blind!"

The news was shocking but not altogether surprising. It had been more than a year since we first noticed odd symptoms—brief sudden cries, sporadic trembling, difficulty jumping onto the couch; almost exactly a year since, in this same cabin, while trying to give him his heartworm pill, I had trouble opening his jaws and finally forced them, causing a terrible, reverberating howl. During this past year we'd taken him to three vets and had had as many diagnoses— Horner's syndrome, temporomandibular joint syndrome, arthritis. Of erratic health even before the more pointed signs of trouble began, over the last year his off days had greatly increased, and while he continued most of his normal activities, it was becoming clear that something was wrong.

Sandy, usually stoic, was crying into the phone, and while this made the situation seem less remote, it caused me to remain composed and cold-hearted enough to feel—in addition to alarmed—disappointed, even a little annoyed. I had so little time to finish one last draft of my novel and savor all I was about to lose: time to stare at the mowing and Mount Monadnock beyond, to listen to that odd dripping sound from the trees, time to happily disappear into the green around me—and having just unpacked my computer, I was now being asked to return home.

"Take him to Angell and call me back," I told Sandy, hoping the vet would tell her she was mistaken, or if not that, would somehow restore Corky's sight just like that. But when Sandy called back a few hours later, Corky was still blind, so I headed back to Boston. En route, I tried to prepare myself. I'd seen that milky blue glaze on dogs' eyes; I'd also seen how normal they otherwise appeared.

But what I found the next morning was anything but normal. There in a ward at the end of many corridors in the renowned Angell Memorial was our Corky, resting in his habitual position, rear legs stuck out behind him, muzzle flat on the floor; and there he *stayed* as I walked eagerly toward him, speaking his name. He stayed there three, maybe five seconds with me in the cage right next to him. Was he deaf too? Finally, he roused himself, but he did not jump up and down, wag, or lick; he did not rub his flank against my leg or position his head so that my hand would stroke it. I had never noticed that he *always* leaned against a leg, but now that he didn't, it seemed his most essential, most defining characteristic. Though he would get much sicker, that moment was the most devastating to me. I burst into tears, sobbing loudly, unabashedly in front of the warden and the couple visiting a splinted dog in a neighboring cage. "Corky," I keened. "It's me. Me!" But still he didn't seem to recognize my voice, my smell, my touch. I put on his leash anyway, sobbing still as we passed the now enviable couple, and I led him through the many hallways, watching helplessly as he banged into walls and corners. The second we were out the front door, he took a pee that went on and on, as if he'd been holding it in since his admission the day before. I ached for him but was also slightly buoyed. Perhaps all was not lost? Pride? Dignity? Overtraining? Whatever it was, that pee broke my heart and gave me hope. Once we were safely down the stairs and in the lot for his walk, though he continued to stumble and bang his muzzle against curbs, car fenders, and tree trunks, though he still did not seem to know me or enjoy the outing at all, I was somewhat comforted by the task I saw before me: I would help Cork learn to get around.

Over the next couple of days Sandy and I visited several times more, sometimes separately, sometimes together. Corky had started the steroids to reduce the swelling of whatever was pressing against his optic nerve. He still seemed depressed, but at least he'd rise when we arrived, he'd sniff and rub. Out in the lot, we studied his movements.

"Did you see that? He can see!"

"What about that? Blind as a bat!"

We took turns playing the optimist. Once, I was certain he could see, but when the doctor shined a light in each eye, he shook his head. "Just learning to compensate."

Yet within a few more days Corky *was* seeing, first just light and in only one eye, soon much better in both. News from the spinal tap wasn't as good: "Abnormal fluid probably indicating encephalitis, inflammation of the lining of the brain. Three to six months." If the disease didn't kill him, the steroids would.

During these weeks, the crisis unfolding outside my belly had more reality than the drama inside. Corky took all our time and energy. Sandy and I agreed: it was disconcerting—how absorbed we were in our dog, how remote the impending baby felt. Privately, I thought back to how I had cried without restraint at Angell. Those shirtwaisted moms on fifties TV—*they* would have maintained a chirpy cheerfulness, especially if the patient had been a baby. Was I up to this? I wondered. Well, at least Sandy and I were proving we could act as a team—gathering information, making decisions, dishing out money, putting the rest of our lives on hold when the health of our beloved was concerned.

Within about a week, Corky recovered enough to spend a few weeks with me at the cabin. I remember throwing sticks and learning to laugh as he scurried around searching for them. Also, his hearing was going. When I called him he would look everywhere but where I was. This, too, I learned to chuckle at. Our walks down the mowing, though still enjoyable, were tainted by my fear that I would lose him. He couldn't see me or hear my calls, and in the tall grass I couldn't see him, except when he leaped. That occasionally he still summoned the élan to leap—this brought a flash of joy, then a sharpened grief.

With Sam due in six weeks, Corky and I, and Sandy part-time, stayed in a friend's house in Hull, an out-of-fashion shore town close to Boston. The beach was scruffy, yet I came to love the somewhat treacherous walks my increasingly bulky body took there with Corky, now nearly blind again. The walks would have been more peaceful if I'd used a leash, but I was beginning to accept the doctor's prognosis and I wanted Corky's last days to be happy, which to me meant free. By shouting above the surf, I, his seeing-eye woman, tried to steer him clear of the craggy rocks and broken bottles, the beckoning dead gulls and fish. I tried to maintain between us the distance that he, with working eyes and ears, would have naturally kept. It was one of the things I most loved about him—that distance. Never, since that first summer, too close to crowd me or too far to worry me. Now, he had to rely on smell and my faintly perceived commands. It was almost a sport, one at which we both quickly improved—though not without stress. I remember once running after him, worried that perhaps I was jostling Sam too much.

It was during that month in Hull that Corky began peeing indoors. Given his heroic control in the hospital, this seemed a bad sign.

For twenty-eight hours I labored and pushed. Then Sam was delivered by C-section. After the astonishment and joy of seeing him greet the world with open eyes and a healthy wail, I felt more like sleeping than tending to anyone else. I wished I'd known this wasn't so unusual. The guilt I felt, the fear that something was wrong with me—these made those first months doubly hard.

During the four-day hospital stay that followed, dog finally took a back seat to baby, though I do remember asking about Corky and feeling grateful that my father was around to oversee his care. When we returned from the hospital with a new baby, Corky was too sick to feel the full sting of jealousy. He had vestibular disease now, a condition affecting balance that caused him to stoop and circle so relentlessly that sometimes it looked as if his head and tail were joined. He couldn't walk straight. He couldn't climb stairs. By day eight, Corky was back in the hospital. I was glad not to have to contend with him during the festive *bris*. The food came from that same deli where I broke the news to my parents. Now they and aunts and uncles and cousins and friends had come to our house to welcome Sam. To Sandy and me it felt like the wedding we never had—not that it was of that scale, but we took it as a celebration of not only Sam, but of us, the loving couple who would raise him.

The guests came and left, as did my parents. Sandy went back to work. Corky came home from the hospital. I, postoperative, began solo care of a dying dog and helpless infant. One morning, in an effort to understand just why I found my days so trying, I attempted to record my activities. Here's my entry from 8:53 to 9:02.

Sammy fusses. I pick him up . . . realize Corky needs heartworm pill. Call Sandy at work. Put Sammy down so I can go to the bathroom. Sammy starts screaming. Corky comes in, upset by the screaming. Screaming increases. I give up on the bathroom idea and go get Sammy . . .

That I was able to write two whole pages suggests this must have been one of the more manageable mornings. The document conveys the frustration and tedium, but it makes it sound funny— writing can do that. It wasn't funny at the time. Even that damn breast pump squirting my milk everywhere wasn't funny when I was alone. In retrospect I think I had postpartum depression. At the time, when someone suggested that, my feminist hackles went up. Wasn't medicine pathologizing a perfectly normal reaction to a drastically circumscribed life? I see now I waffled, sometimes thinking the problem was in me, sometimes sure I was victim to a massive hoax that had led me to expect blissful sunlit afternoons filled with good music and books, a beatific baby nuzzling at my breast, a halo around us. Well, maybe not quite that but not *this*!

Loneliness—that was a big part of it. I joined a mothers' group. Nice people but new to me. One day we planned to meet at the park near Fresh Pond. The weather was glorious. It was a just short walk from the parking lot to our picnic spot on a grassy knoll, but I couldn't figure out how to transport a partially deaf/blind/paralyzed dog and an infant without leaving one or the other unattended. In the end, I lost only my take-out lunch, a rare indulgence. Sprawled on the filthy blacktop, that gorgeous goat cheese and red pepper sandwich reduced me to tears.

There must have been many such times when dog's and baby's needs were in direct conflict, yet I rarely experienced it that way. Caring for Corky I felt relatively competent. Caring for Sam was mostly trial and error. I wanted sympathy from Sandy when it fell to me to take Corky to the specialist in New Hampshire that my father recommended, but in truth I rather enjoyed those long drives. One week we went twice, eighty or ninety minutes each way, Sam sleeping peacefully in his car seat.

We have a snapshot of boy and dog on the bed. Sam asleep, intact, and comfy; Corky, awake, curled up close, looking miserable with drippy eyes, one side of his face slack. How easily Corky, sick as he was, adjusted to our new family, finding his place as Sam's guardian! Touched by the sight, I took out my camera. That night it came to me in these exact words: *This is what it feels like to live a life propelled by love.*

We lived that month in the country of illness. Every day I injected Corky with Gentamicin, gently "making a tent" with the scruffy skin bordering the neck. Gentamicin, Prednisone, Baytril, Clavamox, Tribrissen, abscess, kidney function, spinal taps, tense waits for lab results, phone calls to doctors from restaurants and gas stations, nonstop mental gymnastics and medical detective work. Unspoken questions about when to throw in the towel. And eventually, spoken ones.

One Monday morning when he could no longer open his mouth, walked away from his Campbell's soup, and wouldn't take the pills hidden in peanut butter, we called the vet and made an appointment: 3:15.

I got home from work around two. Corky was lying on the blue tile of the bathroom. I sat beside him, stroking him, silently saying good-bye, until, around 2:15, when he rose and headed into the kitchen and began to eat. When Sandy arrived, we called the vet and canceled. Friends were expected for dinner. Earlier, we'd thought of calling it off, but now we were glad we hadn't. It was good to have a house full of people to celebrate what felt like Corky's resurrection. Sandy and I kept glancing at him and then each other—so happy we were to have him with us still!

But the next day Corky vomited three times, and that night around midnight we were awakened by his labored breathing. We gave him some water and he started heaving as if he were trying to vomit but couldn't. I injected an extra dose of Dex, hoping it would somehow help, but it didn't. He heaved and rasped, obviously suffering, and I thought he might die any minute and I hoped he would. But he didn't. And when I called Angell, the only place that would be open at 1 a.m., I was told they had had a power failure. I didn't know whether emergency lights were sufficient for euthanasia, but I couldn't face driving up to a dark hospital so I didn't even broach the subject. I moved to the futon in Sam's room so I wouldn't have to hear Corky struggling. In my dream, I saw a rowboat, gliding away from shore.

In the morning, he was still alive; in fact, his breathing seemed easier. But we had resolved to make the appointment first thing, and so we did. Even though he seemed to be standing a little straighter. Even though we saw a tiny wag. And then another. That's why we were grateful when Sandy saw that he couldn't eat, not even a spoonful of cottage cheese. I only wished I had seen it myself—that moment he turned away from the bowl.

After delivering Sam to a neighbor, we took Corky to the vet and held him while she shaved his leg and inserted the needle. Then Sandy and I took a walk around Fresh Pond, his favorite local spot. Already it was happening: instead of seeing the stooped oozing thing I'd taken there so recently, I saw him as he'd been in the old days— darting, leaping, his shining red fur making the snow whiter, the pines greener—the whole beautiful world more beautiful.

A friend came over later, brought flowers and muffins. She had the number of a renowned Harvard psychiatrist who led bereavement groups for people who'd lost pets. Though I never even called, it helped to know that some bigwig took my pain seriously. My visitor was sympathetic, both a friend and the vet wrote beautiful condolence letters, but there were many people who didn't seem to understand. My department chair—mother of two children, no dogs—said, "You'll see—how pale a dog will seem in comparison to Sam as he grows."

It's true. Many times a day, I look at his gap-toothed smile. I listen to his ingenious grammar ("John bited me"), his marvelous logic ("I can't wear mine mittens because then they won't swing!" Or, "You know what's really sad, Mom? When an animal dies while it's still living"). I open my arms for his amorous hugs, we whisper in the dark. I teach him what I know and learn what he has to teach. I think: no comparison between dogs and children. Still, "pale" is not the word I'd use, and I will not betray myself by belittling the love I felt for Corky—even if some of it was just the love I felt for myself finally learning how to love so well.

I adore Sam. The love I feel for him is comparable to nothing else. But, except in moments when I drank in his miraculousness, I did not love taking care of an infant. That "bonding" everyone talked about . . . I was angry that so much literature and oral history led me to expect it would happen in an instant. I wanted to hug those who admitted they knew people (themselves?) for whom it didn't happen until the kid started talking. It happened sooner for me, but mothering sure put me through my paces. Kids don't get "trained" in a summer, often not in a lifetime. They rarely keep that perfect distance. More often they're on top of you or out of sight. To carve a path to yourself or anyone else while in their presence is a mighty task.

Sometimes I think back to the earth mother I thought I would be. In college, she was the wife of the bearded professor. Big-boned, wearing a flour-dusted denim skirt, she would manage to feed the whole gang of us fresh bread and apple butter, then disappear into the kitchen where she'd orchestrate a crafts project for a brood of kids. Sandy and I are both professors in need of wives. I've thrown more than a few tantrums since Sam's appearance. Together we struggle to grow up.

It's early July. Soon the mowing will be full of those low-bush blueberries Sandy and Sam and I will pick. As the screen door slams and we descend the path, I'll be thinking, as I do every season, about Sam's first summer here—the summer we scattered Corky's ashes. Heavier than I imagined, they made a long snaky path that lasted and lasted. Days later they were there still, and Sandy and I watched with a mixture of horror and satisfaction as Sam, not yet a year but already so good with his opposing thumb, plucked an ash-covered berry and popped it into his mouth.

———◆———

II

Andee's Fiftieth and the Way We Live Now

For her fiftieth birthday, my friend Andee threw a slumber party—as suggested by her couple's therapist, who happens to be my couple's therapist, too. The party took place at the home of Andee's friend Mary, who had recently moved into a co-housing community. Her home—beautiful and roomy enough to sleep the bunch of us—is among two dozen others spread over twenty boggyish, green acres just far enough from Boston to lend the party the feel of a getaway. Exactly what you want, I think, when you're celebrating what there's no getting away from.

I should know. I, and several of my closest friends, turned fifty around that same millennial period and collectively we'd spent more than a few hours (sometimes with the aid of professionals charging by the minute) thinking about how to mark the event. We knew that the convergence of our private rites of passage and the Christian calendar's major page-turning didn't make us any more important or emblematic than anyone else; still, it was tempting to think so—to put extra effort into planning our celebrations and then to mine them for what they tell us, not only about our individual tastes and distastes, triumphs and failures, choices and defaults, but about those of our whole generation—our whole era, perhaps. In the case of Andee's overnight, or rather those of us—all white, educated, left-leaning feminists—sharing scraps of our life stories at brunch the next morning, I couldn't help noting that not one of us lived in what was once called the Typical American Family.

Let's start with Andee. In her teens, twenties, and thirties, she had an impressive series of seemingly healthy heterosexual relationships; most lasted for several years, yet none led to marriage or children. Then in her early forties, Andee had her first lesbian relationship. At the time of her fiftieth, she was in her third. Liz lives in Boulder; Andee, near Boston. They wear wedding rings but never had a public ceremony. For a while they were talking about having a kid; they even approached some male friends. Andee gave Boulder a try for a year, and, on her sabbatical, Liz came east, but each has decided that, for now, her attachment to home, job, and community outweighs her need to live with the other. They visit about once a month and no longer talk about kids. Liz, now forty, oversees a brood of graduate students and often feels that, given her close involvement in their private as well as professional lives, they will fulfill her need for family. Andee, at fifty, longs for someone who'll be as much invested as she is over which couch to buy, which flowers to plant—and she is keenly sad about the likely prospect of remaining childless. She's also a little bewildered. It's not that she identifies with that cartoon gal who clonks her own head and cries, "Oh, my God, I forgot to have children!" It's just that . . . for so long, kids simply weren't as much of a priority as finding a life partner and maintaining her equilibrium. But even if Andee had been more focused on having children, she doubts she would have done what her friend Ginny did.

One of the brunch crew, Ginny, also had several serious boyfriends over the decades. One she had married, and the two went to Nairobi together to teach. When the relationship ended, Ginny lived communally for several years. She hoped to meet a man, but in her early forties, she stopped waiting and adopted a baby, an African American. Her vision then was to create a family with her daughter and another roommate who also had kids, but that never panned out. Instead, wanting more time with her daughter than her life in Boston afforded, Ginny took jobs in American schools abroad—first in Bangkok, then Damascus, and now Cairo. The adoption has worked out well, but Ginny admits her daughter isn't so keen on all the moving around. Ginny herself is disappointed she has not found a mate, nor has she found the community of people who teach in international schools to be as cohesive and sustaining as she had hoped.

I, like Ginny and Andee, had relationships with men for many years, and then, like Andee, but ten years earlier, I became involved with women. At thirty-eight, after I'd been with Sandy for five years, I gave birth to Sam—conceived by me and an old friend who agreed beforehand that, although he'd see the child twice a month, the child would be raised by Sandy and me.

How I agonized over what Sam's unusual family would cost him. No doubt, surrounded by so many "normal" families, and even more images of normal families—in fables and fairy tales, movies and songs, on billboards and cereal boxes, TV shows and commercials—he'd long for the same. I dreaded the inevitable questions: *Where's **my** Daddy?* (Easy: Vermont.) *How come he doesn't live with us?* (Not so easy.) Imagine my surprise at *this* question posed one cozy evening.

We are midway through a new book, enjoying the splendid watercolor illustrating a baby horse and his mother (referred to as "foal" and "mare"), grazing peacefully in a meadow. "But where," Sam suddenly asks, with all the intensity his toddler voice can carry, "where's the *other* mare?"

"Just on the other side of that mountain," I venture. "Or, maybe, behind that big tree?"

Another surprise: We're in the car, he and his kindergarten friend in the back. "I wish I had two mommies," the friend declares.

And one evening while I was taking out the garbage, our neighbor, in a spirit of one-upmanship, says that a kid in his son's class has *three* mothers—and they're all named Jennifer!"

Of course, multi-everything Cambridge, Massachusetts, is not exactly normal either; and I'm sure, eventually, Sam will have plenty of material for therapy; however, these days—he's now almost eleven— well, this says it all:

"I could never write an autobiography," Sam announced recently, when we were talking about different kinds of books. "Why's that?" I asked.

"Because, there's nothing unusual about me."

I'm guessing Kimberle's child will feel the same way when he's old enough to think about such things. Kimberle, also among the bagel-munchers that morning, is happily, heterosexually married but unable to conceive. She and her husband enlisted a surrogate mother who gave birth to a boy. Things are going so well, the couple is thinking of having another child with the same surrogate mother, who will eventually be known to the children.

Only two of the party guests created families the old-fashioned way—by marrying men and bearing children. In both these cases, the marriages ended, oddly enough for basically the same reason: gross financial irresponsibility on the part of the husbands—at least that's the version I got. One of these guests arrived at the party with a pet baby bunny too young to be left at home, but she and bunny left before the rest of us got up. Jan, the one who stayed, has a new boyfriend now. Her daughter just finished her first year of college, and her son is starting high school next year. The son, Jacob—and his family's response to him—are what make this family unconventional now. He enjoys dressing in drag and lip-syncing to divas, and his family and their friends (Andee included) have learned to enjoy watching him.

Coincidentally, I'd met Jacob just a day or two before Andee's party at a memorial service for a transgender activist. I'd first met this fifty-something pioneer, Penny, when she spoke at the Unitarian church that Andee (and Jan and Jacob) attend. I then invited her to speak about her experiences in the college class I was teaching on "Differences," which she did, bravely, eloquently. A couple of years later, when I learned of Penny's death, I wanted to pay my respects.

At the reception following the service, as I was chatting with a sixty-something man-to-woman cross-dresser in floral dress and heels, she recognized the cherubic Jacob on the other side of the brownie plate. Both had attended last year's "Fantasia Fair" in Provincetown, where Jacob had performed that joyous anthem, "I Will Survive." The older woman complimented him on his performance, then sighed: "Oh, what a different life I would have had if I had done what you did when I was your age!" Her eyes teared, and I could sense the life she'd had instead, its pain and humiliation, its lost opportunities.

As for Mary, who hosted the brunch: At fifty-five, with a pension from teaching high school French, Mary reinvented herself as a successful sculptor and art teacher. Never married, rarely partnered, without children—Mary, now in her mid-seventies, has found community in other ways. She works in an old factory building filled with artists, and at home in co-housing she lives among forty-eight adults and forty kids constellated in a variety of ways. Each unit is self-sufficient, but there is also a community building that houses potlucks, dances, game-nights, and so on. Mary attends about two of these each week and has abundant, impromptu contact with other community members. Cars at co-housing are relegated to a lot near the entrance. This makes the grounds well suited to games, scooters, and schmoozing; and the curvy footpaths connecting the units give the whole place the look and feel of an idyllic Chagall-like village.

As I think about these lives—Andee's, Ginny's, Kimberle's, Jan's, Mary's, and mine—I imagine my skeptical alter ego (who most often turns up in my father's red chamois shirt) grumbling about the "times"—not to mention my longstanding attraction to oddballs. "Let's face it," he says. "What we have here is a bunch of weirdos and sad sacks."

I have no quick comeback. Perhaps somewhere now in these United States there are women at fiftieth birthday parties who once stayed home with their since grown kids, women who for better or worse stayed in relationships without the help of therapists, women who can remain sane and cheerful without the help of antidepressants. As a kid, I assumed I'd become one of those women, but how many of us have the lives we once anticipated?

One day on the phone with my mother, I ask her if she's had the life she expected (which I realize is not quite the same as asking if she has had the life she once craved).

"Well," she says with a little laugh, seemingly surprised by the answer she's about to give, "yes. I guess I have. And I think most of my friends would say the same."

So it's a generational thing, I decide, based on this sample, hardly large or random. Then again, maybe, at least for those of us turning fifty in 2000, the explanation is in the stars. Nineteen-fifty, after all, is a Year of the Tiger. Among our ranks are many incomparables—Karl Marx, Isadora Duncan, Marilyn Monroe, and Marco Polo. Courageous, intense, restless, tempestuous—according to one website, Year of the Tiger folk are especially suited to becoming actors, politicians, writers, race car drivers, and *matadors*.

My friend Judy believes that she and many of her friends who were also born smack in the center of the last century have been caught in the middle. Led in our youth to want only a husband and family, then in our early twenties lured by the prospect of having it all, we have missed out on both ends.

Even so, "weirdo" and "sad sack" aren't the words I'd use to describe the crew at Andee's fiftieth. True, we didn't get it all. We've searched, struggled, compromised, messed up, hurt others, and wept—all the while subsidizing our therapists' vacations. (One of mine claimed her life was transformed by swimming among the dolphins!) We also worked hard to repair rifts with our families, expand human rights, challenge rigid thinking, care for the earth, improve education. Like our mothers, we buy groceries, get Pap smears, vote, and volunteer, and quite often we show admirable ingenuity, integrity, and resiliency. We may not live happily ever after, but the lives we live feel like our own, and, often enough, they're filled with laughter.

We'll be laughing still, I suspect, when the children we do raise end up with lives more resembling their grandparents'.

♦

Yard Sale

People have gone crazy over yard sales. At least I have, and friends in other states say their neighbors have the fever, too: they rise at dawn, ignore stern warnings against early birds, go rain or shine. What's it all about, I wonder—this consuming romance with other people's garbage?

Sure, we're committed to recycling, and we're sick of malls and megastores. And with most Five and Dime stores extinct, yard sales may be the only place ten cents will still get you *something* (*Madeleine* in French, a shoe box of old crayons, a 1989 Monet desk calendar). What's more, since so many of our appetites have been proclaimed unhealthy—if not lethal—it's not surprising we'd be keen on a relatively harmless way to indulge our cravings, be bold and impulsive, even reckless.

Still, I wonder if what really fuels the yard sale craze is our desire to walk about, meet our neighbors, enter their yards, porches, garages—those intermediaries between public and private space. Perhaps yard sales have become our way of communally acknowledging the rites of passage that often occasion them—death, divorce, graduation, and relocation. Whatever the reason, these days I see yard sales everywhere. On both sides of the tracks, in my dreams, even in the books I'm reading.

Take *The Shipping News*, the Pulitzer Prize–winning novel that its author E. Annie Proulx declares in her acknowledgments, "would have remained just a thread of an idea" had she not come across *The Ashley Book of Knots* at a yard sale: price, a quarter.

Take *The Gift*, Lewis Hyde's fascinating book, subtitled *Imagination and the Erotic Life of Property*. Summarizing what anthropologists have said, Hyde reminds us that gifts must create a "feeling bond" between giver and receiver; they must "keep on moving." Doesn't this also shout "Yard Sale"?

Although yard sale bounty cannot properly be called "gifts" because it's purchased—*usually* (I *have* gotten a mortar *sans* pestle, a dilapidated L.L. Bean wood-carrier, and an "Oh My God, I Left the Baby on the Bus" T-shirt, all for free)—unlike most purchases, those bought at yard sales often create a feeling bond. My three-legged, two-tiered oak table? I bought it from a hefty blond with a not-great dye job. Her son made the thing in shop. Who, I wondered, would sell something her kid made in shop? Even if he were grown by now. Even if she knew, as I later discovered, that the thing had a serious wobble? It has gorgeous tongue and groove joints. Proportions as pleasing as the Parthenon's. One of a kind, if it went for a jaunt around town, it wouldn't meet itself coming and going, like I do in my Gap jeans. Each time my eyes alight on it, I wonder about that little carpenter? Big now—with his own kids? Living in a trailer in Idaho? I guess, in this case, we could call it an *imagination* bond.

As for the chair I'm sitting on right now . . . Built to outlast Mount Rushmore, and therapeutic for my sacroiliac, I found it up the road, along with some serviceable smoky blue fabric for reupholstering the seat. Two dollars. The seller was the town's retired minister. Yesterday, when I stopped to buy perennials from her (also two dollars, which, even compared to the chair, seemed like a gift), she said, "You're the writer, right?"

"Yes," I said, "and I write with my rump on *your* chair."

Funny, I still think of it as "hers." With yard sale booty, I often feel more like the caretaker than owner. Perhaps it's because, emanating a whiff of their past, they hint at their future—and mine. I don't know where this chair will end up—but it's bound to outlast me, and unlike me, gain in value as it moves along.

In *Care of the Soul* Thomas Moore advocates "soul work" aimed at deepening the connection we have to "ancestors and to living brothers and sisters in all the many communities that claim our hearts." He believes that soul emanates not only from living things but from "made things" also; and that "If you don't love things in particular, you cannot love the world . . ."

"History is good food for the soul . . . ," he writes. "We decorate our homes with antiques as a way of capturing soul . . ." Furthermore, he says: "Soul loves the past and doesn't merely learn from history but feeds on the stories and vestiges of what was."

So—what else could he be talking about but yard sales!

Maybe I'm getting a little carried away here, putting a lofty spin on what many frankly find depressing. ("All that moldy polyester clothing and hair rollers with other people's hair still in them!") Maybe I'm dignifying what's really nothing more than a desire to exploit some poor woman who doesn't realize that her orange Fiestaware pitcher and Hopalong Cassidy lunch box could buy a week of day care and a mammogram—at least.

Besides: Just how harmless is this yard sale mania anyway? I have heard of at least one casualty. The wife said, "Choose: me or the junk." The husband chose. Now every few years, she or one of their kids, on their way to somewhere else, stops by and says hello to him at the yard sale he gives on some back road in Maine 365 days a year.

Me? I've already mentioned my table and chair, but not this sisal rug and the two small rag rugs, not the three plastic mirrors (ten cents apiece) that make my eight-by-twelve study look a lot bigger. Outside is a gorgeous meadow and view of Mount Monadnock—inside, objects that tell stories connecting me to the past and to people near and far. My soul feels spacious here—well cared for. And today, I'm feeling especially buoyant because tomorrow is Saturday.

I'll rise early to pick blueberries. Our breakfast of honeydew, peaches, and bananas absolutely demands a little blue. I'm aware that given the amount of suffering in the world, my sense of urgency about the blueberries could be viewed as a grotesque distortion of priorities; yet, here, too, Moore comes to the rescue: "The most minute details and the most ordinary activities, carried out with mindfulness and art, have an effect far beyond their apparent significance." I hope he's right. In any case, as with any sport, diet is crucial, and I have found that a beautiful fruit salad is an excellent way to begin a day of yard-sa(i)ling.

I may end up like that man in Maine. My partner, Sandy, is getting nervous and not without reason. In the six weeks since we've been in New Hampshire: a wrist strengthener, a tummy trimmer, a dancing Coke can, Hamilton Beach blender, metal sign that says *Monadnock, Chapter 66*, utensil for getting the last of the mustard or mayo out of the jar, toaster oven that won't turn off, Boggle, Pictionary, popcorn salt, a hot-pink linen jacket, two pepper mills, three wrought-iron monkey-shaped hooks, four breadboards . . . And I'm still longing for that hundred-percent-wool afghan I passed up.

It was made by the seller (moving to her new husband's place) and if I believe her (which I do, absolutely) it won first prize in a crafts fair. She was willing to go down to twenty, but I had fifteen in mind as my limit (so much for being bold and capricious) and didn't have the heart to haggle anymore. Last week I dreamt I went back and there it was still, with its little white tag—and my name on it!

In real life, I'm stuck with Aunt Bertie's ugly acrylic one that's unraveling. I guess I'll just have to give my own yard sale. Yes "give," as in gift or party. Mine will have music and lemonade. Bertie's afghan will sell for a song. But if all goes as it should, I'll someday come across it again. My son or friend or friend's friend will buy it back from the daughter of whoever bought it from me—for she will have mended it, tastes change, and really, while wool is nice, acrylic is less itchy and it lasts forever.

♦

Always Someone!

Barbara likes boar; Gayle, pigeon. Robin is partial to duck. I, Leslie, with my vegetarian leanings, suggest the *pasta con asparagi*, but Barbara detests *asparagi*, and Dee insists on *pasta con tartufi* because "You can't go to Tuscany and not try the truffles!"

Oh, yes-you-can, I'm thinking, for hadn't that renowned gourmet (my mother) given me the final word on the subject. ("Not worth the price.")

"I can't do spicy," Miriam says. "Maybe we should each get our own."

"But that's no fun!" several proclaim in unison.

Fun? Tonight I'm beginning to wonder. Granted, the trip started off well. That first evening in Orvieto, we were on kissing terms with the waiter. The next day our collective brainpower successfully negotiated every surface in the Signorelli chapels. And when we arrived at the archeological museum just as it was closing, no one got miffed. But now it was day three, and just an hour before these protracted ruminations over the menu, we were debating who would ride with whom in which of our two cars and where each of us would sit.

Barbara and Leslie lobbied for the front because they get carsick—or so they say. Robin believes they are simply hypochondriacal prima donnas. The truth, according to Robin—and we know this from last year's trip—is that when Leslie drives, she jerks, and when Miriam drives, she wiggles, but if Robin takes the wheel, the ride will be so smooth no one will get sick. As for Dee, only she is insured to drive the wagon, which simplifies things; but Miriam doesn't want Barbara up front because she can't read a map; and Gayle, being tall, needs extra legroom.

The waiter appears.

"Finally!" Robin says with an all-too-windy sigh. She's convinced we've been denied good service because we are, after all, "just a bunch of aging women." I think the place is understaffed, and slow is the Italian way.

"*Agua naturale per tutti,*" she commands, with a sweeping gesture.

"*Scusi,*" I say, "but *io preferisco 'con gas.'* And it's *acqua,*" I can't help adding. "*Agua* is Spanish."

Robin shoots me a look of mock apology. Probably I deserve it, but what makes her think she can order for everyone!

Between her and me there's a long and complex history. As my ex, she's the one I love—and love to loathe—best.

I feel like a fool. This was my idea—this week in Italy with a "bunch of aging women." What could I have been thinking?

(What a tired idea the nuclear family is, even the "alternative" kind! How nice to have adult time without the usual domestic quarrels! I'm too old to hit the road alone, just me and my backpack!)

This bunch of women is wonderful, of course. Funny, intelligent, creative, mature women—experienced travelers all. No loneliness. No spouses with whom to fight the usual, tired fights. No kids whining *I'm bored.* Probably I was remembering what fun we'd had the previous summer when the same group, give or take a couple, had stayed at a writer's *pension* in France. Foolishly, I had failed to consider that the *pension* had served meals and arranged most of our outings, thus blessedly limiting our options. And conveniently, I had simply blocked out how long it always takes to get anywhere when there's always someone who has to pee or call home, someone who can't pass up a single pottery store, someone who insists on making acquaintance with every passing dog.

But whatever I was or wasn't thinking when I brought up the idea of another trip, I certainly should have seen the writing on the wall when it took two months to settle on dates, and several more of nearly full-time work to find the right country place, one that could accommodate some people's need for private baths as well as other people's need to keep it cheap.

Fun?

No one could say we're not a lively bunch. And very clever. The dinner conversation has us all laughing like we haven't laughed since high school. Furthermore, after one bite, Barbara decides she adores *asparagi*, and I have moved over to the boar camp. But now the bill arrives.

Four of us (after endless email proposals and counterproposals) resolved to try Gayle's system: Everyone puts equal amounts of cash in a kitty and all meals and gas get paid out of that. But, for some reason, Barbara and Dee were not in on that chat and had intended to pay by credit card, thus earning miles for another such fun trip.

Now we spend so much time working this out that by the time we get back to our splendid apartments high on a hill at the *agrituristica*, we need a midnight snack.

And all this is *after* we all agreed to follow Gayle's suggestion for minimizing tedious negotiations: Express a preference only when we feel really strongly about it.

The next night we cook at home. I want to eat outside at the stone table with its spectacular view of the vineyards. Robin, however, is afraid of the bugs, Miriam, of the cold. Taking a quick poll, Miriam decides the "insides" have it. I, a mature, flexible person, resolve not to point out that several group members were absent when the poll was taken. I, a childish, rigid person, must drink several glasses of wine before I stop fuming over how much better it would have been to eat under the Tuscan stars.

Days pass. One, maybe one and a half, but time crawls when you're having so much fun. Maybe it's because I've had a bad sore throat and slight fever, or because I, one of the younger members, have just gotten my mood-enhancing peri-menopausal period. Whatever, while everyone else keeps exclaiming about the fabulous time they're having, I notice I'm not saying much. And after another day or so—punctuated by a spectacular bike ride and a transporting visit to a Cistercian abbey where we hear the monks sing vespers—my weariness with group dynamics has escalated into some ugly spats that have left me feeling a touch vicious and unloved. (I know the two are connected somehow but am feeling too muddled to know which is causing which.)

That night, dinner is at home (inside again!). When the conversation turns to our next trip. I blurt it out: "I'm not so sure I'm enjoying this one!"

Most are surprised; everyone is concerned and sympathetic. They listen attentively to all the little incidents that have corroded my spirit. They listen without judgment or reproach. Not for nothing have we collectively spent several thousand hours on the couch and in t-groups, board meetings, and retreats. We talk a little about how my position in the group might replicate feelings I've had with my family of origin. Someone points out that I've been sick, which could easily explain my heightened sensitivity. Another admits I'm not the first to find her style of decision-making a bit tyrannical. I conclude that trying to follow Gayle's advice has backfired on me. Either because I don't know what I feel strongly about, or, more likely, because I feel strongly about everything, I end up not pushing for anything.

I don't know exactly what does it, but after that night nothing—and everything—changes. My bad throat has turned into a simple cold; my hormones have leveled off. Relieved of the burden of secrecy and self-blame, now I, too, can laugh through our summits and squabbles. And on our last night, when we're once again batting around destinations for next spring, I cheerfully propose another spring in Tuscany for there's so much more to see!

It's not that I've forgotten my misery of just a few days before; it's just that the joy that preceded and followed and even occasionally interrupted it, that joy has been so abundant I'm now convinced I love traveling with a group. I love how there's always someone to get up early and buy the biscotti, someone to stay up late and discuss one's neuroses. Someone who can distinguish St. John from St. Jerome, Puccini from Rossini, who can help me see the poignancy of those early Sienese paintings that used to give me the creeps. I even love what happens when I don't get what I want; for example, when I, a person who would *never* eat a gelato before dinner, has for the sake of the group, agreed to do exactly that—only to discover that the sky doesn't fall, I still enjoy my dinner, and that hazelnut—it's out of this world.

———◆———

Swinging

She flew through the air with the greatest of ease, while *I*, neck craned, mouth ajar, realized I had wasted my vacation. If I ever return to a Club Med, I vowed, I will cut down on the tennis, the lounging, the competitive eating; I'll skip the archery, Trivial Pursuit, and hat-making; and, like this woman roughly my age and shape, I'll devote my time to something really useful like learning to fly on the trapeze.

At the very least, I'll show up for instruction.

And show up I did. It was a year or two later when my parents again took our family to a Club Med. Directly after Monday's lunch buffet (enough to feed a small nation), I found my way to the circus area where for two, maybe three, hours I watched mostly aging Tarzans and preteen Janes climb forty feet, grab hold of a bar and swing through the air, blithely it seemed to me. And not only that, but they did tricks. Club Med regulars, apparently—they hooked their knees and hung upside down. One even let go of his bar and grabbed another on the fly.

There was nothing I'd call "instruction"—no exercises for strength or flexibility, no videos, no step-by-step simulations or visualizations—just a bench on which to sit and watch and wait until your turn came up.

And so I sat and watched and waited, and when my turn came up, I watched myself offer my turn to the next person in line. I did this on Monday and again on Tuesday before realizing that all this watching wasn't helping and I had to *just do it*. Not only had I announced my intention to my entire family, but if I wimped out on this one what could I expect of myself next Monday morning when I began a new job teaching in one of the city's toughest high schools? Courage breeds courage. So on Wednesday I *just did it*.

Sort of. When my turn arrived, I sucked in my gut and buckled up tight. So what if a little fat poked out around the canvas safety belt.

(Where were all the women my age?) I didn't want to risk slipping out of the thing. Not that I could fathom how the rope, attached to the front of the belt—and threaded through a complicated array of pulleys and held by a skinny guy standing next to the net—was going to prevent me from falling at full speed. (Yes, there was a net, but I took little comfort from it.)

"The climb is the hardest part," said the few veterans willing to admit any part of it was hard.

I didn't think I could do it, but the no-nonsense counselor above me, the G.O., "Gracious Organizer" in Club Medese, thought I could. Trembling, eye on the rung just above, I climbed. And then, trembling even more now, so that the whole complicated array of ropes and pulleys and planks and nets seemed to be trembling too, I continued to climb . . . until it was time to take that big, wobbly step onto the narrow plank she was standing on. There she hooked another rope to the back of my belt. Thus secured, I braved a look straight ahead and a little up: Nothing but blue sky, striped here and there by the fronds of the highest palms.

With her long wand, the G.O. hooked the trapeze bar and brought it close.

"Now," she says, putting my left hand on the cable, "reach for the bar with your right hand."

That's when I make the mistake of looking down at the net—so far away, so loosely meshed.

"I've got you," she says, demonstrating with a little tug on my belt. This G.O. looks solid, strong, but she's beltless. If I lose my balance, won't I just drag her down with me?

"Go on," she says with surprising gentleness. "Just thrust out your hips and lean forward and reach."

It seems a foolproof way to lose my footing.

"Go on, now . . . Thrust. Lean."

I have no intention of doing this, but as if her voice is wired to my hips, they go out. And my arms, they reach. The bar is still a slab of sky away. "Lean," she repeats and I do. The bar is in my sweaty fist. "There!" she says, as if I might actually feel better now at this gravity-defying angle. How, I wonder, does one wash throw-up off a net.

"Now step," she says . . . , "Step. And grab with your left hand."

"I'm not strong enough." It sounds like a moan, a plea.

"If a ten-year-old can do it, so can you."

"No!" I say, resolute. In my mind I'm already climbing down.

"Would you feel better," she asks, "if you began with the bar in both hands?"

Something in my face must reveal that I'm considering this. Already she is reaching for the left side of the bar, telling me to take my hand off the cable and grab it. "I've got you," she says, proving it with another little tug at my belt. "Just step."

She says it casually, but they lied: *this* is the hardest part—for what the Gracious Organizer means is I am to remove one foot from its perch, bring it forward, and shift my weight so that my other foot comes off too. *Step.* The word has a *clompy* sound I associate with brick or cement, but I am being told to step into air, invisible molecules, loner-types each keeping as far from the others as possible. My hands are clammy. I failed President Kennedy's pull-up test. As for the net—it's far. It's holey. So what makes me do it?

A childish faith in authority? A latent death wish? An as yet unexplored erotic pleasure in obeying? I do it. I step. *Down . . . Up . . .* My grip holds. *Down . . . Up . . .* With breathtaking *un*ease, but by the third or so swing, I manage to breathe and a thought flies in: *Someday, maybe, if I do this a thousand times, I might come to like it.* By the next swing, my pride kicks in. People are watching—Sandy, Sam, my sister, her husband, my nephews, my parents, strangers, too. I must do more than just *this*. I must gain command of my now floppy legs and tuck my knees up enough to hook them over the bar. *Down . . . Up.* I can't get my legs high enough or at quite the right angle, and already I'm tired.

"Down," I call to the wisp of a guy.

He doesn't try to dissuade me. As with all the others, he guides me through the drop.

"Kick front . . . Back . . . Knees to chest . . . *Now* . . ."

The net is gloriously buoyant. I flop-flop like a walrus, but there's no pain, and in the photo my sister takes, my smile is big.

Once on firm ground, I get in line again.

My second time the climb is still agonizing, the reach for the bar still heart-thumping, the "*just* step"—*that* part is a *little* easier. And after just a couple of *down/ups . . .* , I'm attempting the hook with my knees and this time I manage it. Oh, what single-mindedness a little terror can bring! (Though I've since discovered that a good game of Scrabble can provide the same exquisite clarity of focus.) My knees hooked, I succeed in arching my back so that I feel like an upside-down rocking horse, robust *and* graceful.

The next day, although I'm still scared of the climb, the step, the reach, while I'm swinging I'm pleased. Not because I'm feeling more prepared for Monday morning. Not because I'm showing all the boys how tough I am. Not because it's reassuring to know I'm not yet ready for the shuffleboard set. I'm pleased because it feels so good. There's just something about a swing. And the longer the ropes the more magical it is.

"Please explain," I later say to my one friend who knows a bit of physics.

She draws a diagram. Straight and curvy lines, dots and arrows, "kinetic" scribbled here, "potential" there. Somehow this doesn't help. What helps, I later learn, is listening to jazz.

Vocational schools start ridiculously early. Often the sky's still a bruisy blue as I drive along the Charles River. Perfect for Billie Holiday. Think of her *Come . . . to . . . me*—the way she lags just a little behind the beat, then dangles you on the *my . . .* before pouring out that honey-like *mel . . . an . . . cho . . . ly . . .* How I love that spacious moment before the descent.

————◆————

The Third Hottest Pepper in Honduras

The first time I observed Ms. Taylor's Senior English class they were discussing *Hamlet*.

"Should Ophelia trust Hamlet's expressions of love?" Ms. Taylor asked.

"No way!" Keena called out. Several others also shook their heads.

"Why not?" Ms. Taylor pressed. "Mavis . . . ? Are you with us? No? Tran? Don't look at me. Look at the text."

Keena started to speak, but Ms. Taylor shushed her, making brief but meaningful eye contact with each of the other dozen or so students facing her.

She waited.

I watched. In a few weeks she would be leaving for a six-month stint teaching in Cambodia. I'd signed on to be her replacement.

One boy, with his back to the horseshoe arrangement, had his eyes fixed on the Boston skyline a mile or two away. This million-dollar view was a selling point for me, and I enjoyed the irony of finding it here in Madison Park, a vocational high school in one of Boston's most blighted neighborhoods. The other dreamer, a girl wearing headphones, had her eyes half-closed and inclined toward the ceiling while she mouthed the words to her song. The rest of the students had their noses in *Hamlet*.

"Perfume?" one small voice said.

"Way ta go, Maria." Ms. Taylor said. "Laertes compares Hamlet's words to perfume. But what's so bad about perfume?"

Maria shrugged.

"Look at the text. James? Damien?"

The room was silent. Ms. Taylor waited. Five long seconds . . . maybe more.

"It's sweet but not lasting!" Maria cried out.

"Yes!" Ms. Taylor said, breaking into a big smile.

I had approached this class skeptically. *Hamlet?* The language of Shakespeare is a stretch for most native English speakers and would be doubly so, I assumed, for these students, the majority of whom were born in—you name it—Brazil, Cambodia, Vietnam, Puerto Rico, the Caribbean, Guatemala, Somalia, Nigeria, Cape Verde . . . And it *was* a stretch. When they read the text aloud, even the most proficient students struggled to pronounce the words. Making sense of them required an almost physical effort that left the students thrilled but spent. Yet line by line, under Ms. Taylor's direction, everyone seemed to grasp the story line and give themselves over to the characters' dilemmas. Everyone, that is, but the two tuned-out students. ("Up all night selling drugs," Ms. Taylor later said of the boy. And of the girl: "Bad situation at home." She wasn't just being flip, I later learned—she knew each kid's story.)

"So what *is* Laertes advising his sister?"

"Not to do it with Hamlet?" Russell proposed.

Ms. Taylor nodded. "Exactly!"

I wondered if I'd just hit them on a good day when the subject was spicy and close to home. But subsequent classes over the next couple of days convinced me that much of *Hamlet* was uncannily relevant to these students. For one thing, the violence was familiar. Even the substantial number of students who lived in safe, orderly households were never far removed from the high-drama tales of murder and revenge that appeared in the neighborhood papers and spread through the corridors at school. Furthermore, as Ms. Taylor reminded them, the Prince was seventeen, a student like themselves who studied in a foreign land, far from home. And Ophelia, she was even younger and had all the questions about love and sex and trust that they had. Everything about the way Ms. Taylor approached the material conveyed her belief that Shakespeare was writing for them as much as anyone else, and the students bought it.

I was impressed. Inspired. The kids seemed bright and motivated; they touched and excited me. There was Nadine, an African American with attitude to spare, a novel-in-the-works at home, and a new gender-bending getup every day. (Black lipstick and lacy long johns beneath army fatigues!) And there was Ha. In her native Vietnam she had been severely burned by a kerosene fire and unable to go to school for five years. Now she was on her way to being valedictorian. Slight and quiet, she had the grace of a heron and the tenacity of a bull terrier.

Ms. Taylor assured me the workload would be manageable. A student teacher would take two of my courses, leaving me with just four others—two in Senior English, two in Journalism, all relatively small and each meeting only twice a week. As for overseeing the school paper, Maurice, the student editor, was highly responsible, and besides, the kids knew the routine.

I decided I was game. So what if I was "overqualified," as the dean had brusquely pronounced upon eyeing my resume documenting almost twenty years of teaching writing in colleges and graduate schools. I needed a job. And although this one didn't pay particularly well, it offered adventure, a way to break out of a life that I had noticed was becoming increasingly insular. As a high school girl in Queens, New York, I'd acquainted myself with the wider world by reading—*Black Boy, Black Like Me, The Other America*. I was president of my high school's "Human Relations" club; I participated in exchange programs with students from Harlem; in the summer, I lived and worked on a Blackfoot Indian reservation in Montana. During college and afterward I traveled extensively, physically and psychically. As a college teacher, I attended dozens of panels and workshops with titles like "Dismantling Racism" and "Valuing Diversity." Even so, I'd noticed that although my son seemed entirely at home in his racially balanced school, all the friends he invited home were white. I didn't have to look far to find explanations: my own guests were an equally homogenous bunch, and when my son and I were out on the streets of Cambridge and I ran into people I knew, they, too, were almost always white.

So, yes, I had my selfish reasons for wanting this job—I felt I was missing out by not having more contact with people of color; I wanted to feel more at home in my own multiracial community—but also, I thought I could do a good job. Although my experience with high school teaching was limited to brief stints in largely white, upper-middle-class schools, most of them long ago, teaching was teaching, I told myself. I had a master's in the art of it, and, as a veteran teacher of College Writing, I knew what high school seniors should be working toward. At the very least, I reasoned, I'd do a better job than the disaffected, untrained sub they would otherwise most likely get. Furthermore, I'd have two more weeks of training in which I could learn from Ms. Taylor.

Two years would have been better, but already I had picked up a lot. I had noticed, for example, how physical she was with the kids—hugging the ones she hadn't seen in a while, affectionately clonking the heads of the ones whose attention drifted—unless, that is, she'd made a calculated decision to ignore a particular dreamer or doodler for the day. I saw how she, a statuesque, olive-skinned Jew (I'm a petite, pale one) earned their trust by coaching the girls' basketball team and staying late to teach a prep course for the SATs. How she made it her business to learn about their families, their churches, their talents, and traumas. How her sternness was always mingled with compassion—a compassion so habitual and far-reaching, I once caught her encouraging a bug-ridden computer in the same way she would a troubled student. She'd be a tough act to follow, but I figured that the structures and routines she'd established, and the positive attitudes she'd nurtured, would carry over to me.

My main job during my official training period was to help students with their *Hamlet* term papers. These were a requirement for graduation, one for which Ms. Taylor had lobbied hard because she wanted—expected—a good portion of her students to go to college, and for that they needed experience with academic writing. Of course I agreed, but after a few hours of working with individual students, I began to appreciate the enormity of the task before us. The critical articles they were expected to read and cite were tortuous to most of them. And while several students could relate the play to their own lives in powerful and touching ways—"My father also died and my mother dishonored his name by marrying too soon"—such comparisons didn't add up to an arguable thesis. I figured that the best first step would be to simply chat with students about what had struck them in the play. Laureen and I got off to a slow start, but when she casually called Hamlet a transformer, I thought we might be on to something.

"Yes, go on."

"A transformer," she repeated.

"You mean he has a transforming effect on others?"

She shook her head.

Transformer? Some new pop psychology phrase akin to "enabler"? The only other "transformer" I knew was the metal cylinder on power lines, beaming out possibly dangerous electromagnetic fields.

After a lengthy who's-on-first-like exchange, I realized Laureen was comparing Hamlet to one of those brashly colored, monstrous plastic action figures my eight-year-old had recently introduced me to. Push a button, one head retreats, another pops up; pull a lever, the shoulders sprout wings.

Hamlet. Transformer.

Transformer. Hamlet.

The comparison seemed both ludicrous and marvelous, but before we had a chance to explore it further, the bell rang—at which point, I glanced at the boy next to Laureen whom I'd intended to "help" next, and saw that his paper was shredded. So many times had he erased what he'd written that not a single word remained intact.

By the time Ms. Taylor left, maybe three-quarters of the students had completed a paper she deemed successful. This seemed miraculous, especially considering that several of the remaining quarter had shown up only once or twice since the semester began. (Next to one of those names in the grade book, I noticed the word "incarcerated.") It would be my job to help and prod the ones who still had a chance. This was the only bit of old business I had to deal with. As for future World Lit texts, I was limited by what books were available—Ms. Taylor had ordered Salman Rushdie's *Haroun and the Sea of Stories.* Beyond that I could more or less do my own thing, and Ms. Taylor encouraged me to play to my strengths, that is, work primarily on student writing.

I had what I thought was the perfect first lesson. I would ask students to freewrite on their names, then read aloud or just talk about what they'd written. I had used this icebreaker with countless groups of various ages and levels, and it had never failed to increase people's comfort with writing, with each other, and with me. It also helped people plumb deeply buried feelings and it always elicited much wonderful writing. Now I had what would surely be the ideal group for this exercise—hailing from so many different places and having names both splendid and strange.

I began with brief instructions on what I meant by "freewriting"—my usual spiel:

Write quickly, don't stop. Don't worry about grammar or spelling or punctuation. Don't worry about what others will think of what you're saying. These won't be graded, and you don't have to share them if you don't want to. If you get stuck, don't stop, just keep repeating yourself or writing "stuck" "stuck" "stuck" until a new thought comes. The writing, of course, will be messy and full of mistakes, but that's okay—these are meant as a warm-up, a way to mine your brain. We'll write for about eight minutes. No talking while we write. Any questions?

Usually there are a couple, but this time the questions, the balking, and bitching went on and on:

"Do we write about our first name or last?"

"There's nothing to say about mine."

"I don't have a pencil."

"I sprained my thumb yesterday."

"I miss Miss Taylor."

Most kids, I think, genuinely wanted to cooperate, and in the end, quite a few came up with something interesting—one boy was named after an uncle who died choking on a chicken bone; another, after Portugal's greatest soccer player—but what should have taken twenty minutes took forty-five and a couple of kids produced nothing at all. One had spent his time drawing magnificent cartoons. And another—I had been excited to see him writing nonstop, but when I took a closer look I saw his name, again and again, in giant loopy script—three or four pages of this and just this. He, I later learned, had "special needs," as did many of my students. The term was relatively new then, new at least to me, for colleges had not yet started to admit such kids, at least not knowingly. The phrase clearly implied that *someone* knew what those needs were and knew how to meet them, but if that was the case, no one had shared their knowledge with me.

When it was time to read aloud or just talk about what they'd written, only two students volunteered. Near the end of class, I asked students to exchange phone numbers so they'd have someone to call about the homework if they were absent—creating a sense of community is always my first priority. Well, I was prepared for some flack at the h-word (Ms. Taylor had told me it was hard to get them to do any), but what surprised me were the several students who refused to give out their numbers. "My mother told me to never give it out," one shy Latina explained. Others, I later learned, were worried about calls from the immigration officials or a cousin's parole officer.

The day wasn't a total failure, but I was struck by the amount of energy required to achieve so little. I, too—like Hamlet, like my immigrant students—was in a foreign land. There was a lot I would need to learn before I could demonstrate even a modicum of cultural sensitivity.

Overqualified? I'd had my doubts all along. I had switched from high school to college teaching in part because the latter was a breeze in comparison. Now I cringed at the foolish vanity that had allowed me to bask in the dean's assessment. What use were my elaborate, well-honed systems of responding to first drafts, of teaching students how to evaluate their own work and respond to the work of their peers, if there were no drafts to begin with or not enough trust to share them with others?

Sobered, I arrived the next day with a new bag of tricks: two "Name Your Baby" books and several Xeroxed copies of the book's special section on popular African American names—the Asians had to go it alone. The books created much excitement. "My name means lion," one boy roared. "Mine, king," said another, flexing his muscles. I thought high school students were a little old for such strutting; still I was delighted by the enthusiasm. One boy was so turned on he wanted to Xerox the whole book!

In another class, after trying freewriting again and encountering only slightly less resistance, I handed out an excerpt from Sandra

Cisneros's *House on Mango Street*. This two-page meditation on the name Esperanza had been a real crowd-pleaser when I'd used it with college students and adults. Sensuous and lyrical, imaginative and emotional, it would serve as the perfect model for the revision I wanted these students to do of their free-writing—or so I thought. In fact, several students seemed intrigued, but near the end of class, a girl named Lupita loudly proclaimed: "With Miss Taylor we were doing term papers on *Hamlet*. Now we're doing baby stuff!"

Baby stuff. The phrase haunted me, even though Lupita's "friend" had looked at me sympathetically and said, "When we were doing *Hamlet*, she complained about that!"

The ironies both amused and unsettled me. Here was a Latina female snubbing Cisneros in favor of Shakespeare, personal reflections in favor of term papers. I was reminded of an article I'd read years before. Lisa Delpit, an African American educator, argued that freewriting was all well and good for elite white students who knew standard grammar and needed loosening up, but most minority students, she insisted, needed to learn standard grammar in order to gain entrance into the dominant culture. All that loosey-goosey stuff, she said, was selling them short. I didn't agree at the time: I believed there was room for both imagination and mechanics, freedom and discipline, just as I have always believed there is room for both dead white males and live women of color. But now I wondered if I ought to ally myself with Delpit. I started second-guessing myself at every turn.

Of course, every teaching situation—every student, really— requires one to continually reassess and recalibrate. Jose, one senses, needs pumping up; Franklin a kick in the butt. Last week, Darlene needed time out to cool off; this week, she needs to be pulled back in. Such is the delicate balancing act any good teacher must perform. It requires dozens of little decisions every few minutes with success dependent on one's abilities to read countless subtle cues. Are tears, for example, evidence of too much stress or a calculated ploy for leniency? Is a complaint that work is too easy to be taken at face value or is it a cover-up for embarrassment that what sounds easy feels hard? I'd always prided myself on my ability to assess which students needed what and how hard I should push, but now, unschooled in the culture of poverty and racism and confronted by so many different personalities and codes of behavior, I was misreading some cues and being misread. How else to explain the costly blunder I made sometime after that "baby stuff" complaint?

I had come across an editorial by longtime United Federation of Teachers president Albert Shanker, much of which was in the voice of a straight-A student from the inner city who then transferred to a suburban school where she received Cs for comparable work. Realizing she didn't yet know half of what she would need for success in college, this girl, in a stern but compassionate tone, was trying to warn her brothers and sisters not to rest too easy.

I made copies of the article, passed it out, and we read it together. It seemed like a good way to convey that I, like Ms. Taylor, had no intention of selling them short. I believed they were capable of making it to college, but it wasn't going to happen without a lot of hard work. Probably some students took the article in the spirit I intended, but Nadine—my source for much information, not all of it true—told me later that some students were insulted by it. They felt I was putting them down.

If anyone else had delivered this news, I would have been quicker to shrug it off, but Nadine had some kind of hold on me, and I took the comment to heart. I even considered the possibility that some part of me hidden to myself had *wanted* to put a few of my students down. It was true I'd been feeling frustrated, embarrassed even, by my inability to control the few unruly ones who made it impossible for the others to learn. But no, I concluded, I wasn't trying to get back at anyone. Rather, I'd made the mistake of imagining that these kids would react to such a wake-up with renewed determination—just as *I* would have. Now I realized that *I*—*my* psyche, *my* habitual ways of reacting—might not be the best source of information about how these students would react. I hadn't considered how fragile many of these kids' self-images were. ("Why would you want to teach *here?*" more than one student asked me, bringing tears to my eyes.) I didn't think enough about how many times each day they were dragged down by reasons to give up; I didn't realize how easily they might interpret my attempt to motivate them as my way of saying they were too far behind to ever catch up.

Just how damaging that mistake was, I'll never know. I do know that shortly after it, I seemed to enter a period where I was getting not merely sullenness and lack of preparedness but rudeness and hostility. Take Henry—too handsome for his own good, I decided. Flashing his disarming smile, he'd arrive twenty minutes late and charge across the room, belting, "Yo. Wassup? How's it going?" Take Nadine. From that point on, she seemed out to get me at every turn. When I gave the winner of some class contest a prize (a never-touched blank journal I was reluctant to part with), Nadine publicly proclaimed it a cheap gift. Maybe she'd been hoping to win the contest herself? Or she saw how hard I was trying, how insecure I was, and reacted as any self-respecting adolescent would: perversely. Quite likely, her cruelty and Henry's histrionics and Veronica's surliness were just standard issue—part of a lengthy testing period these students—so frequently themselves the target of abuse—subjected all authority figures to. When I emailed Ms. Taylor about some of my frustrations, she wrote back that it took her "six months to get them to do anything," and she was sorry to hear that apparently they were going to "make me do all that work over again."

I don't mean to imply that those first few weeks were disastrous. They had their bright spots, the brightest of which may have been working with my student teacher. Though it seemed farcical for *me* to be mentoring anyone when I so needed mentoring myself, I loved observing and advising and conversing with Karen, who insisted that my insights and suggestions helped her prevail through some classes that were downright fiascos.

There were also encouraging moments in my own classes. In one I shared my freewriting on my name, saying that my father had changed his so it wouldn't sound so Jewish and hamper his business success. I confessed that while I longed for a name that felt more genuine, I was sometimes glad that I could keep my Jewishness hidden. I'm not sure what the students made of this, but their rapt attention told me they knew I was speaking from my heart. And this name unit that had started so inauspiciously led to several more spirited classes where we discussed an Israeli story called "The Name."

A woman is pregnant and her father wants her to name the new baby after his nephew who was killed in the Holocaust. The woman, on the other hand, objects to all reminders of the horrific past; she wants to give the child a modern, forward-looking Hebrew name. In my more rambunctious class with Nadine and Henry, and others, we debated whether it is better to remember or forget painful events. We listed the pros and cons of each approach. We tried freewriting again. James shared his piece about a fight he'd gotten into with a childhood playmate in Honduras. I don't remember how he'd offended her, but for some reason she was out to get him and did so stupendously by throwing a pepper in his face. "It was the 3rd hottest pepper in Honduras," James wrote. This was just the kind of spectacular detail freewriting often breeds. For me, it was a poignant reminder of all the knowledge this boy had that was common and crucial in Honduras but nearly useless here—except, of course, in its power to delight the teacher. When I got frustrated, as I often did, by just how much some students didn't know—how to address an envelope, where to put the stamp—I reminded myself of all they knew that I didn't.

Our discussion of the Israeli story led us to a poem by the Mexican American Lorna Dee Cervantes. Students enjoyed probing the images and the question the poem posed: What happens to our childhood memories that are "mown under"? Some spoke passionately about the pain of losing contact with their native country and the childhood they had there. They puzzled over what they would find if they dug up those memories—a "corpse" or a "seed." For homework, Celeste, a sixteen-year-old mother (there were two or three mothers in each class and probably as many fathers) wrote about having lost out on all the fun of being a teenager. That period is like a corpse, she wrote, "gone forever." Another student, who was responsible for the care of her severely asthmatic mother—as well as several younger siblings, one of whom was awaiting a liver transplant—wrote that she'd never had a childhood at all.

In these few memorable classes, students saw, as they did with *Hamlet*, that literature could speak to their deepest concerns. They experienced the magic of metaphor, the power of their own voices when they speak their heart's truths. And they saw how a well-chosen detail can evoke a whole, long buried world. They were less inhibited about revealing themselves by connecting to what they read than if I had simply asked them to write about themselves.

These successes sound substantial to me now, yet at the time my pleasure in them was overshadowed by the number of students who came without their homework or didn't come to class at all. And as I moved into what I think of as the middle and most discouraging period of my six-month stay, the victories began to feel more and more piddling. Maybe because my sense of urgency was growing. How would we ever get out even one issue of the school paper? How would my seniors learn even a quarter of what they needed to make it through a month of college? What should I be doing here, anyway? Would college teachers and future employers value a heightened self-knowledge and poetic sensibility as much as I did? Maybe I should put all my energy into teaching sentence structure, vocabulary, the use of the apostrophe? Like Delpit, I wanted to give the students the currency they needed to succeed in the dominant culture, but I had misgivings about concentrating solely on that. As the prominent African American writer bell hooks has said, "Every step into the white, educated world is a step away from the only culture in which minority students have felt at home and validated."

Every good teacher struggles with the problem of too much to do in too little time, but in large urban public schools the needs are generally greater, the stakes higher, and the interruptions and impediments overwhelming. I wanted to scream every time the loudspeaker went on to announce a track team victory, every time we all had to huddle outside because some kid got his kicks pulling fire alarms. During my initial visits, the vocational emphasis of the school excited me. The TV studio and hair salon, the print shop and the student-run restaurant—they all made Madison Park a sexy, happening place. But now that I'd seen how many students didn't know "two" from "too" from "to," didn't even have a notebook or folder where all their English assignments went, I was becoming a back-to-basics fanatic. I started resenting the school's progressive features that I formerly applauded. These kids don't need more stimulation, I thought. They need quiet and calm. They ought to have English every day! Two out of five won't do it, especially because one of those is often missed in favor of some internship, field trip, or special visit from a local business. Better still, they should go to boot camp. The gentle kind, in a pastoral setting, far away from the baby brothers who need to be taken to the emergency room, from the uncles who need translators at court hearings, from the monotonous, deadening after-school jobs that buy them things they need to feel cool. I had an inkling of the psychological cost of leaving one's family and community, but from inside the chaotic world of this school, I was beginning to wonder if there was any other way.

Meanwhile, I seemed to be wasting more and more class time sparring with Henry, who didn't see why we shouldn't have a little party whenever he decided to stroll in, and with Lupita, who refused to put away her nail polish. I remember after one particularly unproductive class, one of the most diligent students said: "My family worked so hard and risked so much to come to this country so I could get an education, but," his eyes welled up, "I can't get one here. Nobody else wants to learn."

My eyes welled, too. I felt he was wrong. There were others, some who would even have admitted it. I berated my "overqualified self" for not knowing how to do right by them. At the same time, I realized that even the most seasoned teacher would have her work cut out for her here because the tone was controlled by those who bragged about their Fs.

I felt sad and fed up. I'd discover that a boy who said he'd gone to his internship never actually got there—had gotten lost and felt too defeated or embarrassed to call for better directions. I'd spend an hour with a kid discussing an alternative to the never-delivered term paper, and he would then disappear for three weeks. I'd try calling the parents of absent kids, but either no one was home or they didn't speak English or I'd leave a message that the student would erase before anyone else heard it. The one time I did actually meet with the parents, they were at as much of a loss as I was. African Americans, they had wanted their son to be proud of his heritage, but now they regretted not busing him to a white suburban school. I was so exhausted by 1:45 when the school day was over, I worried about falling asleep at the wheel. And one day Nadine—always quick to jab me where she knew it would hurt the most—accused me of never staying after school like Miss Taylor did.

What could I say? I *had* stayed a few times near the beginning, but less and less as fatigue and irritation settled in.

And then . . . None of this is easy to reconstruct, but the days got longer, and it wasn't quite so grueling getting up at 5:45. In our Journalism classes, the bare bones of articles came trickling in. Karen and I started working with their authors one-on-one, and it began to look as if we might get out an issue after all. Hilda sweated through five or six drafts of her lead article gleaned from several of Miss Taylor's letters from Cambodia. Nadine and Maurice worked hard to construct arguments for and against Ebonics. Tom polished his jazzy poem on why teachers shouldn't patrol the hallway. (Actually, I was the one who decided it was a poem when I saw the jagged margins; Tom told me he just didn't know how to format on the computer.) There were the usual diatribes against the Walkman Rule and the nasty lunch food, but there were also articles on the lack of black history in the curriculum, on the suspect popularity of Tommy Hilfiger, on abortion, gay marriage, sexually transmitted diseases; on what it means to be a man and on how it feels to live all alone, as this student did. There were reviews of art exhibits and original poems on God and love and Martin Luther King. Although a lot of the writing looked to me like it was done by much younger kids, the newspaper had substance, passion, and pizzazz. I couldn't have been more proud.

By then it was mid-May. Karen had to leave, and the very class that had once tortured her threw her a party with presents and loving, appreciative letters. As for the classes intent on torturing me, small victories continued to occur: when we wrote about my friend's double-exposure photographs, for example, or when we talked about why Rushdie believed so passionately in the power stories have to transform our lives. I can't claim there was any dramatic turnaround. Nevertheless, something started to shift in me.

I'm not sure what did it. Insights from veterans certainly helped. One day over lunch, I admitted to a guidance counselor that some of my students seemed amazingly immature—"amazingly" because I would have thought that with all their responsibility, taking care of younger siblings and working after school, that they'd have been *more* mature. "Yes and no," the woman said. "They've been forced to grow up too fast—and without the nurturing that allows someone to really grow up." And in late spring, during a late spring professional day, a guest speaker said something that stuck: "It's true most inner-city kids are years behind, but don't get angry at them for being where they are."

Perhaps I just got better at picking my battles? Or maybe now that we were in the home stretch, I was simply able to let go a little and relax? All I know is around the time that the newspaper came out and Karen was packing up, I was falling in love with the kids.

They'd gotten under my skin. I don't know how else to describe it—except to croon that line, as I often did then, smiling and shaking my head. Not that the aggravations ceased or even lessened, but I stopped taking them so personally and paid more attention to what gave me pleasure: Eric's pride when he taught me how to cut and paste on the Mac, Celeste's excitement when she told me she'd seen one of our vocabulary words in a magazine. I knew I would miss these kids, even—especially?—the ones who gave me the most grief. And I was full of "if only's." If only I hadn't been so green, so easily thrown off course by a little lip. If only I'd had my own classes from the start and not had to deal with the students' anger over Ms. Taylor abandoning them. If only I'd had more time. Even Ms. Taylor had floundered for six months, and I was convinced I was getting the hang of it now. I went to the dean and told her I'd be interested in a permanent job.

Senior classes end a good month before graduation, and I remember that last month as my best—not because I had only half as many classes, but because I began to see a lot of the seniors individually. They came voluntarily—eager for help finishing long-overdue assignments or for my feedback on their graduation speeches. Many of the students did their best work those last few weeks—maybe because individual help was what they needed all along. Graduation mania was in full swing, and already students were waxing nostalgic about their suddenly wonderful school with all its awesome teachers. Some started visiting me just to chat. Not Nadine, but I swallowed my pride and nominated her for the Intellectual Curiosity Award—which, in spite of everything, I believed she deserved. When she won, she must have found out who'd nominated her because a day or two later, she thanked me. No small victory, that one.

Graduation conflicted with some other obligation I had, but when I heard about what an emotional event it was, I regretted not making it more of a priority. One hot day in late June, I finished up the rest of my grading, cleaned out my drawers, said a few more good-byes and turned in my keys. But all summer I dreamed about the place. I dreamed, mostly, about Henry. He had plaintively begged me to pass him, but I didn't feel I could. I wondered if he'd gone to summer school or just given up on the whole education thing.

In the fall I went back to Madison Park for a visit. While I was hoping to see some of my sophomores and juniors, I went mainly to see Ms. Taylor, who hadn't responded to the messages I'd left on her machine. I was eager to learn what impression she'd gotten of the job I'd done.

When I arrived, she was talking to another teacher in the hall—and she just kept talking to that teacher for a long time, not acknowledging me at all, though I was sure she had noticed me. I was tempted to give a little smile and wave and then disappear, but that isn't my way and besides, I couldn't imagine why she was being so cold—so rude, really. I knew I hadn't been a smashing success, but I thought I'd done pretty well, all things considered. So I kept standing there feeling increasingly foolish until she couldn't avoid me any longer. When we stepped into her classroom, she came out with it:

She was upset that I'd failed so many seniors, especially because among the failures were a couple who had pretty decent skills.

I was shocked. I didn't know how many I had failed—I guessed six or seven, which didn't seem like a lot out of over fifty, especially since a couple of those had never shown up and one had come only once and only, it seemed, to show off the flashy pet iguana he cradled under his jacket. Of the others, either they hadn't done the term paper or they had but they'd done nothing since. None of these even seemed like hard calls—except possibly Henry, and only because he'd begged me and flashed me that smile of his that was so hard to resist.

Still, Ms. Taylor blamed me. Why didn't they come to class? I could imagine her wondering. Didn't you make it exciting enough? Didn't you call their homes after every absence like I told you to? Don't you know what they're up against? How complicated their lives are? How precarious their faith in themselves? How crucial it was at this juncture to give them the benefit of the doubt?

For months afterward, I caught myself rebutting her:

I tried to make some classes fun, but these kids are eighteen years old—they shouldn't expect everything to be fun.

Even if I had stayed late, Henry wouldn't have come, Lupita wouldn't have come. Could you at least give me a pat on the back for the school paper? Several people said it was the best issue ever!

I hated how defensive I sounded. In hindsight, I was sure I could have done better.

All this was years ago, and I've more or less made my peace with what I did and didn't accomplish at Madison Park. I never really pursued a permanent job there; I was offered a position at a prestigious university and I took it. As an adjunct, I don't get paid much there either, but I can teach whatever books I'd like, use their massive library, and stroll through their gardens and galleries. I don't need a key to go to the bathroom, and I don't doze off on my drive home. I have several students of color but few who aren't middle or upper class. Sometimes I miss the kids at Madison Park—their rawness, their hunger and daring: James's mastery of the hierarchy of Honduran peppers, Jose's all too intimate acquaintance with the brutality of the Guatemalan military, Paulina's embodied knowledge of Cape Verdean rhythms. I miss feeling as if I could make a difference in someone's life.

My current students generally come to class, do their homework, and show up for appointments. Many of them will eventually get good jobs, jobs that can make a difference, and I tell myself that I can influence what they will do with the power they will have. I encourage them to live an examined life. I expose them to theories about white privilege and interlocking oppressions. I assign them readings about the lives of kids who go to schools like Madison Park.

◆

III

On the Mowing

July '97

It's a good year for blueberries and I love blueberries, but I'm worried about where such abundance might lead in the long run.

The demise of the mowing?

The mowing is what brought me here, and the mowing—not the cramped, moldy cabin set back among the trees—is what has kept me coming back for more than a dozen years.

I learned of the place from an ad in the paper:

Quiet cabin with view of Monadnock.

"Quiet" was good—I was hoping to complete a novel—and "view" was essential—how else could one bear all those inside hours? But writing is lonely, and I didn't know a soul in New Hampshire. Born in New York City, now settled in Cambridge, Massachusetts, my hunger for country had generally taken me down roads with less dire license plates. Week after week, I noticed—and skipped over—that ad, but after rejecting a slew of too-suburban places in Massachusetts, I finally dialed 603, the "Live Free or Die" state.

The next day I followed the landlord's directions—along the familiar-numbered routes, to the unfamiliar ones, to the ones that had no numbers or names. *Right at the fire station; right again at the little red house; then follow the dirt road.* I followed and followed, through a forest so thick it offered barely a glimpse of rooftop or daylight. I hoped this guy was on the level, and I was beginning to lose faith, when I spotted the promised "Y" with its tree laddered by two-by-fours sporting a variety of stalwart names.

Pulling into the next driveway, I saw a skinny, fifty-something man with thick glasses, looking up from his woodpile. Was that a smile? Confronted by such tentativeness, my own voice boomed. "Are you Harvey Tolman?"

"Yup."

I offered my hand. He dropped his axe. We shook.

"We could take my truck," he said, "or walk up to the cabin through the mowing."

"Let's walk," I said—almost always the better choice, I've discovered, and "the mowing," whatever *that* was, reminded me of "the gloaming," from that song in *Brigadoon* that had once flared all my adolescent longings.

So off we went behind the woodpile, Harvey and I, weaving our way through a thick stand of trees until suddenly we were blinded by an astounding light.

There, sprawling in front of us was what I, raised in Queens, probably would have called a field. And a field, let's face it—even a small, flat, shorn one—is a good thing any old place or time but especially after a long, dark drive. And this one—five acres, ten? I don't have the acreage sense, but it was big. A whole world. Irregularly shaped, climbing and dipping and climbing again, you couldn't take it all in at one glance or guess how far it went. All you knew was the glory of so much tall grass doing what it does best—swaying in the bluesy spring wind.

The cabin was nowhere in sight. But just a step or two into that honey-colored expanse and I knew this was the place for me.

My first June "on the mowing," as I quickly learned to think of it, was cold, buggy, and lonely. Now and again, I saw station wagons parked on the western edge near paths that led who-knew-where but I never met their drivers. The cabin I'd pass near the bottom of the mowing was clearly uninhabited. As for the one about twenty wooded yards from mine, it lay eerily empty except on weekends when a jeep full of rowdy teenaged boys arrived, sometimes with parents, always with rifles they liked to fire at unpredictable hours and targets I didn't want to imagine. Mostly I stayed at my desk, from where I could look down the shaded grass driveway onto my slice of heaven. Often in parka and woolen hat, I sat there from morning until evening, save for a jog or garbage run—both of which took me down the mowing and up it again. At night I'd try to get out, just so I wouldn't get too weird. I'd go to one of the free chamber music concerts held in far-off churches, or to the weekly contra dance in the Nelson Town Hall where, neither welcomed nor shunned, I stumbled through reel after reel and spoke only a few words. More often than not, "mowing" was one of those words. I pictured it as "mowin'." Though I couldn't have told you its precise definition, just hearing the word fall from my lips made me feel more at home and in-the-know—the snob in me judging the in-the-knowness of strangers by how bliplessly the word registered with them.

Whether the excursion had been a balm for my loneliness or salt on the wound, I loved returning to the mowing at night—to its absence, really—its blackness glittering with fireflies. I'd stand at the end of the driveway, the sky above Montana-big, the jaunty fiddles and haunting bagpipes still in my ears, the simple *allemandes* and daunting *hay-for-fours* making my body hum. Still sweaty from dancing—I loved the way the dance progressed, the first couple becoming last and then, eventually, first again—I'd stand there, unable to name the feelings that kept me there long after the chill set in. If this was loneliness, it was delicious. If it was serenity, it was fringed with terror.

That was in '86 and '87. Since then, I've lived on the mowing every summer except one. My friend, the poet Miriam Goodman, now rents the cabin I first rented; I've moved to where the gun-happy family used to be. Set in the forest, it, too, is damp and dark, but all agree, its jutting porch on stilts offers the best view of the mowing and that trumps everything. I've had a nine-by-twelve writing studio built for me a few yards from there. I've also gained a life partner, Sandy, another woman, and given birth to our son, Sam.

"Mowing" is of course the present participle of the verb to mow, but it is also three nouns: the act of mowing, the yield of that act, and the place where that act occurs. Furthermore, in the *OED* it is an adjective—as in, "My little mare had provided for herself by leaping out of a bare pasture into a lot of mowing ground."

No fool, that little mare.

On our mowing, the life of our nontraditional family resembles a Norman Rockwell painting, and however hard I try, I can't summon the cynicism to knock it. Granted, it took Sandy a season or more to warm up to the place—too many mice and bugs, the lake water too cold, newspapers and cafes too far away—but now she's as in love with the place as I am; in love, especially, with the mowing. The mowing is where we have celebrated all but two of Sam's birthdays. Friends from the city come for puppet shows and piñatas, scavenger hunts and pajama relays. The mowing is where we play the kinds of ball games his age demands; where we engage in high-spirited marathons of hide-and-seek tag or attempt to fly one recalcitrant kite after another. The mowing is the permanent home of the tawny beanbag chair we bought at a yard sale—and there Sandy (better at relaxing than I) rereads all of Dickens or roughhouses with Sam. (I'm afraid she's the more fun Mom; I, the teacher and scold.) Both clock and calendar, the mowing is where we camp out to watch the meteor showers, where we spy deer and wild turkeys, eat our breakfast when the cabin is too cold, and drink our gin and tonics when the sun hasn't yet set. It's where the grasshoppers in August announce the coming of fall, where even low-slung city dogs become gazelles, where Augie, Corky's "replacement," leaps over his predecessor's ashes.

It was Nina, Harvey's ex-wife, who first put the fear of too many blueberries in me. It must have been shortly after their divorce. She was still living in the same house at the base of the mowing where I first met Harvey; and he with his new wife, Frankie, had moved to the neighboring farmhouse where he grew up. Walking with me on the mowing, Nina observed that Harvey had been neglecting the mowing, and if he didn't get on it soon—"Here, look!" she tapped her boot on a rock, "You can already see the signs—spongy moss!" She toed a sapling. "Maple trees!" She swept her head around and said matter-of-factly, "All these blueberries!"

"Signs of what?" I asked, already worried.

"Well, if you don't mow a mowing, pretty soon it becomes a forest."

Not such an original idea, I realize, but one that had never occurred to me. I had no more thought to question the longevity of the mowing than I had that of Mount Monadnock. Certainly I know nothing lasts forever, but I assumed that, barring forest fires and greedy developers, large-scale features of the landscape remained the same for generations. Didn't we return to such places year after year precisely because we liked to measure our own fickle selves against their steadfastness?

A few seasons back, I had been startled when a shiny car appeared on the mowing. Out came an older man in city clothes, his clean shirt tucked neatly into crisp khaki slacks. And when I nervously approached (we don't get many intruders here), he explained that some thirty or more years ago he'd summered on the mowing and just wanted to say hello to the place because it's the only one he knows that does not change a whit.

"Now, Harvey's father . . . ," Nina continued, as we stood there contemplating the mowing's future, "to him maintaining the mowing was like a religion. If he had to be out there twenty-four hours a day, that's where he would be!"

Before that conversation with Nina, I often noticed how the mowing would change from minute to minute as the sun and clouds engaged in their operatic battles, and occasionally from day to day, if Harvey or his son Colin happened to be out on the tractor mowing a stretch—an event that always brought mixed feelings since it made walking easier but gazing a little less blissful. Naturally, I also noticed the gradual changes from early summer to autumn. But now, I began to notice changes from year to year.

At first glance each June, everything looked the same—the same graceful descents to the south and east, the same roughly zigzagging swaths of browns and yellows and greens. But on closer inspection, the darker greens seemed to be gaining on the lighter ones, the terrain was becoming bumpier, the bordering trees growing taller and creeping inward, the view of Monadnock shrinking just a bit. "Eh, you're imagining it," others said. But one summer, confirming my sense of a sobering drift, a visiting friend twisted an ankle in a hole hidden by scrub. And whereas once I could blithely pick dozens of wildflowers, now I had to wonder if a handful for me would deprive my neighbors.

And the blueberries! We used to enjoy searching for them during those couple of weeks in late July, enjoy the batch or two of pancakes, the blueberry something we'd bake for Sam's August birthday. (Poor guy, he'd probably prefer chocolate, but I always feel compelled to make use of the berries.) Now with them covering most of the mowing, arriving in early July and staying through mid-August at least, we're wearily searching our cookbooks for recipes that might be enhanced, or at least unharmed, by the addition of blueberries.

Before Nina's comment, I generally regarded the mowing as a beautiful expanse of emptiness, a welcome absence of trees and irritating human and vehicular life. A place for stretching the legs, any old time but especially in the morning and evenings when the light is best and the bugs, alas, are the worst. A quiet, meditative place to rest my eyes when they drift from the monitor.

Afterward, propelled by fear—and embarrassment over the utter lack of curiosity I had shown for everything but the exotic (to me) name of my Shangri La—the mowing itself held new interest. It became not just a place for, but the object of, contemplation. And instead of spending the bulk of my time reading and writing fiction, I combed the local library's history and geography sections. Instead of walking the mowing for sheer pleasure—or to get to the lake or the eggs Frankie sold—I began to tromp around, Peterson guide in hand.

I saw, of course, tall grass, but now I knew that there are over five thousand species of grass. And I knew the answer to that crucial question I had never thought to ask: Why is it that you can mow down grass and it just keeps growing back? The answer, I learned, is something felicitously called the "*meri*stems," the tissues that produce new growth. In most plants, they reside near the tips, but in grasses, the meristems are safely hidden away near the base.

And along with grass, which I had thought of as the mowing's more or less sole component, I saw moss, lichen, twigs, stumps, oak and maple saplings, pygmy bushes, acorns, mushrooms, ragweed, milkweed, tall meadow rue, red clover, and yarrow—not to mention the countless varieties of insects, spiders, and other critters going about their business. Now I understood why one naturalist spoke about the "drama in every bush," another about "a riot" in his nearby meadow. I wondered if I would ever again be able to think of the mowing as a quiet, contemplative place. And I fretted over what all this multifariousness might bode for the mowing's future.

Enter Tom Wessels's marvelous book *Reading the Forested Landscape*. No doubt, "reading the landscape" is not a new idea. It's what hunters and gatherers have done for thousands of years. But the practice, as Wessels rigorously applies it, was new to me—and enthralling.

His point of departure is always a specific landscape. Then the observations and questions begin. Why is that apple tree so gnarled? This juniper so stunted? What can we surmise from this curious mixture of old and new growth? Each question leads to a hypothesis that is usually discredited by some bit of previously overlooked evidence that raises new questions, demanding we look farther afield, and further back in time so that soon Wessels is talking about the Pleistocene era, about Verrazano and John Winthrop and Chief Greylock. Reading Wessels, I began to understand the travesty of teaching about nature piecemeal—by simply identifying and categorizing this or that without wondering how one species impacts on another; and how human inventions, philosophies, and politics leave their marks on fields and forests and streams. I learned, for example, that Napoleon's defeat of Portugal transformed the landscape of New Hampshire.

But I'm getting ahead of myself here.

The indigenous people of New Hampshire were largely nomadic, so that when the "first" settlers arrived in the 1600s, they found almost no clearings—just trees, trees, and more trees. To the Europeans' way of thinking, since the natives didn't clear, enclose, or cordon off land, they didn't own it; and by extension of this bizarre logic, the Europeans concluded that they themselves, who almost immediately starting cutting trees and making fences, did own it.

They chartered the town of Nelson in the mid-1700s—and a rugged bunch they (and of course their predecessors) must have been.

One only has to live in our drafty, wood-heated cabin in early June or late August to start wondering how people survive the winters here now, let alone centuries or millennia ago when there were no shelters, no wells, no roads, no stores, no nothing. According to one history of Nelson, many of the "first" residents "would chop down his acre of heavy timber in a day, and drink a quart of rum, and chew a 'hand' of tobacco while doing it." Clearly these people were made of different cloth than we are today, and there seemed to be no shortage of them. When the British defeated the French and Indian Alliance in 1760, even more people came, and by 1790 Nelson had 7,621 people!

Which brings me back to Napoleon and his defeat of Portugal in 1809. This ended the embargo on exporting Portugal's valuable merino sheep and began the period called "sheep fever," in which half or more—some say 80 percent—of the mostly wooded land was cleared.

In those days, people worried about the vanishing forests; now the process is in reverse. Farmland and pastures and mowings are rapidly being reclaimed by forests. No doubt there are social and historical forces that accelerate this process—the demise of small farms, the overgrazing of pastures, the advent of Polartec and the diminishment of some mowers' commitment to mowing—but apparently this is also simply the way with clearings: sooner or later, they are overcome. "Succession" it is called.

Sooner? Or later? Will this mowing be here in five years? In fifteen? Will Sam, who turns eight this August, someday be that man who returns to the one place that hardly changes at all? Or will he search in vain for the landscape that obliterates the years between his *now* and *then*? For questions about the pace of change here, I always go to Ben Smith. He's the owner of one of those station wagons parked near hidden cabins I didn't venture near until my second or third summer, leery of how my Jewishness and relatively recent lesbianism would be received. But Ben turned out to be a progressive Unitarian. A gentle, handsome man who is now our friend, he has lived in that cabin nearly every summer of his nearly eighty years. When I ask him how the mowing has changed, he says, "Hardly at all." But then he adds, "They used to put manure on it and that made for better hay. Even so, the hay was never that great. Too many rocks.

"And there was an ice house behind the barn. And Harvey's grandmother Mildred used to make donuts. We would get our milk from there—unpasteurized. The mailman brought chickens and eggs.

"Before they had the dam at the lake, you could walk to the island, and that's where we had our sleep-outs."

To Ben, apparently, the "mowing" encompasses all a man might remember about his boyhood summers. I try to rein him in.

"We set up a badminton net," he recalls, "and tether ball. And once I got it in my head I wanted to be a pole-vaulter, so I brought out a bamboo pole and it broke.

"In my mother's paintings, you can see clear down to Harrisville, whereas now that's all trees."

"Was the mowing ever used for grazing?" I ask, wondering how many years we might have before it, too, becomes "all trees."

"Not since I've been here," he says, "but yes—sure—way back. It must have been used for sheep when Ebenezer first came. His house used to be where the French cabin is. Rumor has it some local schoolchildren were doing an archeological dig and located Ebenezer's well there."

The "French" cabin (so named because years ago a Parisian family summered there) is the one that sits near the bottom of the mowing, a hundred yards or more above Harvey and Frankie's place, which borders the dirt road. Ebenezer was Harvey's great-great-great-great-grandfather, I learn. Born in 1748, he fought in the Battle at Bunker Hill and settled in Nelson in about 1787. One history of Nelson quotes Ebenezer's praise for the town's "enchanting hills," but whether he was referring to wooded hills in the distance or clearings in his own backyard, I cannot say. I do know that by the early 1900s the land was probably cleared because that's when Wilmer, Harvey's grandfather, built the five "camps," as they call rustic cabins around here.

August '97

Our neighbor Miriam says the blueberries are nothing to worry about. If they're more plentiful this year, and she's not sure they are, it's merely because we had such a rainy spring.

I feel reassured, until she adds, almost as an afterthought. "Now the blackberries. If you're looking for bad signs, look at them. They're tougher and thornier, and they used to grow just on the borders, but now the whole area near Ben's cabin is covered with them."

It's true, I see one evening as Sandy, Sam, and I walk to Ben's for dinner.

Of all life's pleasures, walking to someone's place for dinner is one of my favorites. In Cambridge, we indulge only during snowstorms, but here in Nelson we do it often. And when we do, with a hard day of work or play behind us—and ahead of us, a feast—the walk offers pause enough to wax pensive. Tonight, I'm filled with wonder and gratitude. How far I once strayed—the drugs, the sex, the Grateful Dead concerts, the near-arrests in D.C., the hitching from Germany to Greece—and here I am, clean and fresh in the perfect light, one hand clasping a child's, the other, a straw basket cradling a still-warm pie.

Yes, wonder and gratitude, but also a touch of alarm, for Miriam is right: the land near Ben's is rife with blackberries.

Sandy and I are setting the table on the porch and here come Harvey and Frankie, first just their heads, their torsos, then their whole lengths as they climb the mowing.

Once we're all settled at the table and well into the meal, we make our proposal—something we've thought about for years, so why not now since we plan to summer here for as long as we can still walk: an expansion of our cabin—a dormer upstairs so Sandy, who's also writing a book (once a professor of economics, she's become leader in the field of higher education) can have a proper study with a view of the mowing!

Harvey and Frankie eye each other. Sandy and I prepare ourselves for refusal.

"That might not be worth your while," Frankie says gently. "Sometime in the next few years we plan to tear down the cabin and build our retirement home here."

For this we are not prepared. I take a gulp of wine. My eyes sting. As the Native Americans know all too well, knowledge, time, and love don't determine a claim's legitimacy, but even if they did, I cannot pretend that my thirteen-year affair with this spot rivals a Tolman's multigenerational intimacy. No, there's no comforting myself with outrage here. I must settle for anger's more difficult sister: pure, inescapable grief.

July '98

Another summer, another dinner with Harvey and Frankie. This time they arrive by car, probably because Frankie has brought her portfolio—bulging with a thick batch of her newest watercolors.

Trying to come to terms with our impending loss, I am practicing a disinterested curiosity. "So, what about all these blueberries?" I ask, nodding to the mowing just beyond the front porch. We have another bumper crop this year, despite a much dryer spring.

It's true, Harvey says, countering Miriam, the blueberries are a sign that the mowing has not been properly maintained. He admits he ought to mow more—fertilize, too. "The fertilizer encourages the grass," he explains, "which discourages all these coarser plants we're seeing now."

I'm surprised he doesn't seem much bothered by this. Could it be they've changed their plans about retiring here; that we, after all, will be the ones to witness the mowing's gradual succession?

After dinner, Frankie brings out her paintings. They are stark stylized landscapes with thrillingly fearless colors, and, having recently done a little painting myself, I feel silly for working so hard to try to capture the exact shade of minty green to indicate the lichen on the two huge trees that grace our porch.

I brave the question. "Is this our last year here?"

"Depends on whether we can round up the cash," Frankie says. "But whenever we do, we hope to find you a place somewhere around here. Would you consider the French cabin?"

"Yes," we say, without enthusiasm. It's already occurred to us, but that place has walls of painted sheet rock. Compared to this place's rustic wooden boards, the French cabin feels positively suburban. And it has no view!

On the tail of a long sigh, I offer up some more pasta, pass around the Parmesan. "Have you designed the new house, yet?" I ask. It is an active, deliberate process—this letting go.

Frankie describes their plans: a long, one-level C-shaped house with kitchen, living/dining room and studio, all facing the mowing.

Until I catch myself, it is *I* that I imagine in that kitchen, in that living/dining room, in that studio, in front of my easel, no longer worried about finding that perfect green.

August '98

"M-o-w-i-n-g-g-g": my first email password.

"The best thing I've ever done," I've more than once thought and said, meaning finding this place.

The first few years I was up here, I looked around for something to buy. I saw houses that were far more substantial, cottages right on ponds; places that cost far more than I could afford, but even they didn't interest me—probably because, as I now read in my *feng shui* book, the ideally located home is the one we have here—protected on three sides by hills or forest and fronted by downward-sloping land. Maybe now's the time to wrap my mind around a totally different sort of summer. Never mind that mine are supposed to be for writing, we should rent a villa in Umbria, drive cross-country, and do the parks.

Daily, on my walks down the mowing, I wander around the French cabin. Lately, it's had only short-term renters, and if it's empty, I venture in. I look out the north window. The trees along the road block whatever view of Monadnock the place would otherwise offer. I imagine building an addition, a porch facing north, and I stand where I would be if I were inside that porch, and I look up the mowing—or the patch of it visible from there. The view's not great, nothing compared to the one from on high, but I remind myself it's the same one I had when I first stepped into the clearing—and that was enough to sell me. I recall that it was good enough for Ebenezer, and that our friend Caitlin who rented the place for a few weeks last season thought it the sweetest.

This summer, bored with my improvised blueberry-peach pie in its gingersnap crust, and even with Miriam's sublime blueberry-lemon teacake, we have attempted a sweet yeasty blueberry *fougasse*. And I'm determined to try a *clafouti*, if only for the name. That still leaves mousse, pudding, bombe, buckle, Charlotte, fool, and grunt.

Happy Birthday, Sam! Ten candles (one to grow on) sink into his mixed-berry crumble/crisp.

I'm buying fewer groceries these days, wanting to use up what we have before we must return to Cambridge. Already a few of the trees framing the mowing are turning red or golden, so I'm feeling my usual mid-August melancholy, but there's something else, too. Sandy hasn't been feeling well—some kind of weird flu.

October '98

Usually, we return to the cabin two or three times in the fall, and, always, we do the final closing on Columbus Day. Packing, cleaning, mouse and moth proofing—it's a big production; we work on and off throughout the long weekend. This year, everything is different. I enlist a generous friend. She and I rush up for a single day of nonstop work.

How much can change in a month! Berries, eviction, succession—who gives a damn about any of it now. Sandy has cancer.

We learned this in early September. Late August, feeling worse, she went to a local clinic that did bloodwork and sent the results to her doctor back in Boston. The next morning, we got a call. Sandy's red count was dangerously low, she needed hospitalization, a bed was waiting for her at Mount Auburn in Cambridge.

Fortunately, some friends staying in the cabin next door were planning to return to Cambridge that night, and they agreed to pick up Sam at day camp and bring him and Augie back with them then. We grabbed some underwear and toiletries and got in the car.

Boston doctors disappear in late August, leaving mostly interns and fellows on duty. The hospital corridors were so empty and quiet, it was as if illness and injury adhered to the same vacation schedule. Sandy was given a transfusion immediately, but diagnostic tests proceeded more slowly.

At first we thought: rare infectious disease. Eventually, we learned it was peritonitis caused by a hemorrhaging tumor on her ovary. Using every contact we could dig up, we began hunting for a reputable surgeon who wasn't at some beach. After surgery, malignancy was confirmed. Ovarian cancer, stage 1C. Ovarian is the bad news; "one," the good—it hasn't yet spread to other organs; "C," bad again—the tumor burst, dispersing the once-encapsulated cancerous cells. The doctor is optimistic. He thinks six rounds of chemo will do it, but the first round was so torturous, it's hard to conceive of five more—and ovarian cancer is ovarian cancer. I've never heard of anyone beating it, not even the indomitable, *It's always something*, Gilda Radner.

I try not to think about any of this as my friend and I step out of the car at the top of the mowing and pause to look. The grass is tall again but decidedly brown, the purple asters rampant, the bordering trees in their full fall regalia. I take a lumpy swallow and a few deep breaths—we have work to do. I pretend I'm being magnanimous, assigning myself the fridge full of moldy cheese and rotten fruit, assigning my friend the job of gathering Sandy's stuff, her better clothes and half-read books and writing projects in-process.

August 2000

The "French" cabin—that's what everyone still calls it, even though the Parisians left years ago and bought a year-round house down in Nelson village. (I like thinking we're all part of some giant contra dance, moving up or down the line—though I don't expect we'll ever return to where we started as one does in contras—and with such a feeling of satisfaction.) Sandy and I are both shocked by how much we're enjoying this place we once scorned. It was so much easier to imagine what we were going to lose—that view of the mowing crowned by Monadnock's long rocky ridge, the exhilaration offered by higher elevations, the scent of mystery and magic lent by the surrounding, creature-filled woods—not to mention all those reminders of our little family's history in every cupboard and corner.

How little imagination we had for what we'd gain!

Dare I start with convenience? We're a shorter walk to the lake, the mailbox, the garbage barrels. The woodstove heats up the smaller living room in a fraction of the time it took in the old place, and this stove is a Franklin with doors that open so we can watch the flames. I hadn't anticipated I'd so enjoy seeing the farmhouse by the road— its cultivated garden and century-old barns and stonewalls, the sheep grazing behind the woodshed. I hadn't realized even the obvious—that we'd have so much more sun—for really, here we don't border the mowing, we're more or less *in* it as soon as we step out the door.

Sandy, of sturdy, resilient Russian stock, had a good year or more cancer-free, during which she took up rowing. But this spring, after months of agony, she learned that the pain in her arm wasn't from a bad back but from cancer in the bone near her elbow. A month of daily radiation cured the pain almost immediately but left the bone dangerously thin and her energy much diminished. Though she keeps her anxieties to herself, even with me—sometimes, I think, especially with me (to protect me? protect herself from my anxiety?)— she has read the literature, she can do the math. Though she's a wiz at denial, I've noticed she's less apt to put things off. A trip with Sam to London. Her own rowing shell. This summer she's enrolled in a watercolor course. With little deliberation, she sprung for one of Frankie's paintings—a stark still life of yellow pears on a table the color of Pepto-Bismol—a clump of four—three standing, one fallen.

If, as I recently read, all landscapes tell a story and all stories are about time, it follows that this story is the same old one—of forests being felled and then creeping back, of life relished and squandered, the farmer getting tired, the dogs dying, the child growing strong and tall, the grown-ups squabbling and making up, the hard truths faced and flung aside. Tonight, basket in tow, we'll head to Ben's for dinner, this time walking more slowly, up the mowing instead of down, still parting the tall grass as we go.

In memory of Miriam Goodman (1938–2008)

———◆———

Enough Tupperware

Finally, we have enough Tupperware. Dare I call this one of the "silver linings" within the catastrophe of Sandy's cancer? No, I don't mean all those colorful, plastic containers with their tight-fitting, burpy lids; I mean that each time I open the cupboard and see the battalion of them, I'm reminded that we're not alone in this world.

You see, as soon as they heard the news, people brought food: comfort food and exotic food and labor-intensive food, like home-made pesto from backyard basil and fruit salads with perfectly round melon balls. Those people (mostly friends but also some neighbors and temple members we barely know) shopped for us, weeded our garden, ferried our child, walked our dog, searched the web, accompanied us to appointments, brought books and tapes and videos and funny hats to mask the ravages of chemotherapy. We had a brigade of sorts, deftly organized by a couple of close friends. They asked me for names of people to be called and tasks that needed doing. I made up lists and handed them over. Sandy, a self-reliant sort, was touched by the outpouring of help but also embarrassed by my willingness to accept and, at times, even ask for it. We exchanged some harsh words. She, rightly pointing out that our friends had stressful lives themselves, wondered why I couldn't manage more on my own. And I reminded her that even when we were both functioning, we barely managed to keep milk in the fridge, and now, not only was she out of commission, but there was a whole slew of tasks that weren't there before—like explaining the situation to Sam's teachers, and seeking out support groups, and shopping for nutritional supplements, and running out at odd hours for the black and white frappe she suddenly thinks she might be able to drink and, and—. "Besides," I said—no, shouted, "People *want* to help. There's nothing wrong with letting them. There's nothing wrong with asking. That's a strength I bring to this situation!" (This latter spin I got from my support group.)

I was tearful by now, protesting too much. I knew there were millions who coped daily, if not with cancer, with poverty, single motherhood, difficult children, many children, ailing parents, prejudice, loneliness, chronic illness or disability . . . and I wondered why I was so weak and spoiled that even with plenty of help I felt so overwhelmed that I was yelling at this very sick person I loved and making her feel like a burden.

Furthermore, I knew such questions were self-indulgent at a time like this—that instead of spending energy obsessing about my own deficient character, I ought to be doing some of the things I was considering asking other busy people to do! Like teaching myself to use the new computer I needed to learn for work. Or returning the borrowed toilet plunger that has been in the trunk of my car for months!

I think there might be something about crises we can't control that brings what we can control into high relief, even if those things are trivial. In this case, that toilet plunger. I knew that when you need a plunger and can't find it, and you're not dealing with a genuine crisis, the missing plunger feels like a crisis, and you're more than a little miffed when you remember who failed to return it. So when people asked what they could do, I often thought: *Well, there is that toilet plunger!* But I never actually said it. Some things were clearly too much to ask for.

Or were they?

It's a tricky matter—this business of asking and offering, of giving and taking; it raises all the big questions about what it means to be in a relationship, to be part of a community. I've spent a lot of time pondering these questions, during those trying months and ever since. Still, I don't know much: only that few of us are immune to the premium our culture puts on self-sufficiency, and yet, when we open ourselves up to being helped, the rewards are many.

I know, also, that our friends' desire to help was genuine, and the opportunity to do so felt like a gift to many of them.

I know that the help we received made all the difference—to me, to my son, and especially to my resistant spouse. She, and many other cancer patients I've recently met, say that the goodness of family and friends had a healing effect.

And I know that those who fear accepting help because it will oblige them to give help in the future are not so off base. Take that Tupperware.

Today, the sight of it is making me uneasy; reminding me of something I've wanted to forget.

It happened just a few months before Sandy got sick. We received a notice from Sam's after-school asking us to bring a meal for another family with a cancer diagnosis. I had already heard the bad news and I definitely wanted to help, but the list of dietary restrictions was daunting, as was the admonition not to send any containers that we wanted back. I remember thinking, *But I don't have any decent containers that I don't want back!*

So what did I do?

I bought take-out.

It was good take-out—and I threw in a pretty card; but now, knowing the solace I got from all those homemade dishes, from the knowledge of all those specific hands picking and peeling, slicing and dicing, I'm filled with shame at the thought of that other family eating food cooked carelessly by strangers. I'm also blushing with the realization that those nifty containers are not, after all, mine to keep.

Not that I must return each to its rightful owner. I could never remember who gave which, and even if I could, I don't think their owners, a more evolved bunch than I, are counting on getting them back. But I am obliged to fill them up and pass them on the next time I learn of someone in need.

That's the thing about gifts. Unlike items bought or sold, they are never simply yours to keep. At least they weren't in many native cultures—as I learned from one of my favorite books, Lewis Hyde's *The Gift*. They were meant to be returned to their original donor, or better yet, to be passed on to someone new. They were supposed to always be in motion.

So much for my loaded cupboards!

But I don't mind. Graced by so many gifts, I'm a different person now. Less grasping. More giving. Or so I'd like to believe.

———————◆———————

Provincetown Breakfast

I've eaten a Provincetown breakfast so habitually, for so many years, and in so many locations that despite its name—rarely uttered but eternally hovering—I rarely remember to pay homage to its origins.

The year was '81, the month January. Poet Robin Becker and I had rented a partially renovated house on Bradford Street, up near the stone clock tower that lends the otherwise colonial Provincetown a medieval air. The idea was to write, and perhaps, more important, to *be*—as one *could* be, in no place better than Provincetown—women in love. We did both, as I remember, with varying amounts of diligence, expertise, and abandon.

Most of the day we wrote—she in one chilly, bare room, I in an adjacent one. Most evenings, we ate in—fillet of sole poached in wine and tarragon, rice, salad, and, for our protracted dessert-time seductions, too many wheatmeal biscuits with brie and ginger marmalade. Surely, this couldn't have been our only dinner menu that month, but I can't remember any other. Writers might well be the most routinized of creatures, and when we find something that works we stick with it.

Such is the case with the Provincetown breakfast. High on Eros as well as our own literary and culinary genius, Robin and I discovered the glories of fruit and yogurt and Grape-Nuts. Probably you've seen some permutation of this dish in every breakfast place in the nation; maybe you even eat this yourself each morning without knowing it was invented by Robin and me that stormy January in Provincetown. We christened it, we codified it (we should have patented it), and with some modifications, it has been a daily requirement in my life with Sandy these sixteen or more years.

As with any great American invention, work of art, or doctrine, the PB is elastic—but only up to a point. Like anything jazzy and sexy, it's a delicate balance of theme and variation. Some liberties can be taken, others are utterly taboo. The fruit, for example, (three types minimum) can vary—indeed, *must* vary with the season and location—but always, always, it must be 100 percent fresh.

As for the yogurt: we started out with Dannon, switched to Colombo, then to Stonyfield low fat, and finally, alas, to nonfat. But, bear in mind, when my father made the mistake of using milk, he was stabbed with disapproving looks.

In our household, the Grape-Nuts long ago gave way to granola, though I still strongly recommend the former to New England types who find that chewing granola isn't quite difficult enough. The granola, I must caution you, must not be too sweet or it obscures the sweetness of the fruit, and I personally disdain the sticky influence of raisins or dates. For years, we ventured weekly to a spooky out-of-the-way Seventh-day Adventist commune that sold granola, but now we use UPS and ship twenty pounds at a time from Gap Mountain Breads in Troy, New Hampshire. Even in such quantities, it's not cheap. Woe to my nephew who, unschooled in the art of modest sprinkling, just poured it on.

Double woe to my father. Just months after the milk gaffe, confusing the dish with his beloved cold cereal and fruit—he put the granola in first! We've rigged up an electronic device to make sure that won't happen again. But just so you know, repeat after me: *Fruit first, then yogurt, then topping. Fruit first, then yogurt, then . . .*

As for color: it counts.

Are you thinking you might try a winter combo of grapefruit, pears, and bananas? Think again. Think of Matisse—the feast of his palette. And the bowls—the bowls. White is safest but certain combos stand up to a bold, fiesta-like solid.

No, this isn't the kind of breakfast you eat on the run. It demands a proper sit-down meal in a sunny spot with strong black coffee and preferably two newspapers to minimize squabbling over the Living section. It takes time and care and love.

Maybe that's why Robin just couldn't sustain it on her own. I think of that January in Provincetown as both the height of our romance and (perhaps this is always the case?) the time when I first had inklings of its demise. We're still pals, however; and once a year, we share a hotel room at an annual writer's conference where I am repeatedly appalled to find, among her things, a stack of little Quaker Oatmeal envelopes!

I thought that would never happen with Sandy. Even more devoted than I, she was always the one to make those late-night excursions for our morning fruit, the one who would get up early to peel and chop and expertly separate the citrus sections from their filmy casings. If I presented her with the option of *huevos rancheros*, buckwheat pancakes, or a blackberry ginger scone, just for a change of pace, she wouldn't even be tempted. And if in the dead of winter I suggested a few frozen Trader Joe raspberries for color, she'd turn up her nose. That's why one of the saddest periods in her now long stint with cancer was when, this winter, she abandoned the Provincetown for, of all things, that pallid pabulum, cream of wheat. (I, losing heart, made do with half a grapefruit.)

But now it is summer. We are on the mowing again. Having changed to an easier treatment, Sandy and I have re-embraced the Provincetown. Though her long-range prospects are no better, each morning, sitting in the sun feasting on what feels like God's food, we forget about what lies ahead.

◆

My June Wedding

Like most girls born in the fifties, my earliest images of marrying a handsome prince in a golden silk tunic and dancing until dawn in a torch-lit ballroom eventually gave way to more contemporary images. First to marrying a handsome doctor-in-training in a tux and dancing until dawn in a country club. Then to marrying a handsome draft-resister, or doctoral student, or furniture-maker in a Nehru, or tweed, or lumber jacket, and dancing until dawn in a rambling old farmhouse, or under a big tent on the beach. Approaching thirty, I was ready to accept that my man might be handsome only to me; I allowed that mid-vow I might notice an irritating stain on his shirt and that there would be a thunderstorm and the tent would leak. But even then, I could never have imagined that the only man at my marriage would be my fourteen-year-old son in sneakers and a shirt in serious need of ironing.

That no other blood relatives would be there, that my father would not walk me down the aisle, that there would be no aisle at all, no rabbi *or* minister, no *chuppah* or veil or glass to smash.

No music.

No dancing.

That the ceremony would take place in a municipal building on a weekday afternoon at 4 p.m., postponed from the previous day because the person I was marrying had to go into the hospital for—and this part is not amusing—complications from the ovarian cancer she'd had for six of the twenty-one years we'd already been together . . . No, this was nowhere among my fantasies. During the last several of those twenty-one years, I'd grown accustomed to hearing about commitment ceremonies for gays and lesbians, about "weddings" performed in progressive churches and synagogues, and even to photos of the newlyweds in mainstream papers. Still, I could never have imagined that legal, state-sanctioned marriage between same-sex couples would be an option in my lifetime. Nor could I have anticipated that I would one day stand in the golden-domed Massachusetts State House with hundreds of other gay and lesbian parents and their children listening to those children (some of them teens I'd known as toddlers) speak with so much passion and poise about why their parents ought to be allowed to marry.

I could never have imagined that along with free, premarital blood tests, the health center at the college where I taught would offer layer cake and champagne and bestow upon us boas and top hats and wedding wands that dispersed bubbles, that the staff there would send us off in a swirl of confetti.

Nor could I have imagined that the city in which I lived would open its main office building at 10 p.m. on a Sunday night so that, at the stroke of midnight, they could be the first in the nation to hand out applications for marriage licenses to same-sex couples. Okay, knowing Cambridge maybe I could have imagined *that*, as well as the handful of sign-carrying protesters across the street, but not all the rest. Just picture it:

Massachusetts Avenue is blocked off to traffic. After we finally find a parking space and are approaching by foot, we see media trucks and TV cameras and *thousands* of supporters. We're too late, I think. We'll never get even close. But then we reach the corner, someone asks if we're there for a license, and suddenly the sea parts. A stranger hands us flowers. Another offers wedding cookies. Swept up the many steps in a wave of cheering, we reach the lobby where we receive our number: 211! Then we fly up another flight to where we are greeted by the open arms of friends. My emotion surprises me. Living in a progressive city, coming from a loving family, I've rarely if ever experienced overt oppression or even negativity, but now receiving not merely approval, but celebration . . . something I hadn't even allowed myself to want! And now here it was from neighbors and strangers, young and old, black and white, gay and straight, from city officials, community choruses, reporters from D.C. and Britain and Germany. I broke down and wept.

As it turned out, we would have had to wait until 4 a.m. to receive our application—out of the question for Sandy who was very weak, very sick—so we left around 12:30 without one. But who knew? As we walked back out the front door, we were blinded by flashing cameras. The crowd cheered. There didn't seem to be any need to correct them. More flowers. And sweets. A bag of freebies from a local bank courting new business. It was *almost* too much. I felt like Princess Diana. What wedding could match this! I thought. But really, it was more than the glamour and fifteen minutes of fame that thrilled me so. It was that our marriage (or impending one, anyway) was, as a marriage should be, a whole community's occasion for joy.

And then a full month later, the ceremony itself.

This is the most astounding part: I, a romantic at heart, someone passionately attached to family and religious rituals, an exasperating, hair-splitting perfectionist who can always find something amiss in every occasion—I found our makeshift ceremony entirely to my satisfaction. In fact, it made me very happy.

How to account for this?

Maybe Sandy's cancer has forced me to finally grow up and see that glass half-full?

The expeditiousness of the affair most certainly played a role.

"Most women have their hair done *before* they get married. I'm having mine done *after*."

How I enjoyed sharing this realization with friends, so emblematic of how last minute this marriage was going to be. Even after May 17th we could hardly believe that somebody (the governor? the legislature?) wouldn't call a halt to it all, and by then we were so damn busy finishing our teaching, preparing our house for its summer subletters, packing Sam for camp, buying film and sunscreen and so forth for a long-anticipated trip to Venice—so busy and so preoccupied we were with Sandy's treatments that we failed to realize our blood tests had lapsed and we'd have to redo them. We considered postponing the wedding until after Italy, but given the uncertainty in our lives—and everyone else's in these post-9/11 days, we nixed that. Which is all to say that there were days when getting married felt like just one more chore to cross off our list.

Did I have no complaints about our wedding, because I didn't have time to fashion any new fantasies against which the reality could fall short?

Had the community celebrations already given me what I needed?

Yes. And yes. And also: only a fool could have failed to love the improvised affair we had.

Its venue—the stately city council chambers with its grand windows, high ceilings, and recessed rosewood.

Our four stupendous friends who canceled their plans that same day to be there and weep.

Those four fabulous bouquets—two brought by the friends, two we grabbed from home on our way out. (With cancer comes flowers—and this kind of ha-ha remark.)

Truth. And Beauty—they were there, too, in city hall. I'm referring to the spot-on statement about the challenges of long-term relationships written by the city clerk for the many veteran couples who wanted to honor their shared past as well as their future. That these words were delivered with such warmth and sincerity by the deputy clerk who told us how moved she'd been by the depth of love she'd witnessed in the dozens of ceremonies she'd performed in past weeks—all this only added to the perfect, well, *wedding* I felt between my own small self and the community in which I lived.

As for Sam, it was hard for him to appreciate the full significance of the event. More than once in the preceding week he said, "I don't understand what the big deal is." I'm sure he was confounded by all the weeping. Nevertheless, he got into the spirit of the thing—just seconds after our *I Do's*, reaching into his pocket and whipping out that favor I'd saved from the little fete at college. With a magician's flourish, he waved that white wand, dispersing dozens of iridescent bubbles that the rest of us, wide-eyed as kids, floated among—until every last one vanished.

———————◆———————

IV

What Can You Do?

Last December in a thrift shop in Silver City, New Mexico, I noticed among the dreggiest of dregs something red and sparkly. Immediately it occurred to me that I should not be interested in such a thing just two months into widowhood. But I was interested. I loved the tomato-red gauzy material, the thousands of sequins and beads glittering in a broad swirly pattern. I loved the wide zigzagging borders on both skirt and blouse, echoing the blouse's low V-neck. I could picture it all on Bessie Smith, but also, maybe, on paler, more diminutive me.

"Fabulous," Laura said when I held it up. We were both on a thrift store high, freed for an hour or more while Sam and David, our teenaged sons, and Laura's husband Howie were roaming the streets in search of cheap CDs and cowboy memorabilia. This impromptu vacation to the high desert had been Laura's idea, a way for Sam and me, and all of us really, to begin to heal from Sandy's long illness and recent death. Our families, Laura's and mine, had been friends since the boys were in day care.

"Try it on," Laura said.

I think she was hoping it would be too big for me and she'd get a crack at it. But it fit—well enough. The top had a tendency to slide off a shoulder, a nice touch, I thought. As for the skirt, the elastic waistband needed to be replaced and the whole thing taken in, but at four dollars (marked down from eight) I figured I could spring for some serious tailoring and still come out way ahead. And if nothing else, I could wear it to the "Red and Green," the annual party our friend Kathy had been hosting for some nineteen years. Originally, it was a Christmas affair, but each year, because of everyone's jammed schedules, it was nudged further toward spring. This year, it was scheduled for April; even so, the food would be mostly red or green, and the getups—often retro, thrift store numbers—the same two colors.

October, November, December. The first few weeks and months after Sandy died, every glance into our shared closet was difficult. Her belongings . . . I thought maybe they'd exude some sort of sheepishness for having outlived her, but every skirt, blouse, scarf, belt, shoe . . . presented itself exactly as before. Maybe that's why I was so eager to get rid of most of it, relentlessly pondering which item would look good on which friend, which friend had the constitution to actually wear the thing, on whom could I bear to see it?

By January, when we returned home from the Southwest, only a handful of Sandy's things remained in that closet: the boxy, black-and-white checked blouse she'd worn during much of our honeymoon to Venice; the soft, squirrel-colored "chemo-shirt" she wore for infusions; a couple of pairs of jeans too worn to give away but impossible to throw out, so filled they were with her shape, her sweat, her determined, responsible caulking and spackling, her joyful digging and planting, her patient weeding and mulching, her ever-increasing hours on the couch without even a book, just the dog stretched out on her chest. Also, I kept the crinkly, lilac tunic she'd worn so radiantly for Sam's bar mitzvah and again at our June wedding in the Cambridge City Hall. But when I hung up my new red dress and my eyes skimmed across Sandy's remaining stuff, I was already pretty good at feeling nothing. I'd had a lot of practice in steeling myself. So many calls to make—insurance, mortgage, credit card companies; so many telemarketers asking for her. "She died," I'd say. The hard thud of those d's satisfied me in a way that the wispy "passed away" did not. Not for this Jew, the comforting notions of meeting again in a fluffy heaven or believing that somehow, somewhere, she knows all those things I find myself wanting to tell her. It seems to me, so far anyway, that death is simply this: the stark, colossal goneness of a once substantial, infinitely complex presence.

Feeling nothing? Did I say that? Often, a few minutes after the phone call, or after seeing her handwriting on the calendar, I find myself wondering why I'm so tired and shaky. Really, it works better to court the feelings as I sometimes do, going through old albums, sinking my nose into her blue woolen hat. The tears come. And then they are over. It's true, what they say: they come at the most unexpected times, but that doesn't mean they don't also appear at the obvious ones. Inhaling that hat, I wonder how long it will retain her smell—and then, when it is gone, what will be left?

This *how long* question has many permutations. How long will we call her place at the table, Sandy's place? Her study, Sandy's room? How long will we keep her voice on the answering machine? That was a particularly tough one. Sam saw no reason to change it, ever, and I loved her telephone voice, so much more inflected, and intimate, than the one she used when we were face to face. How long, I now wonder, will I remember the things I disliked about her? Her ways of keeping distance between us, her rigidity, her silences. Maybe even I, with my fondness for hard truths, will eventually be swayed by convention and ease into remembering only the good soldier, the brave patient and loving mother, the tender and generous heart.

January, February, March . . . I must have glimpsed the red dress nearly every morning, and yet it wasn't until mid-April, until the Friday before the Saturday of the Red and Green, that I brought it to the tailor's—which is just around the corner, is, in fact, the same place where we do our dry cleaning, and I'd gone there several times since Silver City. I don't know why I waited so long. I only know that carrying the spangly material from car to store, another one of those *how long* questions came to me:

How long am I going to keep using Sandy's name here?

For about fifteen years, Sandy and I had been filing our cleaning, or less frequent tailoring, jobs under the same phone number and name: hers, Kanter—probably because her job required far more dry cleaning. This time—well—I don't remember coming to a decision about the name question. What I remember was how delighted the tailor/cleaner was by my find—she with her blunt-cut hair and severe shirts and pants; she who was always there and seemed to have no other life, no other personality than that of efficient, eager-to-please shopkeeper. All these years and I'd never even learned her name. How surprised I was when her face lit up at the sight of my swanky (if a bit musty) dress!

"Beautiful," she said. "Beautiful!" Behind those wire rims I'd always found entirely too big and round, her eyes were suddenly shining.

"You like it?"

"Yes. Yes."

So of course I had to expand my pleasure by informing her that it was used, that I'd gotten it for practically nothing. This seemed to expand her pleasure, too—it didn't seem right to tell her about Sandy then. "It needs some work," I said, "but first, before I forget, I think you still have a blouse of mine. Under Kanter." She nodded, as if of course she knew.

Of course, I thought, as she walked the few steps to the small revolving rack where she kept the alphabetized slips. She found the Kanter one quickly, then pressed the button that started the creaky carousel. For me, this was always a time of high drama. Would my item, or Sandy's, slip past? Would the woman have to backtrack or go around all over again? I watched the woman's finger on the button and her eyes on the passing numbers as I might watch an Olympic skier edging around a slalom flag—too much? not enough?—all the time worrying about the possibility that the item was lost, maybe gone forever, though that only happened once with a sweater I didn't much like.

The carousel stopped, then lurched forward another few feet.

The woman reached for the hanger. Through the plastic I could see my burgundy blouse. She hung it on the rack above the counter, then returned to me and my dress.

"She died, you know," I softly said. "Kanter."

"No!" Her face turned ashen. "Didn't know."

I nodded.

"When?" she asked.

"October."

"Terrible," she said, shaking her head, her eyes on the puddle of glitter between us. I was surprised by how upset she was. "Did you know she was sick?" I asked.

She nodded. "Once came in, told me—bad news, some tests."

I don't know why I thought she might have known—that she did surprised me. Sandy was extremely private. How heartbroken she must have been that day. How undone. On her way home from the hospital, maybe? Or from work, that sometimes merciful distraction. More than once during the six years of her illness, Sandy accused me of not thinking enough about what she was going through. Not true, I thought. Not fair. I thought about it all the time, but mostly had to guess, imagine. She reported the results of each test, each scan, and probably told me more than anyone else, occasionally, briefly, crying in my arms; but all these daily agonies, these little stabbing moments like telling this woman—there must have been thousands of them that she kept to herself.

With the tailor still shaking her head and making small gasping sounds, it seemed wrong, punishable almost, to get back to the business of the dress. But by then another customer had entered, a woman carrying a raincoat. It didn't seem right to keep her waiting too long, and besides, the tailor's upset was stirring up my own. I was touched by how moved she was, but I kept expecting her to recover enough to extend her condolences to me. I'd gotten accustomed to hearing them—from people close to us but also from those with whom we did business, the ones who had clearly figured out our relationship, but also the ones who knew only that I was the executrix, or that we shared an address. *I'm sorry for your loss.* That's how almost everyone put it. The frequent use of these exact words irked me, and yet I couldn't help feeling that they were as good as any—brief, direct, fitting—and even when I heard them from customer service people obviously instructed to use them, I appreciated the acknowledgment, no doubt appreciated it more than most because, as a couple, Sandy and I so often felt invisible.

Now I didn't understand what was taking the tailor so long. Where was her "I'm sorry . . ." Surely she'd figured us out after all these years of dropping off and picking up for each other. Maybe it was the jazzy dress that threw her? Or perhaps it was a cultural thing: she knew but thought it rude to let on that she did? Whatever the reason, via some tortured Mobius strip of a rationalization, I decided that since *she* doesn't seem to get it, *I* don't have to feel the slightest bit apologetic about wearing this dress!

I proceeded into the cubicle next to the plate glass window and put on top and bottom both—just to get the whole picture. When I came through the curtains, the tailor was still shaking her head, her distress so apparent that the lady with the raincoat extended her arm. "Are you okay?" she asked, resting her hand on the tailor's shoulder. A touching gesture—I didn't begrudge her it—but my own shoulder felt suddenly lonely. My hand was clutching the stretched-out waistband, and now the tailor took it from me and held it snug. "This how you want it?"

I nodded. "Now what about this?" I asked, grabbing all the extra material at my hips. "Can you take this in?" She shook her head, pointing and explaining how the pattern of jewels wouldn't match up. I felt foolish for not having realized this myself.

In my street clothes again, approaching the counter, I thought, Now . . . Now she will express her sympathy or at least give me some kind of feelingful look.

But she just kept shaking her head.

"When do you think you can have it done by?" I finally asked.

"Wednesday," she said. "Wednesday okay?"

My folly struck me. I sighed. How could I have thought that tomorrow was a reasonable request! "Is there *any* way . . ." I began, then lost my nerve, then rallied again. "You see, there's a party—tomorrow."

She shook her head firmly, then paused. "Maybe Tuesday," she said with a shrug.

I took another deep breath, then did something I'd never done before and never liked when I saw anyone else do it. I asked, "If I pay a little more?"

She shook her head. "Not the money. Time! Other customers!"

I nodded. Yes, of course.

"Needs ironing too," she announced.

I hadn't considered this. Wasn't convinced. If there were wrinkles, they were barely visible beneath all the sequins and beads. Besides, I thought, if I can't wear it tomorrow, I just might never wear it, or by the time I do, the hanger will have fallen many times and the whole thing will need ironing all over again.

"Are you sure? About the ironing, I mean. This party isn't fancy. It's just for fun."

"Still needs ironing!" She seemed to be enjoying her superior knowledge on this point.

"How much?"

"Fifteen dollars."

I did a quick calculation. Four for the dress, twelve for the waistband, and fifteen for the ironing . . . I nodded my consent and was cheering myself up with the thought that there was always next year's Red and Green, when she startled me.

"I try," she said.

I was confused and must have shown it.

"Tomorrow," she said. "Not promising, but I try."

"Oh!" I beamed. With this sudden opening I forgot everything else. "I would really appreciate that. What should I do, call tomorrow?"

She nodded.

"Around three? Four?"

"Four," she said. "But remember . . . ," she wagged her finger. "Not promising!"

On Saturday, I wasn't holding my breath; still, I had it in my mind to call around four. When, at around three, the phone rang, I was thinking about something else. The voice was unfamiliar. Accented. "Excuse me?"

"It ready. The dress!"

The tailor! I could hear the pride in her voice.

"How wonderful! Thank you! I'll be right over."

It was a happy reunion—the woman looking as pleased as I felt, the dress looking radiant, even under plastic. I paid my thirty-one dollars, briefly considering a big tip but rejecting the idea as insulting. "Thank you so much," I said again. And then again, taking the hanger: "I really appreciate it."

"Did it for Kanter," the tailor declared just as I was about to turn away.

I stood there for a moment just taking it in—her smile broad, her eyes glistening behind her glasses, focusing, finally, directly on me.

"What can you do?" she added, slowly shaking her head.

"What can you do?" I repeated.

"Have to go on," she said and I nodded.

Here's the thing. When I got home and tried the outfit on, the top looked great and the skirt's waist fit fine—and indeed, the ironing brought the whole effect up a notch; but instead of looking smashing as I had envisioned, I looked frumpy. The excess material around the hips and thighs bunched and sagged. I turned this way and that in front of the mirror, but there was no getting around it. I began to wonder about a substitute for the skirt. The first thing I tried did the trick. And that's what I wore that night to my first Red and Green without Sandy—sleek coal-black pants with flickering red top.

Everyone said I looked terrific. No one seemed to disapprove.

April, May, June. I gave away a few more of Sandy's things—a camisole to my sister; to her brother, an antique print of their hometown harbor. I chewed to death a petrified piece of gum found in the leather bag she used years ago; I availed myself of the car wash coupon in her glove compartment. Still, I didn't have the heart to throw out her half-drunk bottle of iced tea, the stuff she lived on when she could no longer eat. As Sam and I were getting ready for our summer adventures—he going to camp and I, again, to New Hampshire, where Sandy and I had had so many happy times—he gave me permission to take her voice off the answering machine. This I did when he wasn't home, but not without first recording it so it would never be totally lost—if, that is, I remembered where I kept it.

While packing my bags I briefly considered bringing the whole red outfit, top *and* bottom, frump notwithstanding. Standards in New Hampshire are looser, and there are, after all, those weekly contra dances. Then I came to my senses. Those dances are folksy affairs. Some women dress up but in homespun cotton numbers. Even if I wanted to go against the grain, the Town Hall has no dimmers, no spotlights or strobe lights to tease out my dress's magic.

Of course it was difficult to return to the cabin—Sandy's splashy blue-flowered bathing suit hanging on the post of the mirror above our dresser, all her medical paraphernalia in a straw basket, her running shorts in the third drawer . . . But what could I do?

I added more windows, wishing I'd done this last summer or the one before so Sandy could have seen the whole mowing from where she rested on the couch. I splurged on an antique rug and rearranged the furniture. I hung up one of her watercolors—two oaks and a portion of a third, beautifully composed and rendered with such a light touch. I walked a lot with our dog, Augie, remembering how she once told me she would look at him and think, not kindly: *He's going to outlive me.*

And so he has. He who lay contently across her chest hour after hour, month after month, though surely the scents of the street or meadow called; he who after she died kept walking from room to room in search. These days, oblivious as her orphaned clothes, he bounds through the woods with renewed élan. And now, almost on cue as I write this, he appears at the screen door, scraggly and drenched. "Oh, I was just thinking about you," I tell him, letting him in, drying him off with her old fleece jacket.

June is always firefly month in New England, but this June, the rainiest I can remember, the bugs are more bountiful and dazzling than ever. That isn't just my perception, either. It was mentioned in the local paper, and New Hampshire Public Radio devoted several minutes to a discussion of bioluminescence. I don't remember much of what was said, only that the lights—so various in intensity and duration—are part of a complex courtship display.

A few nights ago, when the rain stopped just long enough, I stepped out into the mowing to watch the show. I tried to discern some sort of pattern or rhythm to the flare-ups, but soon, realizing it was hopeless, I just stood there transfixed. For the briefest of moments then, it came to me that here, at last, was Sandy speaking to me. But the next night when I stood there again and saw just as many flies, dancing just as jazzily, it came to me with the same certainty that they were just bugs calling to each other in the dark.

———————◆———————

Wonderlust

Excursions through an Aesthetic Education

For all my teachers
and for Barbara Greenberg, especially

1. Dancing Outside the Lines

Ahmed, the son of a camel breeder, leads tourists on excursions through the desert. This is the starting point for tonight's class. Our assignment: to develop a "movement phrase" that is suggested by a word in the sentence. We have each claimed a space on the floor and are trying out steps, often cutting them short—too difficult! too dull!—then starting again with something entirely different, less mimetic. Slower? Smoother? Add a flick of the wrist? Change the order. The emphasis.

"Five more minutes!" Joan, the teacher, calls.

We, the busy phrase-makers, are all female—and I'm not the oldest by far. Most of us are, or were, teachers—me, of college writing; others of kindergarten, graduate school, high school art, middle school science, yoga, and theater. The majority have been working with Joan for years or even decades, but this is my first term with her.

That I find myself here at fifty-two is a case of life imitating art, sort of. Last summer in New Hampshire I gave myself over to a new writing project, a still nebulous *some*thing about the nearly half-century of courses I've taken. I mined my memory and made lists. I read articles, new books, classic texts, my college essays and childhood journals. I telephoned old friends, emailed and Googled long-lost teachers and fellow students. It was fun connecting with them and remembering the person—me—who'd so gamely thrown herself into all those courses—especially that seventeen-to-thirty-something me who loved to dance. Then . . . thanks to the way one click leads to another, I found myself on some Boston-area dance listserv that led me, eventually, here, to this gymnasium in a public grade school just around the corner from where I live most of the year.

The basketball hoops have been retracted, the climbing ropes hooked back up to the rafters. Amoeba-like clumps of dust flit about the edges; forgotten sweatshirts bulge from the folded-up bleachers; the odor of dust, wax, rubber, and sweat pervades. Maintenance men—more often than necessary, I'd guess—traipse through our space to the adjacent gym. I see us as I imagine the young janitors do, as a bunch of old ladies doing that overdramatic modern stuff. I shake off the thought and return to my task.

"Just another minute," Joan shouts.

She must compete with the rumble from the ventilating system and the buzz from the flying saucer–shaped fluorescent lights. Both air and lights, she's been told, are on a timer controlled by someone in Cincinnati. A maddening fact—we're a third of a continent away—but a ticklish concept, one that I think has literary possibilities. Then again, to me right now, *every*thing has possibilities of *every* sort—so high am I on this new way of spending my Thursday evenings.

Sure, I feel pangs about leaving Sam to struggle with his home-work, his other mom, Sandy, too tired from chemo to help him. But I *need* this, I tell myself, uttering the mantra from my caregivers' support group: *If I don't take care of myself, I'm no good to anyone else.*

Ahmed, the son of a camel breeder, leads tourists on excursions through the desert.

This semester-long course is my first dance class in more than a decade. Dancing Outside the Lines, it's called—to encourage people like me who dislike codified steps. Joan's goal this semester is to explore how improvisation and choreography feed each other. The improvisation part is what drew me—I've got plenty of heartbreak to express these days, and it's true: getting some of that out creates space for strength and humor and delight. I'm also finding this cho-reography part intriguing.

Ex-cur-sion is my assigned word and I must say I've taken a liking to it—to its length and outwardness; its muscular beginning;

ornery, doggy middle; fizzy but not fizzling ending. I'm also pleased with my movement phrase. Though short (ten seconds of choreography can take hours to devise), I fancy it captures the word's bold expansiveness. Mother, partner, teacher—lately I haven't had much time to indulge my love of freedom and adventure. When Sandy was diagnosed, we had to cancel our plans to trek in Nepal. We've traveled since then, more than usual in fact, but to tamer destinations. I like thinking about empty spaces dotted by camels. And my quadriceps still have some juice.

But when Joan gathers us together, I must call forth my frayed acquaintance with the Buddhist practice of nonattachment. My movement phrase is not mine to keep. "Find a partner," Joan instructs, "and teach each other your movements, then make the other's your own. Stretch or collapse it, alter the dynamics, the attitude." This is how Joan works, I will eventually learn: juggling the artist's desire for ownership, freedom, and control, with the rewards that can come from submission, limitation, and chance.

Soon we are combining the originals with their variations, selecting the best of the lot, arranging and blocking them out on the floor. We try out one CD, settle on another. To my surprise the version we perform in the last few minutes of class looks not unlike real choreography. It has unity and variety, humor and meaning, too. The horizontals suggest the vastness of the desert. In certain gestures I see something about the awkward relationship between native guides and their privileged charges. Perhaps I'm getting carried away here but, at the very least, there's Hannah's noodly, camel-like gait.

Ahmed, the son of a camel breeder, leads tourists on excursions through the desert. It's a prosaic declaration chosen almost randomly from a *National Geographic*, but the more I ride the words, the more they feel like poetry.

2. Braking for Beauty

A thrilling paralysis, a churning in my solar plexus; these [are] my sole criteria of judgment.

—Bernard Cooper

Today it was the whorly grain of a barn door, the curve of a dusty road; last night, the falling down sign at a deserted gas station, the cockeyed smile on the gawky teenaged boy at the village contra dance. I've long been a sucker for beauty, but the elastic days of summer bring out the glutton in me. This July, especially, I'm called by beauty constantly. Never mind that the nature of what calls me is always shifting, it's the frequency of the summons I'm talking about here: it pleases and troubles me in equal measure. The pleasure is obvious. The trouble? It's hard to get anything done. I'm always pausing, pulling over, leaving whatever I'm doing in order to adjust the position of my potted geranium so that the light shines on its rakish head just so. As an adolescent I scorned those clichéd globs, but I seem to have been born again to their charm. En route to the refrigerator, I stop to take a photo of that glowing geranium. After the print is made, I enjoy cropping it off with my nifty unvirtual paper cutter, so that when I affix it to those blank cards made from fancy ivory paper, I am pleased with the effect. And when it is time to write or pay a bill, I find myself thumbing through my shoebox files of photo cards looking for the right one to send as a thank-you card to Barbara Greenberg.

Barbara—once my writing prof, now my wise and treasured friend—she's the one who years ago suggested I write about some of the courses I've taken. Not only did that lead me back to dance, but it turns out this rummaging around in my curricular life is a lot of fun. And, it feels connected somehow to this beauty craze I'm in; to the conviction I feel—my spot is just slightly higher than the solar plexus where Bernard Cooper's resides—the conviction that if the handle on this pitcher here is at the perfect angle, if all the elements of the picture are aligned and it is framed just so by the window's molding, well . . . well, what?

Is God right here on my windowsill?

Absolutely, some might say.

Then again . . . if She inhabits everything, surely She would not need *my* tinkering to be made manifest.

Or would She?

I'm in over my theological head here, so let's just say, although I enjoy striving for perfection, I distrust the whole notion. Surely, it's subjective—a cultural construct—just as beauty itself is.

Or is it?

With some biologists theorizing that comeliness confers an evolutionary advantage, the jury is still out on that one. Meanwhile, I'm happy fussing over light and shadow, line and shape and scale, though I should probably be doing something more useful. Or kind. Or lucrative.

Which brings me back to those courses I've taken, and am taking still, and again. Courses, classes, workshops, seminars, "intensives." Some cheap, some not, all time-consuming. For a few years in my late twenties, I believed that to be a writer, you had to give up everything else, but those days are long gone. Just last month, I spent a hundred dollars and a beautiful Saturday indoors at an "art-making" workshop. Not long before that I took a full-semester course in watercolor and before that, another in drawing, and before that . . . During a family reunion at a mountain resort, I went to a session on "rock sculpture" and barely left the crafts cabin the rest of the weekend. And that's just in the visual arts. When I was young, most of my classes were in the movement arts. First dance—ballet, modern, and jazz.

Then the martial and healing arts—karate, aikido, tai chi. I've taken workshops in the Feldenkrais Method—to strengthen my bones, to relieve pain from temporal mandibular joint syndrome, to prepare my body and soul for the Jewish High Holy Days! Of course I've tried yoga and Pilates, and I still intend to investigate the Alexander Technique. Over the years, I've explored dramatic improvisation, vocal improvisation, performance art, clowning, trapezing, psychodrama, and several "courses" and modes of psychotherapy. Born in 1950, I was swept up in the Human Potential Movement that surged in the wake of the Vietnam Era. Or maybe I'm just plain curious, adventurous. I've taken Talmudic Textual Study, Syntactical Strategies in Poetry, Japanese Flower-Arranging . . . I've even taken classes in taking classes. Life-long Learning in Jewish Thought, that one was called; it was offered by my son's Hebrew school. Recently, at a fund-raising auction for that school, I bid on six lessons in jazz piano, and to my horror—okay, delight—I won.

Sounds excessive, I know. This is why I so long resisted Barbara's suggestion: I didn't want to sound like a dilettante. But when I expressed this to Barbara over lunch one day, she considered and then dismissed the concern.

"I don't think that's it," she said. "I think you're after something."

3. On Course(s)

After the famous talking horse

A course is a course, of course it is: a unit of curriculum, a part of a meal, a route or path, an area on which a race is held or sport played; a systematic succession.

From *cursus*, past participle of the Latin *currere*: "to run, flow, pursue, hunt"; related to the Old French *cours* (heart), and "courier," "corridor," "succor" (running to the aid of), and "ex-cur-sion" (running out from); not to mention, "recourse," "discourse," "inter-course," and even the humble, taciturn "horse"—though, admittedly, more distantly, via the Greek *khouros* (running) and Old Norse *horskr* (wise).

4. A Want

The house on the corner of Union Turnpike and 212th Street was, like many on the grid of my Queens neighborhood, a sturdy mish-mash of styles with bricks on the lower half and shingles above. What distinguished it were the girls who regularly streamed through the side door. Growing girls, they mostly were, with pigtails and pony-tails, pageboys and flips. Among them also: some fully grown "girls" with lacquered bouffants and beehives. For a few years, smack in the middle of my childhood, my mother and I were among the troops.

We went for Nadja. We called her that: "Nadja." I never even knew her last name. Pronounced *Na*-dja, emphasis on the plaintive "Nah," the name was enchanting to me in those days of mostly homegrown Susans, Judys, and Lynns.

Nadja taught several classes back to back; many of the more experienced girls like my new best friend, Barbara Obadiah, took two, even three, classes in a row. For the novices and their mothers who were required to stay and watch, arrivals were hectic. We hurried down three concrete steps into a dark, narrow hallway. My mother turned left to claim a space on the bench that lined the front of the studio. I rushed ahead into the dressing room—a tiny space clogged with chattering girls flinging street clothes, some destined to catch an exposed pipe and dangle there.

A far cry from the pastel tutus I'd worn in a class years earlier, the clothes at Nadja's were dark and functional. The more advanced a student, the more she covered up. As a beginner I wore a black short-sleeved cotton leotard with a zipper snaking up the back. The more experienced girls wore long-sleeved leotards topped by cardigans and tights topped by leggings—something about the importance of keeping the muscles warm. Indeed, as those girls performed their *pliés*, *jetés*, and *rondelés* in the studio, they shed their layers, tossing them into the laps of their mothers. It was the leggings that most impressed me. They lent an appealing air of hard science to what I'd previously thought of as girlish and therefore frivolous. Usually navy or brown or burgundy, the wool leggings pilled and stretched. Most girls rolled them over at the waist, and still they bagged. In their dolorous, crumpled casualness I recognized things I couldn't have named. Bohemian chic. And, most definitely, seriousness.

The studio had a proper wooden floor, a wall of mirrors, and two sturdy barres at different heights. We were required to buy practice records, boxed sets of 78s, and we were expected to practice every day. Some classes began with an inquisition: *Did you practice every day? Did you? And what about you?*

Did anyone ever confess to laxness? I don't remember. But to this day, if I hear certain Chopin etudes, I am at that barre again—descending in second position, my curved arm sweeping across the floor with all the grace my pudgy body can muster, and then rising up again before both the music and I take a capacious breath, sustaining it an extra beat for drama, and then descending again. And nearly every time I wait at a checkout line or bus stop, or even drive past a bus stop, I think of Nadja because, according to her, *pliés* were the answer to just about everything and one should do them in every position, with arms and without, every chance one gets: before going to bed and after rising up, at the checkout line and while waiting for a bus. A multitasker in the days when one could still imagine doing one paltry thing at a time, Nadja taught me that art requires discipline. She herself, in the old days, would rise at four in the morning to do her *pliés* on the cold floor, and then, when her fingers had warmed, she would practice her piano scales for an hour, all this before her morning chores.

This wasn't a turnoff. Ambitious, eager to please, I wasn't scared of hard work, self-sacrifice, even a little pain. But I wasn't sure I had that other quality Nadja implicitly campaigned for. I'm talking about what it takes to do *pliés* anytime, everywhere: an indifference to appearing bizarre. I was, after all, in the fifth grade of Public School 188, a mostly Jewish, all-white school where the wrong hair or socks make your life miserable. Even so, a part of me enjoyed the *thought* of doing *pliés* at the bus stop on Union Turnpike where all the world could see. I must have sensed, even then, that I wanted a life that took me beyond the conventions of my cookie-cutter neighborhood. Nadja's unorthodoxy, her odd clothes, even the feel of her name in my mouth—they all gave off a whiff of something enticing.

Ostrich-like, she had a big bottom, jiggly thighs, and a long cordy neck, accentuated by the way she wore her apricot hair piled high, and by her long, dangling earrings. When Katharine Hepburn died and the papers were full of her pictures, I was reminded of Nadja. Hepburn was more beautiful, but they had the same regal bearing, the same cheekbones and sly, inescapable eyes.

Rumor had it that Nadja had once been in Martha Graham's company. No one knew how old she was—and I'd guess not much older than I am now—but Nadja's dancing days were apparently over. Though she generally wore twirly dancer-like skirts, netted or tinted hose, and, always, ballet shoes, I don't remember her demonstrating a single step. For that she'd call on one of the more advanced girls in the front row, who would perform with a stony face, again and again if Nadja requested.

I had always assumed that the frigid floor of which Nadja spoke was in Russia, but Barbara Obadiah says Nadja was born and raised in the states. Wherever she learned her teaching methods, they wouldn't

wash today. I'm surprised that even then none of the mothers object-
ed. Once when Edie, a pretty, dark-haired girl whose father owned
the candy store across from Nadja's house, asked in the middle of the
class if she could go to the bathroom, Nadja said no. A few minutes
later, when Edie asked again, Nadja again said no, assuring Edie she
could wait. What surprises me now is even after I saw, we all saw,
the widening puddle, the silently weeping Edie rooted above it, my
faith in Nadja remained unshaken. I never questioned her approach.
When we were engaged in the never-ending quest for a better turn-
out in first position, she would plant her slippered foot against my
instep and force my knee out with hers. And once, when I was on
my knees, my torso leaning backward, my spine not cooperating with
her orders to arch, Nadja grabbed me by my ponytail so that the full
weight of me hung from it. Initially stunned by the pain, within a
long second or two filled with Nadja's surprisingly gently commands,
my back found its way into an arch. Pain, I learned, can be useful,
and I can bear more of it than I thought.

My allegiance to Nadja and her methods extended to the second half of that Saturday class, the hour devoted to choreography
and dance history—which seemed to include music and art history,
too. It was at Nadja's that I first heard the exotic words *baroque* and
rococo, the names Balanchine and Thelonious Monk.

Classes at Nadja's were ongoing. One paid by the lesson, putting
money in a coffee can near the Victrola. With no specific starting or
ending dates, new students often joined classes of more experienced
students and had to get with the program without much orientation.
In one of my first classes, I and another new girl were instructed to
choose some music from our home library and perform a dance to
it the following week. Nothing to be nervous about, Nadja emphasized, just a way of getting to know us better so she could select an
appropriate record for us to buy for future compositions.

Sitting on the carpet in my parents' bedroom, I searched through the yard-long stretch of albums snug in the cabinet my father built for them. Mostly I found show music—*South Pacific, Kismet, My Fair Lady, Oklahoma!*—but also some movie scores, several Gilbert and Sullivans, a Harry Belafonte, Judy Garland, Renata Tebaldi, and a smattering of the more popular classical concertos, symphonies, and ballets. I don't know how many I considered, but I ended up with a selection from *Around the World in Eighty Days* and was pleased with my choice.

Next class, when it was my turn, I gave Nadja the album, and she placed the needle on the first of the chalk marks I'd been instructed to make. I'm sure I was nervous, but when I heard my music, I blocked out Nadja, my mother, the other mothers, and all the girls sitting Indian style beneath the barre, and I danced. On my toes, into the air—I sashayed and *jetéd* and spun around as I pictured the hot air balloon flying jauntily, the giant pages of the calendar tearing free and floating away, day after day. I danced for maybe forty seconds (it seemed an eternity) until Nadja lifted the needle. Flushed and sweaty, I returned to my spot beneath the bar and awaited the "criticism," which I had already learned could include the good as well as the bad.

"Nice levels," one of the girls said, a popular compliment.

"She covered the whole floor," another remarked.

"But she should have held it longer at the end to make it more dramatic."

"And she didn't have . . . ," the young critic struggled for the right word. This part I remember well. "She didn't have . . ."

"A want," someone else called out. "A want, a want." Once the word was out it was volleyed back and forth. "Every dance needs a want!"

A what?

As the discussion continued, I came to understand that dances performed at Nadja's were supposed to be "choreographed." Which meant? A lot of things: repeatable moves, some sort of shape, a beginning, middle, and end. You got this shape with its parts, by creating a story. A story had a character who had a want, something she usually got at the end but sometimes didn't. I came also to understand that by choosing the theme song to *Around the World*, I'd committed another error. Music written to accompany a movie, ballet, or play was "program" music. Granted, *it* had a story, a want, but that was precisely the problem: the want belonged to someone else.

Although I had danced my heart out and gotten the most basic things wrong, I didn't feel humiliated. Nadja was most pleasant about the matter and seemed to regard the assignment a success. Based on who knows what—my dance? the album I selected?—she now knew exactly what music I was henceforth to work with: Bach's *Goldberg Variations*. And not just any recording but only the one by Glenn Gould.

The other new girl? I don't remember what album she brought from home, but I remember that for her Nadja assigned Bartok's *Romanian Folk Dances*. In subsequent classes, I was envious. The Bartok featured a passionate, lilting violin that gave the music a dancey feeling, whereas Gould's *Goldberg Variations* had a single steely line of piano plunks as jaunty as a bread slicer. How Nadja got from *Around the World in Eighty Days* to the *Goldberg Variations*, I'll never know but, to distract me from Bartok envy, I decided that the Bach was more grown-up, and that's why Nadja so wisely chose it for me.

After something even then? I seemed to want everything Nadja had to give me.

5. Plank

It is beauty that saves me, that makes the voyage from day to day possible and sometimes a treat.

When I wrote this in June of 2003, my days truly had that voy-agey feeling—arduous, perilous. A month before, we had learned that Sandy's cancer had come back: round three. Just a few days follow-ing that news, when I received some mail announcing a Saturday of "art-making" in the "Kate Ransohoff way," I tossed the flyer into the recycling bin. I'd never heard of Turtle Studio, where the workshop was to be held, and I certainly didn't have the time or mental clarity for a whole day of anything—let alone anything good for nobody except, just possibly, me. Still, the name Ransohoff lingered. Wasn't she the one who had mentored Mary McClane, a sculptor friend of a friend with whom I'd taken some workshops about five years ago? And hadn't I attributed one of the happiest summers in my life to those workshops that taught me about the role of play in creativity? That summer, instead of adhering to my usual no-nonsense writing regimen, I gave myself time to play, to *potchkying*, we might have called it in Queens—dismissively. On my initial drive up to our cabin, I stopped at a yard sale and bought a doll-sized chair made of twigs. This became my totem of sorts. I found moss to cushion the seat, a pygmy pine branch and tiny wildflower to weave through the back. I placed the chair on the ledge above my computer, and each morning before writing, I assessed its state. For weeks, the moss remained a moist, luscious green, but the branch and flower tired quickly, requir-ing frequent forays into the woods for replacements. This cost me time, but when I settled down to writing, my senses attuned, I felt filled with wonder for nature's miniature gifts; the writing time that followed seemed more productive, so much so that I felt entitled to quit working early so I could play around some more, this time with bigger branches and stuff I found by the woodshed—rusted tools and chains, defunct stove grates, ax handles, brooms. (New Hampshire folk are famous for the way they both save and dump. Deep in the woods, jalopies and wringers molt, their skeletons serving as plush hotels for spiders and mice.) A bricoleur now, I turned junk into relief sculptures—amateurish for sure but with a quality of aliveness that pleased me; and despite my clumsy, low-tech methods of affixing my creations to outside walls, they survived that winter and several more.

And so, I retrieved that flyer from the recycling bin. Read the description again. Remembered the single session I'd had with the therapist recommended by a friend in a similar situation. I'd been coping, yes: managing to teach my classes, get dinner on the table. Sam was still growing and learning and enjoying his childhood most of the time. Sandy had wonderful doctors and nurses, good health benefits, and still plenty of unused sick days. We had an amazingly generous community of family and friends who did and did and did for us. But Sandy hated asking so much of others; she didn't see why I couldn't do more. I didn't see how I could do more. We had some ugly fights about this. Only a monster, I thought, fights with someone so sick. And it's not as if I wasn't still seeing friends, walking in the park with the dog, taking a dance class for God's sake! All this and more I told that therapist, and what she said is simply this: "When your bank account is empty you need to refill it." And then she asked me what fed my soul.

It was a tense moment. My soul? I concentrated on my breathing so that I wouldn't cry, and then, in a scared, small voice, I tried this out: "Picking things from the garden and arranging them in a vase?" As I said it, I knew it was true. I remembered how this used to delight me, though I couldn't remember when I'd last done it. And I was pleased with myself for coming up with something that was relatively modest, that wouldn't make me sound horribly shallow but was still, under current circumstances, out of the question.

But this esteemed psychiatrist gave me permission, more than permission; she made me feel as if it were my *duty* to replenish myself. No, she didn't exactly sanction a whole Saturday of "making art in the Kate Ransohoff way," but "my account felt empty." I sent in my check.

. . . beauty that saves me, that makes the voyage from day to day possible and sometimes a treat. Beauty I see in that harsh, rough rope with its stiff tiny hairs that can hurt.

Like Mary's workshops, this one at Turtle Studio provided a big space, a long stretch of time, and an unfathomable array of materials—the usual arts and crafts stuff (remember pipe cleaners, clothes pins, popsicle sticks, cigar boxes, feathers, fabric scraps, shells, pollywogs, beach glass) along with plumbing, electrical, and office supplies, and all manner of industrial widgets and whatnots. In the "Ransohoff way" we played around, then talked about the results of that play, usually tangible, then wrote about and photographed our creations before dismantling them. (*Poof!* A-plus in nonattachment; now you're a Buddhist monk.) I have my snapshots and jottings still. That "harsh rough rope" was heavy and thick and loosely wound around the lintel of a yard-high wooden post-and-beam structure I assembled. On the floor beneath this doorway of sorts (it reminded me of the stocks I'd seen as a kid in Amish country—and the rope, of course, suggested a hanging—thus, I suppose, my title for the piece, "Torture Tent") I tossed three pieces of cloth the colors of earth and sea. Like Jackson Pollock, I threw these down in extravagant motions, surrendering to chance, but then cheated a little, adjusting some folds so that the light and shadows pleased me. On the most sea-like color I placed a boat-shaped gourd and, in its cradle, scattered some dry white beans that spilled over the sides and onto all three overlapping cloths. I also built a bridge—a gently curved branch that I rested on two big rocks.

Was there really beauty there in those spiky threads that could hurt? In that stocks-like doorway that I associated with punishment? To me in that moment, the whole assemblage looked reasonably like art. Good or bad art—I didn't much care. I was pleased with what I saw. It seemed to me that I'd found some rough equivalent of the landscape of my psyche. The resonance between outside and inside soothed me.

But now I have to wonder if it was really *beauty* that saved me each day?

Even at the time I wrote that, I had my doubts. My jottings continued. Maybe it's really truth that saves me? Hard as it is to confront, it offers a kind of comfort, or at least relief from the strain of denial . . . I was thinking there of the no-nonsense tone in my support group for women with partners who had cancer. Of the people—and there were enough of them—who didn't try to prettify Sandy's suffering or prognosis.

Or maybe it's friendship? I continued. *A kind of beauty, that outpouring of generosity from so many*, I wrote. I was also thinking of those unflinching friends who gave so much by simply listening to me in my most despairing moments. *Mostly, it's Augie*, I continued, *our soft, scraggly mutt whose joyous boundings in the park each day give me the energy to go on.*

Beauty? Truth? Kindness? Frolicking ball of fur? No need to choose. But weighing in on the beauty side is the memory of that winter of Sandy's first chemo treatments, before such treatments became a way of life. How hard it was seeing that once sturdy dynamo so depleted, stationary and miserable there on the green couch; how hard to manage my teaching as well as all the household tasks that even with two healthy parents often felt beyond me. How false my chirpiness felt when Sam and I had our meals without her. He was nine then—confused, scared, angry. How strained our "normality" when Sandy managed to get off the couch and join us at the table. She'd sit in her usual place but not eat; sit but not cajole Sam or talk of her day, her work, her take on national politics, or her garden plans for spring. Yet each morning that long winter when I came downstairs I saw, within the hibiscus plant beside our kitchen table, a new vermillion blossom, sometimes the star of the show, sometimes just the latest addition to a miraculous profusion.

"A plank amid the waves," Augustine called this lifesaver, beauty. I held on tight.

6. Beauty, the Treacherous

Fall 2004: I was in New Hampshire, taking a break from all the packing and cleaning entailed in closing up our cabin for the season, a task that for the first time in eighteen years I was doing without Sandy. I climbed partway up the mowing, plopped down on the path, and drank in the ocean of tall grass, the riot of purple asters, the comforting shape of our cabin below. I looked beyond that, to the curve of hills and then the mountains. How? I wondered, how does anyone say good-bye to this?

I wasn't thinking good-bye until next year. I was thinking about Sandy, now too sick to travel, on a drug I was shocked to discover the internet called "palliative." I had no answer to my question. I rested a few minutes, squeezed back the tears, threw Augie a few sticks, and went back to work. Surveying the cabin an hour or so later, the car already loaded, on a last-minute whim, I grabbed the painting off the wall of the porch so Sandy could have a reminder of the place. It was that bold watercolor of pears that Frankie, our landlady, had painted. Sandy had bought it that first summer after she was diagnosed. She was an impulsive shopper and I didn't always approve, but now I could see that this purchase was an act of faith; a prayer, perhaps; her plank. Surely it would be a comfort—just as those hibiscus blooms were for me. And those morning bowls of brilliant fruit. And those Maria Callas arias I'd once thought so over-the-top but whose emotional pitch now felt just right. All those forms of beauty felt like emissaries from the sublime, assuring me that even if God was not on my side, or Sandy's, or Sam's—even if there was no God at all—life was good.

Back in Cambridge, after unpacking the car, I proudly presented the pear painting to Sandy. She burst into tears.

"I'm never going to see that place again," she said.

7. Wired for Beauty?

When I was ten or eleven, old enough to have my own key, about twice a week when my mother played cards I came home from school to an empty house. On one such day, I felt something odd as soon as I walked in. From the tiny vestibule, I could see past the darkened living room into the adjacent dining room: our old table was gone, a new one in its place. The old table was oval, or rectangular with its flaps folded down; this new one—I went to investigate—was perfectly round, and instead of being a single shade of a purplish brown—I turned on the light—this new one was more of a reddish, golden brown with a finger-length band of blonder wood around the perimeter. Unlike the old one's thick, waxy finish that we shined before company came, this new one's finish, if it had one at all, was invisible, and the wood seemed to shine from within. Most striking, I could see that it had once been a tree. The border had traces of grain and greenish/yellow flecks. Even the darker middle had some variations that made it seem alive. And it was exactly the right height. I did not have to reach or bend at all to rest my hand on it. And maybe because of its burnished look, because it had a single central base rather than four protruding legs or because the outer circle seemed to amplify its roundness, the table sang of spinning things—records, tops, planets. And so I had to walk around it, my fingers grazing lightly over the greenish-yellow band, around and around until its roundness was humming inside me.

I've been thinking about the way we're sometimes struck by beauty. Is that capacity innate? Learned? Universal?

I've been asking friends: "What is your earliest memory of being struck, stunned, arrested by beauty?"

We were visiting a friend of my family's, a painter, says Donna. There was a circular brick entryway, a calm hush inside the house, the smell of linseed oil. And out back, a circular pool of goldfish. I felt safe. Mesmerized.

It was at the beach, says Helen. I remember the feel of the wet sand beneath my toes. I was watching the shells fill with water as the tide came in, and empty as it went out. There was a sense of safety and adventure, too, of being contained and being free. I think maybe it had more to do with the fact that this was a place where my mother was happy—a rare occurrence.

This sample is tiny, but already some things seem clear.

The eyes are not the only, nor even the widest, door. For Donna, beauty is ushered by—or nestled inside—a hush, a pungency. The squish and grit beneath Helen's toes figure in her memory; for me, the feel of the table and my kinesthetic sense of its shape loom large. My friend Miriam who speaks of her childhood trips to the symphony recalls little about the music or even the look of the concert hall, but her palms can still summon the feeling of the railings' plush velvet. Multisensory, synesthetic affairs—odd that I never before connected "aesthetic" (from *aisthetikos*, meaning "perceptual") with its opposite, "*an*esthetic"—some of these memories also suggest a cognitive element. The mind seizes patterns, likenesses, and differences—the circular brick entryway, the circular pool, the shells repeatedly filling and emptying.

The emotions also play a role—or maybe I should say the nerves, or adrenal glands—those sentries that send us into fight or flight, neither conducive to aesthetic experience. Both Donna and Helen speak of safety. Donna's experience seems a consequence of her perception—beauty not just as plank but as a whole private island. For Helen, a sense of safety just might be a prerequisite. Her account suggests that beauty can't enter until she feels secure enough to shed her usual vigilance. But Helen also implies that safety (the feeling of being contained) is most delicious when served along with the chance to break out.

For my friend Jeff, the only male I questioned, an alluring sense of danger—he'd ventured beyond his usual childhood territory into forbidden woods—seemed to magnify his pleasure in what he found there: a smashed juke box, sunlight bouncing off hundreds of fragments of colored glass that turned the leafy canopy above into a shimmering cathedral. Like most I spoke with, Jeff's perception of beauty seemed to arrive in a single blow, but his narrative suggests that, well, that a narrative is necessary: the moments preceding the perception play a crucial role in readying us.

Today a class of painters is scattered on the mowing surrounding my writing shack, so I venture out.

It happened in a college art class, says Polly, a student in her fifties, when I discovered that blue and orange made gray. For some reason this absolutely thrilled me. Something about the transition between warm and cool. I remember running back to my dorm to tell my roommate, but it turned out she wasn't much interested.

It happened when I was in kindergarten, says Dale, the teacher of that class, also middle-aged. It was in New Jersey, and the teacher took our class out to draw the George Washington Bridge. We stayed there for some time, and when the teacher told us it was time to leave, I got really upset. I felt hurt. I believed in that drawing! And now felt as if I were being literally wrenched from it. She pressed her fist against her sternum.

Just as Bernard Cooper said ("a thrilling paralysis, a churning in my solar plexus"), the thrall of beauty is somatic. Polly's moment of thrilling paralysis was immediately followed by a compulsion to run and tell. For Dale, it seems the drawing *became* the bridge and both entered her body. For me, my orbits around the table drew the table's marvelous circularity into me.

As for courses, the trigger for all this musing, clearly they are not prerequisite. Most everyone can—and does—get hammered by beauty at some point. Glowing brain scans suggest we might just be wired for beauty. Even so, in my life, teachers—even the scolders and hair-pullers—have often been the ones to turn the current on.

8. A More Modest View of the Power of Teachers

This willingness continually to revise one's own location in order to place oneself in the path of beauty, [this] is the basic impulse underlying education. One submits oneself to other minds (teachers) in order to increase the chance that one will be looking in the right direction when a comet makes its sweep through a certain patch of sky.

—Elaine Scarry

9. Me and Georgia O'Keeffe

Visual descriptions are an important part of writing, I told myself in my teacher's voice, already sensing where this was heading. It was winter in Cambridge. I had just picked up Sam from day care. His teachers there were geniuses to my way of thinking. When not negotiating conflicts between toddlers, fierce and menacing as Khrushchev in his shoe-banging years, these teachers were artists—dancers, musicians, actors. Sam's lead teacher was a potter. When I mentioned we were planning to spend the summer in Taos, she told me she knew a terrific teacher out there who taught a course in landscape painting. Lois Tarlow was her name.

Back in the car with Sam strapped in, I had half a moment to think: Could I allow myself six full days away from my precious writing time?

I imagined my sturdy legs singing as they tromped around the desert; I smelled the sagebrush, and off in the distance, I saw a clay red mesa. On top of that mesa, I could make out a figure, a wide-brimmed hat, *my* hat, *my* loose cotton shirt rolled up to the elbows, my uncertain hand poised in front of a canvas held up by a rustic easel.

It will pay off in the long run, I told myself. You'll learn how to see better.

As the only rank beginner among six well-schooled painters, several already showing and selling, I did learn how to see better. At least a little better. There's so much to consider, not the least of which is deciding *what* to look at—in many ways my favorite part. The first day or two, we worked from Lois's deck in the foothills, but each day after that, we'd pile into her van and drive to one of her favorite spots. And that's where the tromping came in. Across dusty roads and dribbling rivers, up mountains, past proprietary wild bulls, down slippery scrabbled valleys, through fields peppered with scarlet penstemon, to the base of those craggy clay boulders that O'Keeffe had her way with. All this in search of what? A spot big and flat enough to hold our two feet, our three-footed easel, our box of paints and brushes or, in the case of this ingénue who didn't know how to draw, my box of charcoals and pastels (Lois's orders), a perch from which we could see something that called to us.

How much of that something? That, also, was a key question. The answer: not much. To see better, I learned, it's best to see less. First by employing a small, handmade cardboard frame the same dimensions as one's canvas—Lois's low-tech way of deciding what goes in and what stays out. Then by using the squint—a marvelously simple way of erasing excess detail to highlight the predominant shapes. And finally, by simply deciding to excise whatever might be too difficult, too cute, too much. This, for some reason, felt like the most radical lesson, requiring me to make peace with that thrilling but discomforting feeling of choosing among nature's countless darlings. I loved the fierce, jagged boulders. I loved the scrub. I loved the mirages on the roads, the vintage jalopies on the sides of the roads, the cacti I couldn't name—such attitude they had! And I loved the mountains. And the mountains behind the mountains.

So much for the *what*. Then there's the *how*, starting for me with the humbling task of exiling all those images I'd had since kindergarten. No, the sun does not look like a circle with spikes. Clouds are not white, tree trunks not brown. Leaves on a distant tree don't have the shape of those pressed against your childhood windowpane. But what *does* the sun look like? What color is a cloud? A tree trunk? A wand of penstemon in a field of weeds? And, more difficult still, suppose one knew these answers—with whatever faculty knows such things—how would one make that color from the thirty-six lined up in the box?

How does one mash three dimensions into something paper-thin?

And I must not forget the matter of how to hold the charcoal.

No, not the way I did, my elbow hugging my torso, my tight little fist clutching the stick down near its point, pressing hard and continuously, often breaking the tip. Lois held her stick loosely, on the end closest to her. She'd stand a bit away from the paper, engaging her arm in a graceful arc; yet the strokes she usually made were short and fast. However she did it, the resulting line looked effortless, elegant, alive.

What else did I learn from this workshop?

One must never neglect the matter of tools.

And one should never discard old pajamas, their soft flannel so perfect for blending pastels.

I learned that when painters discuss what to cook for dinner, their conversation eddies around which shape of pasta will best complement the shape of broccoli. That after ten days of drawing or painting you can have more or less ten completed pictures you can line up against a sofa or vehicle for critique; whereas, after ten days of writing, you're lucky if you have a scrap of something that, though easier to transport, is less likely to become someone's treasured possession. I learned a little about visual artists' critical vocabulary, learned they used literary terms like "vocabulary" when alluding to their various strokes (lines, squiggles, dots); they even used that most basic literary term, "to read," as in "that section of the painting where the fence borders the river is hard 'to read.' " They borrowed terms from dance and music—a painting could have "kinetic energy" or a "harmonious" design. Of course, musicians use the term "color," and writers talk about "texture." These days, such crossovers seem old hat to me, but at the time they were revelatory.

Another revelation: I learned why there are so many beautiful older women in Taos. Why? Because they're not really older, they're young—with great bone structure but desiccated skin. Most of all, I learned the heady pleasures of being a beginner, in which every effort, no matter how fledgling, is praiseworthy; where there's no place for apologies or posturing or shame, where one can work joyfully and recklessly without much fear of consequences and where, years away from any plateau, your learning curve is steep. I loved allowing myself to like what I did. I could see that the perspective was way off, the penstemon too big, the mountain too small; from the stiff line of my tree trunk, I could tell I was holding the charcoal too tight. But I could also see that something about the shapes and positions of the boulders gave them character, a lilting whimsical quality I liked.

I can't say for sure that this workshop improved my descriptive prose, but I never regretted those six days under my wide-brimmed hat, teaching me, if not exactly to look in the *right direction*, to find in *every* direction something worth looking at.

10. On Beauty and Justice and Becoming a Horse

"Wittgenstein says, when the eye sees something beautiful the hand wants to draw it."

This from Elaine Scarry's *On Beauty and Being Just*, a treasure of a book that serendipitously presented itself to me—displayed as it was near the cashier of my local bookstore. How could I resist? Ever since my college days, when the crowd I hung with spent more time discussing Marx and Marcuse than we did Joyce or Kandinsky, I've been trying to reconcile my love of beauty with my desire to do good. Also: the book was so small, so slim, so *beautiful* with its cover of lovingly painted birds' eggs, twenty-five of them arranged in rows of five, each egg different from the rest—but you had to look carefully to discover the differences.

"Beauty brings copies of itself into being," Scarry continues. Broadening and modernizing Wittgenstein: "It makes us draw, take photographs of it or describe it to other people. Sometimes it gives rise to exact replication and other times to resemblances and still other times to things whose connection to the original site of inspiration is unrecognizable." This belief in beauty's inherent "forward momentum" is the starting point for Scarry's thesis that beauty and justice are linked. I cannot hope to do "justice" to her intricate argument, but her logic goes something like this:

The perception of beauty inspires us toward a "more capacious regard for the world." It does this by taking us out of ourselves, or, as activist-philosopher Simone Weil puts it, by forcing us to "give up our imaginary position as the center." Arrested by beauty—or absorbed in the process of trying to replicate it—we are transported to a state where we sense ourselves to be "adjacent" to the main site of interest or importance. Scarry explains: "It is not that we cease to stand at the center of the world, for we never stood there. It is that we cease to stand even at the center of our own world. We willingly cede our ground to the thing that stands before us." And here, paraphrasing novelist-philosopher Iris Murdoch, Scarry adds: "All the space formerly in the service of protecting, guarding, advancing the self (or its 'prestige') is now free to be in the service of something else."

In other words: Struck by beauty, experiencing ourselves as just a little *beside* the point, we are infused with a generosity of spirit; we become more altruistic and other-directed. We are impelled to create more beauty and to make more of the whole stash available to more people.

It's a lovely, seductive idea. And certainly when I have been "taken" by something I've just read, even if the hour is late, I'm tempted to telephone all my kindred spirits and say: *You must read this!* I'm inclined to grab my camera at the sight of a crocus pushing up through the snow. And who among us can resist pointing up and shouting *Look!* so that not just our companion but *everyone* in the vicinity can see the flight of a red-tailed hawk? As the saying goes, pleasure shared is doubled, so why not spread the wealth.

Still, sometimes sharing means halving, or worse. It could easily mean no more private beach for you, no more secluded cabin for me. As evidence of our impulse toward "justice," toward wanting beauty available to all, Scarry points out that we have an environmental movement, and that we take pains to ensure that great art is preserved so that it will be available for future generations. Scarry doesn't directly take on the question of class, or of whether other goodies aside from beauty—food, shelter, freedom, education—should also be spread around (the implication is, of course, yes); nor does she raise the question of how much we're willing to personally sacrifice so that beauty, and other nurturers of body and soul, are more equitably distributed. Rather, she implies that this latter question is almost moot, saying, "People seem to wish there to be beauty even when their own self-interest is not served by it; or perhaps, more accurately, people seem to intuit that *their own self-interest is served by distant peoples' having the benefit of beauty*" (emphasis mine). Ergo real self-sacrifice is not necessary. She expands on this only briefly and not entirely convincingly—as if perhaps a bit of wishful thinking were at play here.

My sculptor friend Toby Bornstein works mainly in wood, carving behemoth figures, mostly mothers and children, from mature tree trunks. When I ask her about her process and the role of beauty in her own desire to create, she responds in an old-fashioned, handwritten letter to me: "It was never beauty that drove me. Rather, an obsession with love. First it was a hunger for the children, to hold and own them entirely, to love and (less intensely) to be loved. And then I learned there was more love than I could express in reality . . .

"The sculpture is not a story," Toby continues, "but starts with a feeling, an obsession, a secret that sometimes even I don't know, just that I feel the scalpel must go this way, and it may be days that I sit and stare at it and then know the solution and the feeling finally comes through the wood and I know the passion inside me eases down and it is finished. It is a miracle to me each time."

Toby and her scalpel seem to be infused with something like Nadja's "want," a tension impelling them in a certain direction. "A secret that sometimes even I don't know." I feel that, too, in my solar plexus, inclining, propelling me forward, whether I am writing this or gluing a branch to a rock or dancing "outside the lines."

"These days," Toby continues, " 'beautiful' is an old-fashioned way to describe art and I know no one who is working to make something beautiful. . . . And another thing you didn't ask me, the more I think about myself the less art I can do. The best working is when I'm completely oblivious to myself, it is only the working."

"Only the working." This—this luscious gift of self-oblivion garnered in the state of "flow" while creating—as well as while encountering beauty already extant—this is what Scarry, Weil, Murdoch, Dale (the kindergarten bridge-drawer), and so many others describe. In *The Zen of Seeing*, the sublime artist Frederick Franck explains: "In order to draw a horse, draw horses until you practically become a horse—not 'horses in general,' but always that particular horse . . . until you feel the tense curving of its neck in your own neck." Once a horse, of course—a particular horse, that is—no longer are you *you*; nor are you quite *not*-you, but, rather, as Franck says, "outside and inside are unseparated."

This deep embodiment of the other, the fusion that happens when we're perceiving or loving or duplicating, surely this state—and even just the memory of it—inclines us toward a "do unto others" code of behavior. At the very least, it expands our capacity for compassion. How far that inclination and capacity take us remains a question for us to wrestle with daily.

For now, let me just test out the sound of this:

Much—*if not most*—of what's best, most just, most generous in me was sown by the beautiful things I've heard, read, and seen. (Oh yes, I think. Yes.)

11. The Good, the Bad, and the Pretty/Beautiful/ Wild/Disgusting

In September of 1964, a few months shy of my fourteenth birthday, I began to keep a diary in a spiral notebook. *Personal*, I printed on the rough cardboard cover, just above the RiteWell logo. *PERSONAL!* I wrote again, this time in caps, below the logo.

As if that were not enough, beneath that I wrote:

If anyone dares to look in this I will NEVER speak to you again. I am trusting you without a key. Live with your conscience. Thank you for your honesty.

And then I put a carat above "anyone" and inserted: *That includes you, mother!*

Clearly the power of understatement eluded me.

Wanting to learn more about—okay, I confess—about *me*, but also about how *any* of us come to apprehend beauty, be arrested by it, recognize it in uncommon places, and, most important, act on that yearning to replicate it in some way, I've reread this old journal in its tedious yet touching entirety.

The first page explains its genesis:

I was just speaking to Linda and telling her my problems when she suggested poetry as a form of escape and relief. I realize I am untalented in that field so I decided to just plain write.

And just plain write I did. Over the course of a year and seventeen days, I wrote eighty-seven pages of careful, schoolgirl script.

Linda, by the way, was what we then called a "tramp." I knew this the minute I saw her cakey eyeliner, black fishnets, and big, teased hair. She had a husky voice and tough broad demeanor. She was also very smart. I knew this because of the things she said in class and because in private she told me she loved Shakespeare. Although we became friends, hanging out at lunch and after school, I don't remember her ever coming to my house. Perhaps I never invited her, suspecting my mother would have raised a brow, just as she would have had she *dared* to look inside my *(Personal!)* notebook and read this:

I pulled my turtleneck out from my pants. Then his hand was under my bra on my back near the side . . .

This time his hand was very near the side, but I really don't know how far, but quite . . .

The hand belonged to my then-boyfriend Seth. A year older than I, he was exceedingly popular among the girls at Camp Che-na-wah. Blond-haired, blue-eyed, and bony, he had an adorable goofy smile, a fuzzy dimpled chin, and a fetching gap between his front teeth. He liked to imitate Froggy of TV fame—*Hiya, kids, hiya, hiya!*—and blow tiny bubbles off his tongue—no easy feat. I'm not sure why this charmed me so, but it did, though what got to me even more than that, more than the chin and teeth, was that the previous winter his father was diagnosed with leukemia and died within a week. I only got glimpses of the big raw wound within Seth, but I took it for granted that someone who had experienced such a thing immediately became a person of great depth and sensitivity. I was crazy about him and believed he had feelings for me. But a month or so after the summer ended, he seemed to forget all about me. Thus those "problems" I told Linda about, and the journal's excruciatingly detailed accounts of us getting together, breaking up, and venturing toward each other again the following summer. Scattered among those lengthy passages, I dropped asides about schoolwork (*I have to cut out articles on what Goldwater and Johnson think about Nuclear Power*); The Beatles (*I saw them on TV and really like them*); a hootenanny at the high school (*Pretty good but Mu Sigma boys sat behind us and acted like they owned the place*); ski trips (*On the bus ride home I was sitting with Haydan who was holding my hand*); and temple dances (*the tramps and hoods went extremely wild and were disgusting. I danced too, but not like that*). Finally, here and there among all of that something else poked through: signs of a more reflective, curious, creative person emerging.

I am growing up, I say right there on page 1, *and believe me it's every bit as hard as everyone says. I myself can notice the changes in me.*

On page 2, after listing my best friends that past summer, I add: *And I mustn't forget myself, for I found myself a friend more than ever before.* I learned to enjoy my own company.

I feel this new intellectuality in myself, I write on page 64. *I have more appreciation for pretty and intellectual things, and it makes me happy although I'm not happy otherwise* (page 65).

No doubt the very act of keeping a journal prompted some of these changes—or at least my awareness of them. And it wouldn't be surprising to Scarry that my erotic awakening would be accompanied by an explosion in my appreciation for "pretty" things and an urge to experience and create other pretty things.

I just read over all I wrote tonight. I am a little disappointed. It isn't really beautiful, but then where I try to make it pretty like with "the longing within me," well, that just doesn't sound like me and I want this diary to be truly me because that is what a diary is (page 9).

Still, I don't stop yearning for some pleasing expression of my summer of love. Halfway down page 17, I make an aborted sketch of Seth and me sitting on a rock looking out on the lake. On the next page, I explain: *A couple of nights ago I got the urge to paint a picture of that from memory and to give it to Seth for his birthday. I imagined it all beautiful n'all, but then I came to reality and I knew I could never do it well.*

Maybe out of desperation, in spite of my earlier declaration (*no talent in the field*), I tried my hand at poetry. My early attempts were about Seth, but soon I was on to all the Big Subjects: Innocence and Experience, Racism, Travel, Adventure. Sometimes I wrote when I didn't have the journal with me, and I clipped the stray pages to the back cover. Both the poems and the just-plain-writing give glimpses of a soul searching to get hold of a rapidly changing "truly me," and she is asking versions of the same questions I'm asking still. In "What is Joy?" she writes:

> *Joy is nature and humans combining forces,*
> *forming beauty.*

I'll spare you the other nine stanzas but not my critique:
I think my thoughts are good. But there is really much more I'd like to say and I should know how to say more in less words. I should try to say things in a prettier way.

Later in the journal, which increasingly becomes an accounting of my burgeoning interest in books and art, film and theater, I seem to be questioning the premium I have put on "prettiness" as I find other ways of thinking about what I read and see.

About Herman Wouk's *Marjorie Morningstar* I say, *All thru the book, she loved this guy Noel. Then she marries another man. I really can't explain the tragedy of this in my mind.*

About James Agee's *A Death in the Family*: *Good but strange and slow . . . I kept thinking this is what Seth went through.*

And about Gabriel Marcel's *The Philosophy of Existentialism*: *Read about 8 pgs first nite then next nite read them over. I understand parts but it seems contradictory and makes little sense.*

I start going to Manhattan with Barbara, the friend who turned me on to Nadja.

I love it there so much, I write. *You see so many intellectual people. We went to the Guggenheim museum. There was an exhibit on Calder (Mobiles). I loved it.*

I report on the dark "films" that my parents, oddly enough, started taking me to. (My sister was now away at college, and I'm guessing they felt bad about leaving me home alone.) Of *The Night of the Iguana* and *Toys in the Attic* I write: *Both good but very depressing!*

I comment on a much-talked-about production of *The Trojan Women* that my parents also took me to: *Interesting.*

I'm surprised I don't say more about that play. I remember how excited I was to be going to Greenwich Village, to an "avant-garde" theater, the Circle in the Square. I remember the strangeness of such a small theater without a stage, without scenery. Mostly I remember—in fact *all* I remember from the play itself—is a bunch of women in white tunics stomping their bare feet and wailing. Just a few yards from the action, I was frightened by the intensity of feeling, by those deep, agonized voices echoing off the theater's bare walls. This was not pretty. And yet, unlike the girl who two months earlier had declared the wild dancing at the temple "disgusting," I did not recoil from these keening, flailing women. I must have suspected that, like Nadja and Linda, they had something to teach me, and I found myself leaning forward in my seat.

I wish that I could throw my shoes away . . .

So begins my next-to-last poem in the book, though I doubt that at the time I connected the image with the Trojan women.

> *Dance about on my bare feet*
> *To a wild, never-ending beat.*
> *Kick the damp dirt,*
> *Feel how the roughness can hurt.*

12. Rediscovering the Goldbergs

When we are struck by beauty, be it in the fissures of Janis Joplin's bluesy voice, the smile of the boy next door, or the unexpected gesture of kindness from a stranger, we are utterly convinced that our awe is justified—no critic or scholar can talk us out of it. And so pleasurable is this absolute faith in the beauty of the voice, face, or gesture that, in the words of Elaine Scarry, we "ever afterwards . . . wrestle with the world to locate [other] enduring sources of conviction—to locate what is true." This wrestling, this searching for truth, is what Scarry means by education.

The year is 1973, and the place, New Haven, Connecticut. I am twenty-two or twenty-three, having finished college and a year-long master's program in the teaching of high school English (my way of serving beauty and justice, too). I'm living in a house I share with three others. My bedroom there is the biggest I've ever had, and for the first time in my life I have the freedom and resources to make it my own from the ground up. I have sanded and stained the floors and painted the walls several times until I found an acceptable shade of mustard yellow. Tonight I am in for the evening. It must be the weekend; otherwise I would be tearing through a dozen teaching books searching for a way to ignite my students' interest in *Beowulf.* I am sitting on the floor beside the shelves I built with bricks and boards, shelves for books I love (Mann's *The Magic Mountain*, Woolf's *To the Lighthouse*, R. D. Laing's *The Politics of Experience*) and for my new turntable, receiver, and giant Advent speakers—graduation gifts from my parents. I picture a glass of scotch, but maybe I just have scotch on my brain because of the scotch tape on the album jacket (named for its whiskey color? or the thrifty, resourceful Scotch people?).

The album? Bach's *Goldberg Variations.*

I must have come upon it while going through the house in Queens for things I wanted to take with me now that I was finally out of school, with a job (North Haven High), and the chance of staying in one place for more than a year. I hadn't taken it with me to college. In fact, I doubt I'd played it since I left Nadja sometime in junior high (not out of any disenchantment, just because I had too much schoolwork). I don't remember using the album much for choreographing, though its bandaged jacket suggested it had been handled a lot. Maybe I'm stuck on scotch because of the album jacket, a checkerboard of black and white photos of Gould, all tinged amber. In each he wears the same white shirt, but his position, his gesture, his expression is different: theme and variation.

I'd gotten quite an education in the previous few years—not only about the arts, religion and politics, but about "atmosphere"— about the kind that's conducive to romance, and also, extending that junior-high discovery, about the romance of solitude. I had learned about the loveliness of earth tones, about Indian print bedspreads and prayer plants, candlelight and incense, about altered states. In this quiet moment, everything is of a piece—all the golden, flickering tones in the room in harmony; the parallel and perpendicular lines from books on shelves, from window frames and ledges, from my newly stained floorboards—all somehow in sync with the album jacket and its checkerboard of images of Gould at the piano. And, of course, the piano keys themselves—I cannot listen to Gould without picturing his fingers on the keys.

In my Nadja days, when I put on a variation, all I heard was one steely plunk after another, but this evening I can hear the notes in relation to each other. I can hear Gould's quirky timing, his distinctive way of striking the keys. No wonder Nadja would admit no other recording, and my mother and I had to scour Manhattan for it. With Nadja, when I composed dances, I'd compose to a single variation or possibly two (the chalk marks were still there on the vinyl), but now I listened to all thirty-two variations in one sitting.

Once I had thought the music chilly, monotonous, entirely without melody; now I began to hear its beguiling geometry. And over the more than thirty years since then, I have continued to listen to the *Goldberg Variations*—so that now I can hear what Gould in his liner notes called their "luxuriant vegetation," their "gravitational pull" (their "want"?). Such clairvoyance that Nadja had—to choose that piece for me! She was probably just trying to yank me away from the schlocky *Around the World in Eighty Days*, but I like to indulge in the fantasy that Nadja sniffed something in me, some nascent ability to perceive pattern and subtlety—or whatever it is that makes someone into an ardent lover of this piece. Now if I had to choose a single CD for my desert island, I would choose Gould's *Goldberg Variations*. Either that or Casals's Bach's solo *Cello Suites*.

In my fantasy Nadja was prescient. She knew that in AP English Mr. Jacobson with the glass eye would read the finale of my poem about *The Tale of Two Cities* aloud (. . . *slumber Sydney slumber.*) and declare to the whole class: "Now that's real poetry!" In my college years, after seeing the sexy movie *Sunday Bloody Sunday*, I'd hunt down that mournful Mozart aria the rejected bisexual lover played obsessively. I'd fall in love with the music in Roethke and Yeats and listen to the sounds of my own swallowing during John Cage's "silent" *4'33"*. One spring day I'd watch those dance students outside on the green, positioned in a wide V, ever-so-slowly shifting directions in unison like a flock of geese. (Yes, in learning to listen and see, quite often less is more.) The preternatural Nadja even knew I would someday come to experience sexual desire—its exacerbation, attenuation, dissipation, rejuvenation, consummation—and that this knowledge would contribute to my ability to inhabit a line of complex music—but contribute not quite as much as did that funny-looking guy who presided over Oberlin College's legendary Music 101.

13. Crisscrossing

I was attracted to Oberlin because it was the first US college to admit blacks and women, and I was intrigued when I heard on the radio that its students had surrounded an army recruiter's vehicle and wouldn't let the guy out, even to pee. I chose Oberlin because when I visited in October the weather was perfect, the trees in Tappan Square ruddy and golden. A nice boy sat under one of those trees, and he invited me to go with him to hear Ravi Shankar that evening. Shankar sat cross-legged on the floor of the stage in the magnificent Finney Chapel. Having never attended a concert of Indian music, I didn't know that sitar players always sat on the floor. I was delighted by the informality of this position, the intimacy it created. I felt on familiar terms with "Ravi," even as he played a kind of music that was entirely unfamiliar, music that blasted open everything I knew about music up until then. I chose Oberlin because that blast thrilled me, that boy was gentle, smart, and interesting. Everything I saw and heard that weekend gave off a scent of what I think I was after then and am after still: that perfect combination of adventure and safety, individuality and community.

My senior year in high school, I read a lot about racism and poverty, about loneliness, alienation, conformity, and rebellion in American society. I thought I'd probably major in sociology, but it turned out that the prerequisite Intro class met at 8 a.m. so I never took a single sociology course. Instead, I took later-starting courses upperclassmen recommended. "You *must* take Suskin's 101," several told me. That this squat, pale, frizzy-haired Jewish man with geeky glasses was not the target of mockery but, rather, a beloved icon—this was proof enough that in choosing Oberlin I'd done a good thing.

Suskin's first assignment was to attend a classical concert and write about it—a frightening prospect. Luckily, we were allowed, encouraged even, to write about the whole "experience"—a hot word in those days but still a good one when it comes to art and beauty. The concert hall, the lighting, the pianist's clothing, movements, facial expressions—I remember commenting on these and also on some of the images that went through my mind while I listened. I don't remember if I said anything about the music itself—I didn't have the vocabulary—but this assignment has stayed with me because it assured me that no matter how sophisticated a work of art is, one's humble observations and reactions are fair game. Learning surely helps, but those initial perceptions are a good place to begin. This is my approach when I ask students to react to a piece of writing, and it's an approach that gained legitimacy when the "reader-response" school of literary theory came into vogue. I remember this assignment also because it introduced me to the phenomenon of "synesthesia," what Scarry calls the "crisscrossing of the senses."

I loved going to Suskin's class. To enter the Con(servatory) designed by Minoru Yamasaki, who later designed the World Trade Center Towers, one passed through a Japanese garden whose pond reflected the building's latticed façade. The bars of the façade also suggested piano keys and organ pipes and maybe, too, a musical staff placed on its side. Passing through that garden with its little fountain, pygmy maples, craggy rocks, and lily pads, I would be snagged by its hushed beauty, before remembering that class began in two minutes.

Much of Music 101 was devoted to Mr. Suskin's exuberant embodiment of Mozart's Symphony no. 40 in G minor—at least that's the part I remember best. That sprightly man, already adorable to me, would stand on the stage, tap on the projected score with his pointer, and talk, sing, and *dance* his way through a few measures of the piece. This—and under headsets later that afternoon—is where I learned about theme and variation, repetitions, reversals, transpositions, keys, rhythm, dynamics, embellishments, and how the opening bars might go underground only to surface again and again in such surprising yet gratifying ways. This is where I learned that you could love the most aural and abstract of arts with your whole body.

14. How I Became an English Major

My English professor, the poet David Young, escorted us through a door that led to the courtyard of the King Building—another granite and leafy Yamasaki creation, this courtyard fully enclosed, more intimate than the one outside the Con. Even in northern Ohio, spring eventually arrived, and this pungent April afternoon seemed just made for Theodore Roethke's loamy, sonorous poems with their celebration of youth and Eros, their crisscrossing of the senses, and all those tantalizing paradoxes embodying the anti-intellectual, Eastern-leaning Truths ("We think by feeling. What is there to know?") that in 1969 we nineteen-year-olds thrilled to.

People like to knock their Intro courses, but I loved many of mine. Never since have I been so enthralled with the present moment, yet so eager for it to end, as I was sitting there on the sun-drenched stone listening to Mr. Young read Roethke's pulsing lines ("Light takes the Tree . . ."), while I slowly traced those barely budding branches with my eyes, something I had learned to do in Intro to Art History, where our first assignment was to draw the outline of a potted plant while looking at the plant, but not at our drawing hand, not at the paper. Seeing was the point—the outcome, incidental. Now, during that English class, all my senses awakened, I wanted the moment to last forever; at the same time, I was itching to get up and go, leave my skin, turn myself inside out. Spring fever, or simple horniness? I had a date right afterward to play squash—another new discovery: smashing that heavy black ball against any number of blinding white walls, sometimes crashing into one's sweaty new lover. Fever? Lust?

Both—and also this thing called poetry. Yes, I knew about syllabics, alliteration—remember *Slumber Sydney*—about personification and onomatopoeia. On another early spring afternoon in high school, after the school day ended, my best friend from that AP class sat with me on the school yard pavement and together we reveled in e. e. cummings's "puddle wonderful" world. Cummings was cunning and playful, sexy too, but this Roethke guy—on that day, especially, in the courtyard of King—his lines seemed to be oozing Eros.

Thankfully, Mr. Young didn't push us too hard toward analysis that day. Sensing our distraction perhaps, he allowed us to wallow in the poetry's "luxuriant vegetation"—Gould's words for the *Goldberg Variations*, but they seem apt here—to just ride along with its "gravitational pull."

I wake to sleep, and take my waking slow.

The poems' rhythms got tangled in the rhythms within me. Two of my most brilliant writer friends once discussed how they regarded their bodies simply as vehicles for their brains—a shocking idea to me, almost unholy.

I learn by going where I have to go.

That afternoon I thought: If this excruciatingly delicious aliveness is what literature is all about, I want it my whole life long.

15. Consider the Float, the Glide, the Slash, Dab, Wring

Who would have suspected that so many of my formative experiences would take place in church basements? This one lay on the edge of New Haven, and it was there that Donna Blank taught modern dance in ways entirely new to me. Her warm-up on the floor, for example, easy and boring at first, became harder and more interesting the more I did it. The challenge was to do the sequence slowly, fluidly, feeling all the connections between bones, muscles, and joints; to control which part initiated, which part went along for the ride. When Donna asked us to make adjustments, when she traveled among us and said *No!* or *Yes!* I was suspicious. Could the minuscule modification I'd attempted actually be seen?

Donna also attempted to teach us rhythm, something I'd lost in junior high but suddenly, miraculously, found again at the Oberlin discotheque where I realized not everyone—in fact, probably *no one*—was paying much attention to me when I danced. Donna had recently returned from Senegal where she had spent several months eating scrumptious peanut soup (funny, the details you hold on to for forty years), and where she had danced for hours on end with the Senegalese who, Donna said, regarded dance not as performance but as an essential part of everyday life. She brought back a drum and had us march around to the beats she banged out:

One, two, three, four, *onetwothree, onetwothree* . . .

Or, *onetwothreefour*, one and two and three and . . .

She made us clap or skip or do a little two-step as she introduced more complex rhythms and syncopations, gradually—quickly, really—moving us from kindergarten to graduate-level Eurhythmics. But the part of Donna's class that was most revelatory to me was the part in which we learned about the work of Laban, and Irmgard, and Birdwhistell. Donna came out with these names often, and it was some time before I got them straight.

Laban, Rudolf Laban, created a method of movement analysis used for dance notation in the years when we had no film or video to preserve choreography. Irmgard, Irmgard Bartenieff, Laban's student and Donna's teacher, furthered Laban's method, using it to train dancers and to rehabilitate the injured and disabled. Ray Birdwhistell, an anthropologist, applied Laban's work to his study of visual communication or, as it came to be known, "body language."

Imagine putting a ballet on a page as you would a symphony! Consider the simplest component, a solo: feet doing one thing, torso another, shoulders and arms and hands another. Consider the timing of each movement, then its relation in time to the other movements. And what about that slight upturn of the chin? The way the third sweep of the hand is performed just a bit more languorously than the first two? It's complicated business, this problem of notation, as is the language of "Effort/Shape," as Labanotation is sometimes called. Simply put, there are four components—Body, Effort, Shape, and Space. All are equally important, but the Effort part—that's the part that excited me. Not the *what* of movement, or the *where*, but the *how.*

In a direct or indirect path. With weight that is heavy or light. Quickly or slowly, in a sudden or sustained way, and most intriguingly, in a way that is bound or free.

These categories are just the beginning. Consider the Float—a dizzying combination of light, free, slow, sustained, and indirect. Or the Punch: strong, sudden, direct, free. Imagine the Glide, the Slash . . .

The real payoff of Donna's methods came near the end of each class when she set us free. I still couldn't do a split or pirouette, but I was taking risks, maintaining my balance, sustaining my energy, feeling those connections, playing with complex rhythms and a variety of efforts. Language doesn't just reflect experience, it creates it. Suddenly, I was slashing. I was dabbing, I was flicking. Finding new ways to move felt akin to finding new ways to feel, to be.

The tension in this dialogue builds to a crescendo.
This poem operates on the principle of theme and variation.
The ermine on the queen's collar echoes the white porcelain
on the mantle.

In college I'd learned to use the language of music to talk about poetry and drama. I'd heard the language of painting in discussions of music, as in Debussy's "colorations" and Bach's "ornamentations." But music is abstract and painting is two-dimensional. Movement is concrete and three-dimensional—or, rather, four, because it unfolds over time. For me, the body is always the best teacher. What we learn there sticks. In that church basement, wringing, carving, gliding, dabbing—I thrilled to this new lingua franca, my Esperanto, that would bring together everything I loved.

16. Traveling in the Dark

Another church basement, also in New Haven, housed a "Teacher's Center"—some ratty couches and Formica tables, shelves of books, manuals, and art supplies, and a crowded bulletin board, one post commanding: BREAK THE LECTURE HABIT!

I didn't have the "lecture habit." Twenty-two, in my first year as a teacher of high school English, I didn't have any teaching habits at all. I went to the center in search of ideas and in hopes of befriending other scared fledgling teachers who stayed up way too late sweating over lesson plans. Something about this BREAK THE LECTURE HABIT ad caught my eye. The jaunty slant of the paper? The humble but bold, hand-printed lettering?

And it was only six sessions, twenty bucks total.

Four others showed up for the first meeting: one veteran English teacher, one novice drama teacher, one visual artist, one therapist.

Kenneth Maue, our teacher, was twenty-something, skinny, shaggy, and loose-limbed, with the thickest glasses I'd ever seen. I remember not liking his shirt—polyester, a loud harlequin pattern.

A musician, a composer with an expansive sense of what constitutes music, and an educator interested in experiential (that word again) learning, Ken explained that we would "perform pieces" he'd composed. Today's was called "Travels through an Imaginary Landscape." He provided one master sheet of typed instructions. I'm excerpting this version from *Water in the Lake: Real Events for the Imagination*—a collection of Maue's pieces published about six years after we met.

> Spread out several common road maps. To begin, each player cuts out three sections of map . . . (no borders, legend, etc.) . . .
>
> Players attach their map fragments to surfaces in the available space. . . . Choose just the right places, locating them with care.
>
> Now begin to travel about the landscape, in this fashion: Make string roads between the map sections. . . .
>
> After the road-building is underway, players begin to leave written records of their imaginary experiences in the imaginary landscape on 3x5 file cards taped to places where the imaginary experiences have occurred. . . . A player coming to . . . an experience reported may add another card reporting a related experience. In this way, chains of experiences may evolve . . .

And so on, for a full two pages.

Eager for the "traveling" part, I wasn't looking forward to the fussy prep work, but deciding which sections of which maps to cut turned out to be more interesting than I would have expected—as did all the odd steps comprising Maue's pieces. By what criteria should I choose a section of map? Shape? Color? Scale? Could a small fragment of the Himalayas be followed by a larger one of Manhattan's Lower East Side? Already people were "mapping" the floor. Was a tabletop also a kosher "surface"? We weren't allowed to ask—or consult with other players. That alone—the required silence—was especially interesting. If we met another player along a road, we were instructed to negotiate our passing "gracefully, without talking or signaling . . ." But the file cards—that's the part I loved best.

Is it possible that in eighteen years of schooling I had never been asked to imagine anything? One social studies teacher urged us to contemplate the life of a Puritan or a slave. "These were flesh and blood people," she repeatedly said, a line we liked to mimic when she wasn't looking. I remembered an English teacher imploring us to envision that "ribbon of moonlight," "the highwayman came riding." But the raw conjuring of experience? And in this moldy basement with people I'd just met? The prospect might have panicked me, but all that cutting, pasting, and threading Maue demanded—now I could see how it eased the way. My imagination began to hum.

Stopped at a rest area here, someone wrote on a file card.

Saw a dead dog in the woods on my way home from school, I wrote.

Stopped here for gas and discovered the attendant was my old college roommate.

These—mine too—I'm inventing now, but what I remember well is how events started piling up, converging, crisscrossing, and splintering through time and space—all this, years before the internet or the play that popularized the six-degrees-of-separation notion. Video games existed, but few of us knew of them then. What fun it was inventing—and bouncing off each other and ending up where we never expected. (Like life, I guess.) I loved getting glimpses into strangers' psyches. I loved the push and pull of restriction and freedom—the latter more exhilarating because of the former.

We traveled silently through our imaginary landscape for more than an hour. Maue's instructions on how to end the piece were both explicit and vague. "Tune into a sense of when the piece is 'beginning to end.'" Then "shape the activities remaining . . . according to this sense." We did as instructed the best we knew how. After the last player pronounced the end, we stayed silent and motionless for several more seconds—spent, refreshed, reluctant to leave what felt almost like a postcoital state. Eventually, we formed a circle and "processed" what had occurred. The following week, every one of us returned.

After the six sessions, we contracted Ken to lead us for the rest of the school year. When Ken moved away the following year, the rest of us, along with a few of our friends, continued to meet weekly, taking turns to create our own pieces. Then I left New Haven and high school teaching and went to Vermont to write. Until then, I'd thought I would be a poet, but, inspired by my travels through that landscape, I began to write fiction.

I never did develop the lecture habit. Over the years, I have used my own version of the Imaginary Landscape piece with beginning fiction writers, and I've devised other structures as icebreakers or lessons in literature and creative writing. It's true that in the eighties and nineties, as the students became more conservative and I became more interested in a steady income, my teaching became less daring. On the other hand, with Maue in my brain these days, I recently took my college composition students to a large grassy expanse and we marked out a map of the world, roughly to scale. Then we positioned ourselves on the place we considered home in order to gain a visual and kinesthetic sense of one of our "Differences," the theme of the course.

To be creative you have to be willing to travel in the dark. Of all the things Ken taught me, this is the one that has really stuck. It is what I tell my writing students when they want an easy ride, what I tell myself while wandering through these decades in search of threads. No longer so resistant to fussing with my hands, I remember Ken's words when I play around with rocks and branches and rusty mop frames. I remember them when, with a sustained sweep of an arm or leg, I'm searching for a movement that might suggest "excursion." Ken's words give me the courage to invite friends to dinner at the last minute. Still on the phone with them, I open the fridge: leftover salmon, red pepper, asparagus, goat cheese . . . Already it's coming into focus: tonight's rendition of pasta primavera—Norwegian style.

17. Rooms to Dwell In

Beauty is a bit of a bore.

—William Somerset Maugham

Lately, I've been thinking a lot about Kenneth Maue, not only because he taught me so much about teaching and living and making art, and about how the lines between these can blur, but also because, on the recommendation of a student, I've been reading Mel Alexenberg, who reminds me of just how ahead of his time Maue was.

A cyber and public artist, as well as an art theorist, Alexenberg, author of *The Future of Art in the Digital Age*, gives me new lenses through which to view my own obsessions and forays. Drawing on the work of the theologian Thorleif Boman, Alexenberg contrasts the Greeks' adoration of unified and stable "space-centered" art forms with the Hebrews' preference for multifaceted, dynamic "time-centered" forms. The Greeks, he believes, view the spiritual as existing "above the mundane," whereas the Hebrews aim to "bring the spiritual down into our everyday lives." Furthermore, Alexenberg contends that in our postmodern digital age we are going through a paradigm shift from Hellenic to Hebraic consciousness, a shift Maue foresaw in the seventies. "We are going through a profound change in our orientation within the world," wrote Maue in *Water in the Lake*, "from a consciousness organized around structure to a consciousness organized around process."

(You don't have to be Jewish to have a Hebraic consciousness.)

"The story of the Jewish people," Alexenberg reminds us, "begins with movement . . . with '*lekh lekhah*,' a journey away from the safely familiar towards adventuresome freedom." A psychological as well as a physical expedition, this trek takes us from a place of "narrow-minded thinking to a place where [we] can freely see." Alexenberg continues: "The Hebrew word for 'God,' YHVH, is a verb not a noun, an action word not a thing." He translates it as "*Was-Is-Will-Be* or *Will Bring into Being*."

This leads Alexenberg (again channeling Boman) to another of his distinctions between the Greeks and Hebrews. The former, he claims, with their commitment to mimesis, charge their artists with making beautiful, harmonious replications of God's glorious *creations*. The latter, with their emphasis on movement, want their artists—all of us, really—to replicate God's work as *creator* and become "*co-creators*." So maybe it's not so far-fetched to think He? She? needs my tinkering to be made manifest.

What's more: Alexenberg describes Hebraic aesthetics as being "primarily about . . . opportunities for dynamic dialogue, expansive integral thought, and interactive experience"—precisely the same kind of opportunities Maue's *pre*–digital age pieces provide.

Take "Non-Sequiturs," a Maue piece I performed more than thirty years ago involving actual dialogue, albeit in an unusual form.

A group of players holds one-to-one dialogues in which each remark follows the preceding one in no perceivable way. . . . Let the sentences be of as wide a nature as you can invent in terms of content, tone, and manner of expression.

"It's sunny today," your partner begins.

"Bears like blueberries," you say, immediately realizing your tone (flat), your manner of expression (declarative), even your number of words is similar to your partner's; furthermore, in content, there's a discernible link—sunny days leading to bountiful blueberry crops and happy bears. So now you try harder, reaching for sentences from galaxies different from your partner's. But alas, you are also becoming increasingly adept at finding links between these seeming non-sequiturs, so much so that you start to feel as if every thing is connected—every uttered fact, idea, or sentiment, yes; but also every body—animal, vegetable, or mineral.

I still remember one line from the dialogue I engaged in all those years ago: "When I was five my mother died and that same year my father was diagnosed with Parkinson's." These words, uttered without inflection by my partner, followed some vapid, factual statement I'd made. Though the rules of the game did not guarantee that our statements be true, I felt sure that my partner's was, and I yearned for some permissible way to convey my sympathy. I don't remember what non-sequitur I came up with, only the feeling that I'd succeeded as well, or better, than I would have with a more conventional response—if only because the prohibitions forced me to wait longer and think harder before speaking. I remember the feeling of closeness the dialogue engendered and I wondered if this was what Maue intended.

What *did* Maue intend—with this piece and others? One piece asks you to say aloud the name of every person you ever met. Another tells you to put a book in your freezer and leave it there. Another to simply "vocalize" by dredging forth nonhuman or rather prelinguistic, a-musical utterances, largely grotesque but embedded with kernels of gorgeousness.

In his essay "What Cage Did," Maue says, "Cage's music is like rooms to dwell in: places to be, less important for themselves than the life occurring in them. It doesn't lift us out of our lives, into the artist's feelings; it gives us who we are." And so it is with Maue's own pieces: Though they may not always fly in conventional settings, they give us who we are.

So who am I? Or, for starters: Where do I stand on the Hellenic–Hebraic spectrum?

With my still strong appetite for sublime "space-centered" art that displays the old classical virtues such as coherence, balance, harmony, and grace, I haven't yet abandoned the Greek ship. However, I think it's fair to say I have at least one foot on the deck of the Hebrew one and may well be about to leap on. I'm wild about Maya Lin's Vietnam Veterans Memorial, not because of the beauty of its static form but because of all the Hebraic values it embodies. If a "viewer" sees merely the black slabs carved with names of the dead, she might say, as many have, "*This* is what won out over fourteen hundred others?" But if she goes there and takes her time, approaches from afar, enters the roped off pathway, notices the sudden hush, walks silently until confronted with the first slab; if she reads the names, pronounces the names, touches the indentation of a name, notices the reflection of the trees in the stone, notices her own reflection or that of a weeping woman, sees the boot left at the base, the bouquet, sees a child rubbing a name, feels the heat of the sun or the bite of the wind—she will experience Lin's genius; she will know this is a monument that gives you not just itself in steadfast granite but *yourself* changing as you move through time and space; it gives you not just the dead but the living in community with others and the material world.

Also calling me toward the Hebraic ship is Frank Lloyd Wright's Guggenheim in New York and Frank Gehry's in Bilbao, both of which Alexenberg mentions. The kinetic energy of those buildings affects the way I experience the art they display, much of which, in Bilbao especially, demands physical interaction, Hebraic style. Not much of it would be deemed "beautiful." A lot of it aims to provoke and incite change. Some of it aspires to unite, to heal. Says Suzi Gablik, an artist Alexenberg quotes: "We need an art that transcends the distanced formality of aesthetics and dares to respond to the cries of the world."

Once I might have been skeptical of art with a social or "healing" mission, but the cries of the world feel so much closer now with my own grief, and Sandy's too, still reverberating. "I'm never going to see that place again!" she sobbed, when I brought her Frankie's pear painting. *That place* was the mowing, I'm sure. And she never did see it again.

18. My Digital Age

Unlike Alexenberg, an avid maker of e-art aimed at *tikkun olam*, "repairing the world," I have been slow to embrace our digital age. But without it, I could never have extended my belated thanks to Professor Suskin of Music 101, or Donna Blank (Effort/Shape), or Randy Coleman, the Oberlin prof who took us to hear John Cage. As for Ken Maue (now Kenneth)—it took years to track him down, but finally I scored. What's he been up to? Here's a partial list:

Performing solo piano and theater pieces.

Writing for a philosophical journal.

Doing art photography.

I'm reminded of Donna Blank, the dance teacher I called a while back. Movement analyst, therapist, sculptor, too, she's having fun "following her nose." I'm reminded of the speaker in that Roethke poem "going where [he has] to go." Kenneth, like Alexenberg's desert journeyers, likes going "away from the safely familiar, toward adventuresome freedom."

As for me, the course horse who studied with them and so many others—I, too, vote for the unknown, even if it means being a beginner, being lost or outside the lines. Dilettante, *schmilettante*, is what I say now. Who wouldn't want to be one! From the Italian *delittare*, "to delight," and the Latin *delicere*, "to allure, to entice."

19. Changing Course Course

The Art and Language of Transition, this one was called. "Useful for individuals in the midst of career or personal transition," the description read. That I was such a person had only recently occurred to me. When Sandy died, I knew I was entering *some* kind of in-betweenness, but in the more than two years since then, I had devoted my energy to maintaining as much continuity as possible for both Sam and me. In a few months he'd be going to college. I'd be living alone. Having inherited Sandy's retirement fund, courtesy of the Commonwealth of Massachusetts which permitted us to marry shortly before she died, I could afford to think about changing course. And so on a lark (it was spring vacation, a week of no teaching) I registered for this workshop taught by Kendall Dudley, a longtime friend and teacher I admire.

I was far from a model student in this one. I didn't do the reading, didn't complete the homework, took scant notes, and showed up without the requested art materials. But show up I did, for all three sessions—and those weeks turned out to some of the more exhilarating I'd had in years. My rabbi, Rim Meirowitz, has said that God is whom you thank when you're in the right place at the right time. By that definition those weeks were divine. At lunch with a colleague, I would learn about her new program catering to returning adult students—an interesting teaching opportunity for me. At the local café, I'd run into an old friend of Sandy's who was working in a program intended to create "a culture of writing" in the Boston Public Schools—they were hiring. When I began this odyssey in search of what it is I seem to be after, I didn't know it would lead me to reconsider how I want to live and what I want to do; yet that's exactly where I find myself now. In the college writing courses I teach, I use material aimed at expanding compassion and understanding differences. It's good work, but I'm frustrated by how many students want to learn only what they deem applicable to their future careers. I've become timid about trying more radical pedagogies. And I often wonder if I'd have more impact teaching a less privileged population. As for writing, I doubt I'll ever stop hearing that call, but I'm interested in working more collaboratively, using other parts of myself, especially this body of mine while it's still my friend.

Once while I was taking Kendall's course, I went to a dance performance that incorporated text and I thought: now there's a new direction for me! Another performance featured computer-assisted choreography—I was even open to exploring that. I heard about a graduate program in "Interrelated Media," which, in its vagueness, sounded just right. Also inspiring was an exhibit of William Wegman's non-Weimaraner work. In one piece, he videotaped himself wearing nothing but his underpants and ladies' pocketbooks of every variety. Wearing eight or ten of them dangling from his arms, legs, and neck, he walks into an empty room and starts shedding purses. It's very funny—or was to me and my friends. It got me thinking about gender and clothing and accessories, bags and burdens, outside and inside, away and home. Now here's a guy who's not afraid to follow his bliss, I thought, or at least his oddest ideas.

I have some odd ideas, too, I thought. And then I remembered something the novelist Michael Cunningham said in a workshop I'd taken with him: "Ten or twelve Hummel dolls and you've got some tacky *chotchkes*; seven hundred Hummel dolls and you've got a show in the Whitney!" Maybe the only thing that separated Wegman from me was *chutzpah*! Suddenly I felt that I might be able to cultivate more of that. In fact, I was feeling so ignited, so game, so *able*.

Spring break ended. It was back-to-school. I told myself I'd better forego that lecture at the Radcliffe Institute and prepare for my class instead, but at the last minute I got on my bike and pedaled to Harvard Square, arriving just as Anna Schuleit, a recent MacArthur genius grant winner, was being introduced. First she showed her drawings and paintings, and oh, I thought: The MacArthur people got it right with this one—such lightness of hand, such complex, suggestive, *alive* forms! But it was Schuleit's public art that really seized my imagination, especially *Habeas Corpus*, the sound installation she had created at an abandoned mental hospital. *Habeas Corpus* was the culminating event of a two-day commemoration. Schuleit recruited volunteers to place 102 speakers in the hospital's broken, iron-barred windows and, at a specified time, Bach's Magnificat resounded. The video of the event was so moving, I wasn't the only one in my row who was tearful. The loose trail of people trudging in their overcoats up a hill past November's naked branches and overgrown weeds—they looked like pilgrims, their strides weary, purposeful. Scattered among the merely curious were several who'd clearly had some truck with the place. They were lame, awkward, palsied, somehow not "normal" but maybe not insane either; maybe merely too dreamy, fat, passionate, visionary, poor, or androgynous? Now, oddly enough, at the emptied, impotent house of memories, they no longer seemed like misfits; they seemed in possession of their full share of human dignity. And when the Magnificat began and all raised their faces up toward the abandoned institute's open windows, it was these people who wore the most intense expressions. Some wept, some simply stared, some rocked back and forth, some hugged their loved ones and wouldn't let go. Yet not just these but all the people there seemed moved and ennobled by Bach's twenty-eight minutes of glorious music in defiance of the dreariness, tedium, injustice, ignorance, fear, chaos, insanity, violence, and, especially, loneliness that once lived inside this hospital and, to varying degrees, afflicts the soul of everyone alive.

This is what I want to do! I thought, once I'd regained composure: create public art events like this one, events that stir people and unite them with lost parts of themselves and with one another. It's what Ken does, what Alexenberg does—*tikkun olam*—and I can do it too!

Maybe.

With a little more *chutzpah*.

Imagine my joy when I learned about *Landlines*, Schuleit's next public art event. It was taking place in a few months in Peterborough, New Hampshire, just a short drive from where I would then be living. Talk about being in the right place at the right time! Remembering what my rabbi said, I beamed a little prayer of gratitude.

20. My Story/Your Story

In the many years that I've been taking Dancing Outside the Lines, we have moved from that buzzy, over-lit gym to another school's leaky auditorium stage, to a cold church basement, to a state-of-the-art dance studio at a university, to a padded space designed primarily for toddler play . . . Through all these venue changes our membership has remained largely the same. Some semesters we focus on choreography, but mostly we practice improvisation.

Of course the two cannot be easily separated. I've seen how chore-ographers will videotape an improvisation in order to isolate interesting moves they couldn't have come up with in a more deliberative state. As I've learned from Stephen Nachmanovitch, improvisational violin-ist and author of *Free Play: Improvisation in Life and Art*, every artistic composition has its improvisational component. You mess around with your materials until they speak to you and you speak back. I had never equated drafting a piece of writing with "improvising," but I now find the term both comforting and apt. In fact, Nachmanovitch believes all creations—human-made bridges, theorems, and democracies, as well as mountains, rivers, and continents—are improvisational in that they arise "from the power of free play sloshing against the power of limits." It's a compelling idea. Even so, it isn't the results of improvisation that thrill me most; in true Hebraic spirit, it's the process.

Joan provides the "score"—the structure, rules, or "limits" in Nachmanovitch-speak. Generally, these are scant, the ratio of limits to options being about 1:1 zillion. Certain parameters are always assumed: We behave according to our unspoken, evolving standards of decency and safety. If there's music, our dance can continue after the music stops. We confine ourselves to the space we have contracted. Further limits might demand that we work in trios, incorporate a prop, include stillness or a phrase spoken in a foreign language. Maybe our task is to convey the feeling in a particular photograph or the tone of an excerpt from *The Heritage Cookbook.* How to explain my joy in what then occurs?

"For art to appear we have to disappear," Nachmanovitch says, and I suppose that's the crux of it—and the bliss. I imagine it's like the loss of self that yogis achieve during meditation. Improvisers are in "the surrender business," Nachmanovitch explains. We "must give up our expectations and a certain degree of control." We must "give up being safely wrapped in our own story"—I love that phrase—

conveying the risk and hinting at the reward: the expansion we feel when we avail ourselves of stories not our own. Improvising demands keen awareness, not just from the senses but from the mind that must perceive a lot of things simultaneously—our current partner's fluid movements, her melancholy mood, the music, the figure in the corner of the room, the size of the space between us—now what were Joan's instructions? We sense, we perceive, we choose to extend what's occurring or modify or shatter it. What's most exciting is when perception, impulse, and action occur almost instantaneously and our responses surprise us yet feel inevitable.

"You're *so* alive when you dance," Joan once told me. I wanted to cry. *This*, I thought, is what I've been after—to be *alive, alive* and recognized as such. A modest goal for the living, but how rarely we fully achieve it; and with illness and violence all around, every scrap of vitality seems all the more miraculous.

Picasso said he spent a lifetime learning how to draw like a child. What he meant, I think, is learning to combine the knowledge, skill, and habits of mind he'd developed throughout his life with the self-forgetfulness he'd had before all that. When my dancing is alive, my body makes split-second, seemingly instinctual decisions informed by those hours under headsets listening to Beethoven quartets; those days studying the negative space formed by my arrangement of rocks, feathers, and twigs; those years in front of the computer, rocking back and forth (like a Jew at prayer) to the music of syllables, portioning out stories about wanting and getting and not.

Joan didn't mean I was a "good" dancer—strong, graceful, buoyant. What she meant, I think, was what my sculptor friend said. When I'm *on*, there is no *me* dancing, there is only dancing. What she meant was what Franck said about his drawing a horse, "Outside and inside are unseparated." Call it animal absorption; call it bliss. It's what we had as children, but better.

21. On Beauty and Dying

A sudden, agonizing blood clot in her leg sent Sandy by ambulance to the emergency room. It was a Sunday. Her own doctor was out of the country. My parents were visiting. For several hours a team struggled to get her pain under control. They wouldn't let anyone in the room. Meanwhile, two young men took me into a small office—one of them a resident, the other a specialist who'd been called in for Sandy's case. He was in jeans. He still had his jacket on, a tough-looking leather one. I wondered if he was gay. The jacket—or maybe I was just looking for a connection, some way to feel better about the weirdness of it all: the tiny room, the wrong clothes, the sense of urgency. We'd had emergencies before, but never this room with two men, one with papers in his hand.

The specialist did most of the talking. He held a Do Not Resuscitate form.

Hadn't we taken care of all that with our wills and powers of attorney shortly after Sam was born? Since her diagnosis, no one had raised the issue with me. If they had with her, she didn't tell me. Sandy was an optimist, a denier, a survivor. She'd had cancer for six years. Her doctor, a research man, always knew of some promising new drug. True, in the week or two preceding this blood clot, a "bridge" nurse visited to broach the subject of hospice care. She mentioned Chilton House, a highly regarded place right in the neighborhood.

Death was in the wings, but not here. Not now.

The specialist was soft-spoken, gentle—they both were. They saw how shaken I was.

"Are you saying she may not make it out of here?" I asked the specialist.

"It's quite possible," he said.

They both opened their arms for me while I wept.

I asked more questions. Then I signed.

Soon after, Sandy was wheeled out. Heavily drugged, but conscious. No longer in pain. She slept. The rest of Sunday and all day Monday, she mostly slept. By Tuesday morning, she was out. "In a coma," I heard my father tell someone on the phone. "She's not in a *coma*!" I said. "It's the pain meds!"

Later her doctor, now back from abroad, came to visit. I asked him. "She's not on that many pain meds," he said.

Tuesday afternoon, a meeting was arranged—me and the Palliative Care team. I brought along my sister, a close friend, and a close friend of Sandy's. A decision to sign on would mean a peaceful, hospice-like atmosphere within the hospital.

"But she wanted to die at home!" I said, remembering that moment after the bridge nurse left. Such pain on Sandy's face, "Please don't make me go to Chilton House," she pleaded as if she were a child.

"She might not survive the trip," one of the doctors was saying now. "And even if she did, it would be harder to keep her comfortable there."

"There," I knew, would be our den where for the last few weeks she'd been sleeping in a hospital bed—where I had been sleeping too, catty-corner, on the green couch. It was a beautiful room with a slightly pitched roof, a fireplace, pine floor, two bands of fir molding lining the butter-colored walls. Tall windows looked out onto the garden she had created and tended. Glass doors opened onto the deck where we'd enjoyed so many meals. I imagined death would be gentler there among greens and golds and honey-colored wood.

At least in this meeting I didn't feel rushed. I wanted "there"— that room, that light—but it seemed foolhardy, a fantasy, maybe not good for Sam, maybe, at this point, more for me than for Sandy.

I asked the team more questions.

I asked my sister, my friend, Sandy's friend. Everyone agreed. I signed.

"She's a beauty!" the chief of Palliative Care said shortly afterward when he came into Sandy's room. She was bald, pale, even a little scary-looking to some, but he must have seen what I'd always seen, more apparent now than ever: the magnificent architecture of her face. A beauty—yes.

As it turned out, there was beauty enough in the hospital. One of the nurses was a professional singer. She sat by Sandy's bedside, right near her head, and sang a Yiddish lullaby. It wasn't one I knew and I doubted Sandy knew it either, but the cadences were familiar, the tones deep and haunting. I imagined them traveling through Sandy's ears into her mother's, her grandmother's, her great-grandmother's, traveling all the way back to Russia where the earth is rich with those plain old potatoes Sandy loved.

There was beauty, too, Wednesday evening, when Sam and I and friends sat vigil—candlelight, poetry, a guitar. When we got word of the miraculous comeback by Sandy and Sam's beloved Red Sox winning the pennant, our guitarist started strumming "Take Me Out to the Ball Game." For a second I was uncertain. Was this okay? Was it right? But as we all joined in and the song gained life, I knew it was perfect.

22. With Sam in Wonderland

And of ourselves and of our origins . . .

—Wallace Stevens, "The Idea of
Order at Key West"

It's been longer than I care to admit since I began singing this song of myself and of my loves and their origins. Let's just say Sam, a kid when I began, is now in college—at Oberlin! After my first visit I immediately called my parents—they'd met at Cornell and would have liked me to go there. "Forgive me," I said, "for not giving you the joy of seeing me where you once were."

Are you sensing you're in for one of those gloating holiday updates? Indulge me, please. Picture Sam and me stretched out on Tappan Square, the same tree-filled green where I met that nice boy who took me to hear Ravi Shankar. Now there's a burrito place across the street. Everyone is out—the jugglers, the Frisbee players, the couples in love, and the oh-so-Oberlinian ensemble of Renaissance recorder players. Sam's phone buzzes. The editor of the school paper. There's going to be a candlelight vigil tonight in support of local immigrants arrested during a raid. Will Sam take photos? Of course he will. A friend stops by to chat. We eat our burritos. We manage to get a little studying in. I click on Sam's laptop, music floats out. This beats those stuffy cubicles we had in my day—those headsets so heavy they gave me a headache.

"Second movement," Sam guesses correctly.

Later I borrow a bike and we crisscross the campus so Sam can give me a tour. The art museum has a new wing devoted to photography studios. We stop there to see Sam's work—first a series of Oberlin's jazz musicians (he likes Beethoven but loves Coltrane), then the pictures he took in New Orleans where he helped rebuild homes destroyed by Katrina.

Finney Chapel has changed mercifully little, though there's now a new Sunday night ritual: students can lie on the stage floor and experience the vibrations from the new organ—4,014 pipes strong. We pedal past Warner Gym. (How strong my legs still are, thanks to all the dancing I've been doing.) Warner is where Sam and his crew from his Intro to Dance performed his first bit of choreography. Warner is where contact improvisation, my latest favorite dance form, was born the year I graduated. We stop at King Building so I can peek into the courtyard where I fell in love with poetry.

I get to take a nap while he goes to his trumpet lesson—a brand new thing for him. Thankfully, though we share Oberlin, the nose Sam is following is his own. (I swear, I never, not once, took a trumpet lesson! And he's majoring in history.) Still, I enjoy seeing he's a bit of a dilettante after my own heart, delighting in a variety of pursuits and in the ways they speak to each other.

"Arranging, Deepening, Enchanting" is the title of the lecture I attend while Sam works on his history paper. The words are from Wallace Stevens's "The Idea of Order at Key West," a poem I studied with David Young, the professor who turned me into an English major. Like his predecessor, DeSales Harrison is a genius at making his students feel like co-creators of meaning. With Harrison as our guide, we parents and grandparents, the audience for this lecture, travel through Stevens's enigmatic lines until—*aha*! Suddenly it's perfectly clear: Like the singer in the poem who walks by the sea, all of us are the "artificers" of our world—"artificer" not in the sense of "falsifier" but in the sense that our minds are always *arranging* our perceptions, our imaginations are *deepening* and *enchanting* our experiences. Furthermore, as teachers and students, writers and readers, artists and appreciators—we live to share the meanings we make. In fact, DeSales holds—from the quiet gasps in the lecture hall it seems most of us buy it: *This* is what it's all about—this very costly, not entirely practical but nevertheless sublime, in-the-path-of-beauty process known as a liberal arts education.

And this less formal, postgrad education of mine? Hasn't it been about these same things?

23. Like Art, Like Life

There are still a few vacant front-row seats when I arrive at the MacDowell Colony for *Landlines*, the culminating event of the artists' colony's yearlong centennial celebration. Six or seven papier-mâché telephones the size of bears hang suspended over the outdoor stage where act 1 will take place. It's a gorgeous summer night, warm but not hot, dry, bugless, and perfectly clear. Nevertheless, I am worried. Behind the pink Princess, the classic black rotary, the boxy payphone with coin slots, a million-watt sunset makes it impossible to look at the stage for more than a second. Knowing Anna (Schuleit)—as a *Landlines* volunteer, I now feel we're on a first-name basis—she has anticipated this problem. Knowing Anna, she knows the exact second the sun will slip behind the mountain this August 11th, 2007, in Peterborough, New Hampshire, "Our Town," as it is often called, after the Thornton Wilder play it inspired.

I've been doing my shopping and café-sitting in Peterborough for twenty-one summers, but only now do I feel a part of that "our"— proof that even before it has officially begun, *Landlines* has succeeded in one of its main goals: community-building. As a member of the Tree team, I ate the donated noodle salad and ferried empty water bottles to the recycling dumpster. I learned how to splice telephone wires—blue to blue & white, orange to green & blue—and I helped string the wires from tree limb to tree limb. Tonight I proudly wear my *Landlines* T-shirt.

"Is that seat free?" I ask a woman in the front row. Turns out she's a current MacDowell fellow. "I do public art," she tells me.

That's it! A sign. "*I'm* interested in doing public art," I tell her. "What kinds of skills would you say are requi—"

"Business skills," she says, all business-like. "I spend a good fifty percent of my time on the phone."

I nod as if I expected as much, and really, I'm not surprised. My time on the Trec team gave me a sense of the dizzying number of tasks involved in just the last few days of an event more than a year in the making. Even so, I feel deflated. There goes my fantasy. Inspired by Suzi Gablik, the artist Alexenberg mentioned, I had imagined creating a Boston event that "responds to the cries of the world." I imagined a day of public grieving—people walking through Boston, stopping at sites where teenagers were killed by gang violence. At each site, there'd be shrines, portraits, requiems . . . But alas, do I want to trade a life of writing, teaching, dancing, and course-taking for a life on the phone?

The public artist and I return to studying our programs. So long in the planning, so short in the happening, site-specific art events tend to breed a maniacal preoccupation with documentation. This program includes the species of 100 trees, the names of the antique phones installed on them, the miles of telephone wire used (38), the estimated manpower hours (4,269), and, my favorite: the number of eggs in the Centennial Cake (guess!). By the time I'm finished reading, the obliging sun has slipped behind the mountain and Anna has climbed onto the stage.

She welcomes us warmly and thanks the heavens for the weather, explaining that part of the challenge—and charm—of public art is that some things are beyond our control. One makes contingency plans, but there's *always something.*

It's surprising therefore that act 1, "On the Stage," goes off without a hitch. In a dozen brief scenes that celebrate the art of collaboration, local children present original puppet shows, jazz compositions, videos, you name it, each inspired by the work of a former MacDowell fellow and created this summer under the mentorship of a current one. The skits are whimsical, they're delightful, they're sometimes moving, and even when they are a little hokey, they still give a juicy taste of how much art has been created right here, and of how emerging artists continue to be inspired by the generations who have come before them.

Right on schedule, act 2, "In the Woods," begins. The concept here is in the Maue-Alexenberg spirit: multifaceted, time-centered, interactive, full of dynamic dialogue, and ideally soul-enhancing. Into the woods we stream, *lekh lekhah* style, for not only are these acres unfamiliar to us (even to me who worked on trees deeper in), they're normally off-limits to anyone who's not a current MacDowell resident. Now they are dark, lit only by acorn-sized bulbs lining the pine-cushioned paths and by small halos of light forming "booths" surrounding each "tele-tree."

While most people walk in couples or groups and I go it alone—often the case in these post-Sandy times—tonight I don't mind. The mood is electric. I feel lucky to be part of this once-only event. Quickly, my eyes adjust to the darkness, my steps become more confident, I can imagine some of my favorite artists—Aaron Copeland, Milton Avery, Spalding Gray, Meredith Monk—walking these same paths, dreaming, ruminating, despairing, rallying, maybe praying in their fashion. Because of the hush and the darkness, my senses are heightened. I feel the tingle of August air on my face; hear the crunch of needles under my feet, the *swish-swish* sounds of trousered legs. What I'm *not* hearing are any telephones ringing. I tell myself not to worry, to just keep walking, taking in the musky smells, the whisperings around me, the last melancholy calls of the hermit thrush. I'm into this sensuous haze when I'm startled by—that inevitable *something* Anna alluded to?

Thunder?

Terrorists?

We all seem to get it at once: Here in the "Live Free or Die" state, July 4th fever lingers all summer.

Poor Anna! Sixteen months of work wrecked by fireworks junkies.

(Lucky me, getting such a clear signal that, despite my distant stints with the Buddhists and more recent practice in the surrender business, I do not have the stuff from which public artists are made.)

And yet . . . *All* is not lost. My fellow travelers and I are taking this something in stride. First we moan, then we laugh, then we start pointing to the splashy flowers in the sky. Between the booms we chat with each other—*Where are you from? What brings you here?* We're having such a good time we hardly notice when the booms begin to subside.

Sssh! What's that?

A telephone ringing.

Hard to tell from where, but our footfalls get faster; someone grabs a receiver and says a breathless, *Hello.*

Hello?

The program has told us what to expect: a voice from the past or the present; the former via a recording of a famous work written by a MacDowell artist, the latter, one of the thousands of former fellows who has been sent a request to call in at precisely this time.

Hello! the voice says again, all of us listening with him.

No one's there! he finally says. The receiver lands in its cradle with a dejected thud.

Ten, maybe twenty seconds later, there's another ring from another tree. More footfalls, *Hellos, Hellos,* disgruntled mumblings, another unhappy thud.

Another something!

A snafu in our splicing? A key wire ravaged by a squirrel?

The phones are ringing now, and people are finding them, but the line seems dead, or crackling. I'm just about to privately declare act 2 a fiasco when someone with a *Landlines* T-shirt bellows: "The switchboard is flooded, the operators tripping over each other. You've got to be patient. Hold on longer."

And so we do. I'm never the first to reach a ringing phone, but I hold my breath and listen.

Hello . . . . ?

Hello . . . . ?

Seconds pass—how long they seem! Then someone tentatively says, *Yes?* Says, *Hi!* Says, *Marian.* Says, *Jonathan.*

The fireworks and switchboard glitches were a good thing. By now, we all feel like old friends. Keeping a semi-respectful distance, we gather around each booth in use and wait for the report.

Some amazing music by Leonard Bernstein!

Some far-out choreographer from Brooklyn!

Soon I hear other fractured reports of calls from L.A. and Beijing, Nebraska and New Orleans, Berlin and Jerusalem. Calls from the past and from the present; from sculptors and filmmakers, writers and composers, genre-crossers and -crashers; from young and old, famous and not. Some read or perform but most just want to *talk*, share stories.

The phones are ringing, the woods alive with laughter and conversation.

Hello . . . . ? Hello . . . . ?

Sssh! Listen!

Human voices, each distinct, eager, hopeful, wanting, *wanting*, art *or* life, both divine, when they happen to land in the right spot at the right time.

But now it's my turn. *I* want a call to a tree near me. *Hello!* I'll say. And I won't even have to be patient.

Hello, she'll say. I'll recognize her right away—Sandy, my Sandy—her voice cheerful, robust, wanting to know what she should pick up for dinner.

♦

At the Donkey Hotel

Walk until the day becomes interesting. That's the approach to travel that Rolf Potts suggests in his book called *Vagabonding.* It's also my preferred approach—although I didn't dare use it my first day in Fez. Founded over a millennium ago, Fez, Morocco's second largest city, has 9,600 alleyways—or so I was told by several proud Fassis eager to guide me through the maze. Fear trumping pride, I joined two women at my guesthouse, and we hired one of these guides. *She* (a rarity among guides—and bare-headed!) marched us through miles of dizzying, donkey-clogged streets, instructing us in the Five Pillars of Islam and the Six Articles of Faith. She pointed out the tiny windows through which women, once not permitted to show their faces, could peek out. She led us to the famously smelly tanneries—rows of ancient stone tubs holding dyes. As non-Muslims, we were not permitted to enter a mosque, but we huddled by the entrance of the fountained courtyard and watched the men perform their ablutions. We also poked into a defunct *fondouk,* meaning hotel, in this case for caravanning merchants and their camels, too. Predictably, disastrously, near the wearying day's end, we drank mint tea with a rug merchant.

Now it was day two, a Tuesday. I had spent half the morning at the post office with the rug merchant's cousin who helped me ship my new Berber carpets—all four of them. (It's an old story, I learned too late: jet-lagged, eager-to-please tourist unfamiliar with the currency pays way too many *dirham* for rugs she doesn't need and no longer even likes.) Yes, I had a serious case of buyer's remorse, but, with the deed done, I was determined to put it behind me and venture out on my own. No, I told the cheerful young man who must have noticed the lost look on my face as I stepped out of the PO, I did not want him to take me to *the* best restaurant (his uncle's.) I would visit the library and Jewish quarter on Thursday when my tour group arrived.

Today, I was going to—how I wished I could say it less haltingly—
L'Ho-pi-tal Vet-er-i-naire.

"Why there?" The young man asked.

How could I explain? I'm a vet's daughter. As a kid I watched
my father pull slimy puppies out of a neighbor's poodle. As a teen, I
helped out in his hospital, holding small animals in awkward positions
while he did things they didn't like. More to the point, my parents
have been traveling the world longer than I've been in it, and early
on I learned that every trip, whether a state or continent away, will
prove more interesting if it includes a visit to a veterinary hospital.
What's more, this *ho pi-tal* made it into my *Lonely Planet*, which said
the clinic was funded by the SPCA of Massachusetts, my home state.
Surely that would increase my chances of getting a warm welcome.

"Just interested," I told the puzzled youth. "Do you know where
it is?" I pointed to the entry in my book, just then noticing that
visiting hours ended at 1:00. So much for walking. It was already
after 12:00. "Do you know where I can get a taxi?"

Less cheerfully, he led me to a nearby plaza just outside the
carless *medina*. A taxi pulled up. I opened the door. *L'Hop-i-tal Vet-
er-i-naire?* I sputtered to the driver. He seemed to know it.

Shukran, I said, looking back to thank my escort.

"But there's nothing happening there!" He said it so plaintively,
I hesitated, but just for a moment before climbing in.

Barely a minute later, it seemed, the driver pulled up in front
of a long white stucco building. On one side of the grand arched
opening, a tiled sign read "American Fondouk"; on the other side,
the equivalent, I presumed, in Arabic letters.

L'Hop-i-tal? With its American and Moroccan flags and scruffy
shrubs, it looked more like an embassy in need of a landscaper.

The driver nodded.

A slender man in work clothes appeared, greeted me in Arabic and French—Azami was his name. He led me into a large courtyard splotched with shadows from five or six leafy trees—more than I'd seen in one place since I'd arrived in Fez. Maybe that's what gave the place such a tranquil feeling, that and the hush and absence of people and carts piled high with—you name it: camel heads, olives, snails, herbal concoctions (one called "Viagra Turbo") . . . Or maybe it was simply the donkeys—one lounging under a tree, another munching on hay, a few others in surrounding shadowy stalls. True, the muncher had a cast on his leg, the lounger a stitched-up flank, but compared to the overburdened, dust-crusted donkeys crowding Fez's alleyways— these looked as if they'd landed in a—*fondouk*! on the Riviera.

Alas, tranquil is nice, but within seconds of scanning the scene, the boy's parting words came back to me. *Nothing happening there . . .*

Well, I told myself, you never know. I'll poke around, take some pictures, maybe attempt a photo essay—a new form for me.

Mass-a-chu-setts, I said to Azami, tapping my chest. He nodded and grinned, apparently recognizing that mouthful. We stepped into the first alcove bordering the yard. "Farrier," he said, tapping his chest, then pointing to the wall arrayed with antique tools and all manner of equine shoes.

Ah, un blacksmith!

He nodded. I mimed the act of writing, in the old-fashioned way.

Ah, un journaliste! Like many of the Moroccans I'd met, his whole self came to life, even during the most basic exchange, as if, unlike many Americans, he was not already a little sick of the whole business of conversation. Likewise, the housekeeper who let me trail her on her rounds—up some stairs past the head vet's residence to a roof garden and storage area. Though she spoke no English and little French, we had a great time trying to converse and shared a hearty laugh over the napping "guard" dogs—the first dogs I'd seen in Morocco. "Muslims don't believe in having animals for friends," Kareem, my friendly innkeeper had told me. That's how I guessed that the hospital's director wasn't Muslim. Through her filigreed front gate poked the sleek nose of a Saluki, an elegant breed.

On ground level again, after checking out the office, classroom, and lab, I chatted with a vet. A young Moroccan, she explained in her perfect English that the Fondouk was a free clinic catering to working animals. And yes, we agreed, it was a sad irony that animals lucky enough to recover in this hotel returned to miserable lives of punishing labor. After watching while she and a technician set a mule's broken leg, I figured I'd leave, but by now the building's entrance was closed. Just as I was wondering where Azami was, he flew past. *Emergencie!* he announced, then turned his attention to opening the massive wooden door. Urgent voices, the sound of a truck pulling away. In walked a shepherd-like figure in a dark, flowing *djellaba* and sandaled feet, his broad arms cradling a dark brown animal roughly the size of a greyhound. As he approached, I got a better view: a baby donkey with gangly limbs.

As Azami led them to the farthest corner of the quad, a tall woman in scrubs came running down the open stairs. Clearly in gear, ready to take charge, she nevertheless paused before me.

Gheeghee, she said, hand outstretched. *Like Gigi, but in the UK we make it a hard G.* With her strawberry blond hair tied in a scrunchie, her breezy British voice, flushed cheeks, and hale and hardy demeanor—if this hadn't been Morocco, I'd have guessed she'd been out tromping over the moors. I gave her what had become my stats: a writer from Massachusetts, daughter of a vet. As we hurried toward the examining area, she filled me in.

For its first two days, the donkey seemed perfectly healthy, then on the third, close to death. Sounded like a classic case, akin to what happens to newborns whose blood is incompatible with their Rh factor mothers. The newborn starts gobbling up its own red cells.

The foal now lay on a mat on the ground. Already one of the technicians had shaved his neck. Gigi and I, the contracted vet, and two helpers huddled in close. The farmer—he spoke only Arabic—stood outside the circle, silent and calm. The patient looked awfully sick: limp, immobile, eyes sallow and glazed. I studied his long, comma-shaped nostrils . . . his chest . . . I had a history of perceiving death in sleeping pets and people, but everyone was proceeding as if this donkey were alive. And then he defecated, which I deemed a good sign.

While the lumpy pile kept drawing my eye, the others ignored it as they concentrated on inserting a pesky IV. Once satisfied it was properly connected, Gigi reached for her iPhone and almost immediately began reading aloud in English—a jumble of chemical names and numbers, weights, and measures. This wasn't the first time the new smartphone had wowed me. (When mine was brand new, I asked Siri the meaning of life. *I don't know*, she said, *but I think we have an app for that.*) It was, however, the first time I saw how wide the gadget's reach had already become, saving the day, I imagined, for doctors in Zambia, arborists in the Amazon.

On another phone now, Gigi punched in a number. "I don't always have all the answers," she told me cheerfully, waiting for the connection, "but I know who to ask."

In this case: her mentor from Scotland. The question: Use fresh blood from a horse that had recently been ill? Or two-day-old refrigerated blood from a healthy horse? Donkey blood, Gigi later explained, posed the risk of another rejection.

I was pleased to learn a transfusion was in order. From living for years with a partner who had cancer, I was familiar with how quickly a transfusion could make her rally. My Fondouk story (now photos *and* text) was already writing itself as I envisioned its ending in a sped-up film version: Inert donkey twitches, then stretches his limbs; his eyes clear, his head lifts; he belts out a healthy bray—at which point, all of us encircling him burst into cheers, praise Allah, and embrace.

Gigi relayed the Scottish vet's recommendation: Use the refrigerated blood, but not just yet. Force in more fluids first, so the donkey can pee out the toxins that have built up.

"Any idea of his chances?" I asked.

"Slim," she said, sounding, for the first time, brusque.

After that it was a waiting game. One of the technicians cleaned up the donkey's mess, then disappeared along with the others. "Might as well put you to work," Gigi said, pointing to a second mat hanging sideways from some contraption. I rushed to it. My eagerness garbled my fingers but finally I managed to detach the thing, and, together, Gigi and I slipped it under the foal to cushion his spindly limbs.

As Gigi scribbled some numbers on the whiteboard, I took a few pictures (permission granted earlier) and then got out my notebook. Minutes passed. Then Gigi called: "Could you come here again." Something about the IV was bothering her. "Hold it here, just like this." She traced the length of the tube until she found the offending bend. Now this *is* important, I thought, already imagining how much my parents would enjoy the story. At eighty-eight and ninety they were beginning to accept that their days of exotic travel were over— no more performing emergency surgeries on dogs in Bangladesh, no more mushing escapades with Huskies in Lapland. Now I could reassure them that they'd taught their daughter well: she was brave and resourceful and could sniff out the genuine article, the unscripted, unmediated, once-in-a-lifetime experience, and even be of some use. I liked this thought, but as I clutched the tube, I didn't like what I saw: only the faintest sign of breath, just a dribble or two of pee.

This wasn't the first time I'd sat vigil like this. First with my partner, then, in quick succession, two close friends—but in all these cases, by then I'd accepted there was no hope of recovery.

Gigi replaced the tube with a new one. I went back to my notebook. As he had throughout, the farmer sat in a fold-up chair next to the sink. I glanced over at him now and then, drawn to his stillness, his dignified bearing. Given what Kareem had said about Muslims not befriending animals, I assumed the farmer's grave look was less about a sentimental attachment to this nameless, three-day-old foal than about feeding his family. A donkey could live for thirty years. In sprawling, carless Fez, donkeys carried crates of tomatoes, sacks of couscous, computers, refrigerators, whole extended families. Losing a foal was like losing a future pickup truck, plow, mower, dolly, wheelchair all in one. And of course there was no such thing as donkey insurance. I told myself all this, but when my eyes met the farmer's, I thought I saw something more than bleak calculations. Though I figured I was as mysterious to him as he was to me, and probably more suspect, I still wanted to offer some fellow feeling. When our eyes met, I hoped mine conveyed something like this: *I know my stake in this life is much less than yours but still, I am here with you now, rooting for you.*

And because the farmer didn't look away, I felt he accepted my humble offering.

After that, things were calm for a long time, so long that I started wondering just how long this could go on. I scanned the scene—the sleepy courtyard, the shadowy stalls, the gigantic metal scale labeled "Horseweigh." Would I stay all afternoon? All evening? I certainly didn't want to leave before witnessing the transfusion's magical effect. (Old dreams die hard, I guess.) My eyes returned to the donkey. By now I'd gotten used to seeing hardly, if any, signs of life, but this time, at almost the same moment, Gigi, too, sensed an absence. She rushed over, knelt down. She placed her ear against his ribs, *one second . . . two . . .* then reassembled herself and did something I couldn't have predicted. She laid her left hand on the donkey's chest, just behind his front limbs; she cupped her right hand around his snout, pressing her fingers firmly against his left nostril; and over his right nostril, she placed her mouth. She inhaled deeply and blew with great effort, and then pumped his chest.

Breathe in . . . Breathe out . . . Pump . . .

In . . . out . . . Pump . . .

Of course I'd seen depictions of mouth-to-mouth resuscitation—drawings and photos on pamphlets; handsome men on the TV screen working their magic on bikinied blonds they'd plucked from the sea. I'd even performed it myself about fifty years back while training for my Senior Lifesaving badge. But I'd never heard of the procedure being used with animals, never even thought to wonder about it; and seeing it now, a few feet in front of me, in a life-and-death situation—well—such leveling between human and animal, such a stark expression of our kinship—the shock and beauty of it took my own breath away.

Gigi's lungs didn't fail her. She kept blowing and pumping for what seemed like a long time—long enough for me to start wondering how dead was too dead? Was it really still possible to bring this donkey back? Long enough for me to look over to the farmer and catch his eye again, both of us shaking our heads now—it was over, done.

Finally, Gigi, too, gave up. Stood up. No one said a word. The assistant vet escorted the farmer out. Before I knew it, the donkey was gone, too—carried away by the technicians. There seemed to be nothing for me to do but leave. Wanting to give my condolences, I walked over to the sink where Gigi was washing.

"They almost never make it," she said, "but I'm surprised he went so soon." Her voice faltered, "I can't help wondering if I shouldn't have just given him the transfusion right away." Her eyes tearing, she turned away, grabbed a paper towel. "I'm going to get some lunch," she said, her voice regaining its chipper tone, but her steps were heavy as she climbed the stairs.

The assistant vet reappeared. "The farmer was very sad," she told me. "He cried." This seemed both surprising and not at all so. We nodded in unison.

I said my thank-yous and good-byes. Azami offered to call me a cab, but I felt like walking. The route was straightforward, but what the *petit taxi* had done in seconds felt long and arduous to me. Stiff weeds clogged the road's rutty shoulder. The sun was hot. The donkey was dead. I had my story but it had the wrong ending.

A taxi, and then another, pulled up alongside me, but I politely waved them away. I kept wondering about the farmer. We'd been through something together, and now, having barely been outside the city wall, I couldn't even conjure an image of where he went, or what he would do when he got there. First his abrupt disappearance, now this blankness, I didn't like either. I felt bereft. So I turned my thoughts to what *I* would do next.

The answer was easy.

I would do what the living do. I was hungry. I would eat.

Two days later, my official tour began. We were nine, plus our guide, Mark, an American who decades before had come to Morocco as a Peace Corps volunteer and decided to stay. I liked everyone immediately, so of course I was eager to tell them my story, yet every time I sensed an opportunity, I let it pass. There wasn't enough time or the mood wasn't right, or—? I puzzled over my hesitation. Was it my story to tell? Would I somehow be betraying the farmer, the donkey, Gigi?

The days passed—about ten of them. We meandered through miles of souks in Marrakech. We explored Aït Benhaddou, the magnificent earthen city where parts of *Lawrence of Arabia* were filmed. There we watched a small crew videoing for a TV series on the Bible—the costumed actors looking exactly like "my" farmer. Most thrilling, we galumphed up and down sand dunes, me atop a camel named Jimi Hendrix, according to my teenaged Tuareg guide. I must admit I was flattered he deemed me the Hendrix type. Yes, for this major excursion, we had guides, and cooks, and porters, and I was thankful.

During our next-to-last breakfast as a group, reluctant to leave our sunny rooftop, we started sharing our most memorable moments from the trip. I considered our desert excursion, that middle-of-the-night pee, just me and the wind-whipped sand and indifferent stars, but I chose to risk the donkey story and was glad. No one seemed impatient during the lead-up, and when I got to the mouth-to-mouth part, their jaws dropped, they were rapt, and then moved. I broke the silence afterward by asking if anyone had heard of using that kind of CPR on animals. None of them had.

"Are you sure," Mark said, "that it wasn't just for show?"

I was slow to comprehend. I suppose I was angry. "I mean . . . ," Mark said, noticing, perhaps, how I was staring oddly at my hand. (Was *it* just for show? Was the coffee cup I was holding *just for show*?) "I mean maybe she was just trying to reassure the farmer that they'd done everything that could be done?"

I pictured Gigi's lips cupped over the donkey's closer nostril, her fingers pinching the other, her palm's hardy thumping; I heard the *whish* of her all-out breathing. No way was it "just for show"! But as I strenuously shook my head, I remembered a moment of doubt about the tightness of the seal—the donkey's nostrils being so big, the doctor's mouth and fingers so small. Even so . . . No!

"I suppose it's possible?" I added with a shrug. *Anything is possible!* That's long been my motto, and of course, I knew from personal experience how comforting it is to believe that everything that could be done was done. If that had been Gigi's motive, I wouldn't have faulted her. I gestured to the person on my left—her turn to talk.

I'm not sure why I didn't simply dismiss Mark's idea. Because he'd been in Morocco so long? Because he was a man and a big one at that. Because I've always been an assiduous truth-seeker?

When I got back to the states, I couldn't resist a quick internet search: *donkey mouth-to-mouth.*

Among the top headlines:

In Numbers, "the Lord opened the donkey's mouth."

"Doctors Sadly Do Not Recommend Doing CPR to 'Staying Alive.'"

So much for that. I studied my photos again, the careful placement of Gigi's lips and hand, her tender, earnest gaze. That should have settled it, but I dug out the email address Gigi had given me and composed a delicately worded message thanking her for her good work and the honor of witnessing it. I mentioned that I'd just sent off my donation, (true!) and I asked her, for the sake of the piece I was writing, to confirm my understanding of her diagnosis and treatment. Near the end of a rather lengthy paragraph, as casually as I could, I relayed Mark's question, and asked if there was any truth to it.

When, after a week or two, I still hadn't received an answer, I checked the address again. It looked right. I reminded myself that I sometimes lose track of the messages *I* intend to answer later. I considered writing again but instead began another internet search, this time Googling "equine CPR" with much better results. Several reputable sources affirmed that CPR "mouth-to-snout," it was called, can be, and *is*, performed on equines (and dogs, too). One post included a video, and, although that one showed the use a plastic tube attached to an accordion-like pumping gizmo, another text-only entry described breathing into the "up" nostril and closing off the "down" one. This—along with my *near* certainty that, had Gigi been faking it, I would have seen it in her face—this settled the question for me. Still, as the months passed, I kept wondering: What if it had been just for show? Would that have changed everything? Anything?

I dropped my college philosophy course after the first class. (What do we *mean* by knowledge? What do we *mean* by "mean"?) As it turned out, I became an English major, and now I find I keep thinking about "A Worn Path." Written by Eudora Welty, the story describes an arduous journey that Phoenix Jackson, a very old woman, makes each month by foot in order to bring back medicine for her sick grandson. Struggling through thickets, over logs and barbed wire, she reaches the clinic, the nurse dispenses the medicine, the old woman starts the journey home, and that's it—the end. The story is often included in textbooks, and often, along with it, appears an essay Welty has written in response to the many letters she has received, letters asking if the grandson is, *actually*, dead. Welty's response?

No—maybe—it doesn't matter. "[T]he only certain thing at all," she says, "is the worn path. The habit of love . . . remembers its way. . . . The path is the thing that matters."

So, what matters here in my Fondouk story—experienced, told around the breakfast table, written here? What matters to me, I guess that means.

You could say that I (petite, fearful by nature, raised before feminism's second wave) have worked all my life to be brave enough to find my way alone to a genuinely foreign land. So I'm proud of that and glad I made it to the Fondouk. Even when not much was happening, I found things of interest and engaged in spirited conversations with strangers. Then, when the day turned really interesting, for an hour or more, I was no longer an infidel standing outside peering in, no longer a bareheaded woman seen mostly as a source of *dirham* or even as a writer greedy for material. That the donkey died, that matters, too. Nonetheless, for a time I had a place within a small circle of rich and poor, dark and light. And when Gigi funneled her breath again and again into the donkey, we, all in the habit of love, breathed along with her.

———————◆———————

Selected Bibliography

Adams, Robert. *Beauty in Photography*. New York: Aperture, 1996.

Alexenberg, Mel. *The Future of Art in a Digital Age: From Hellenistic to Hebraic Consciousness*. Bristol: Intellect, 2006.

Booth, Wayne. *For the Love of It: Amateuring and Its Rivals*. Chicago: University of Chicago Press, 1999.

Cooper, Bernard. "Just What Is It That Makes Today's Homes So Different, So Appealing?" In *Open House: Writers Redefine Home*, ed. Mark Doty, 55–72. Saint Paul: Graywolf Press, 2003.

Dell, Cecily. *A Primer for Movement Description Using Effort-Shape and Supplementary Concepts*. New York: Dance Notation Bureau, 1970.

Franck, Frederick. *The Zen of Seeing: Seeing/Drawing as Meditation*. New York: Vintage Books, 1973.

Hyde, Lewis. *The Gift: Imagination and the Erotic Life Property*. New York: Vintage Books, 1983.

Maue, Kenneth. *Water in the Lake: Real Events for the Imagination*. New York: Harper and Row, 1979.

Moore, Thomas. *Care of the Soul: A Guide for Cultivating Depth and Sacredness in Everyday Life*. New York: Harper Perennial, 1994.

Nachmanovitch, Stephen. *Free Play: Improvisation in Life and Art*. New York: Penguin Putnam, 1990.

Rich, Adrienne. "Split at the Root: An Essay on Jewish Identity." In *Visions of America: Personal Narratives from the Promised Land*, ed. Wesley Brown and Amy Ling, 90–105. New York: Persea Books, 1993.

Scarry, Elaine. *On Beauty and Being Just*. Princeton: Princeton University Press, 1999.

Tanizaki, Jun'ichirō. *In Praise of Shadows*. Stony Creek: Leete's Island Books, 1977.

Tharp, Twyla. *The Creative Habit: Learn It and Use It for Life*. New York: Simon and Schuster, 2003.

Wessels, Tom. *Reading the Forested Landscape: A Natural History of New England*. Woodstock: The Countryman Press, 1997.

Questions for Readers

The following questions can be used in the classroom, by book groups and spiritual groups, and by solo readers seeking to deepen their engagement with the material. Many of the questions can serve as writing prompts for students in creative or expository writing workshops or gender or multicultural studies classes. Similarly, other groups might want to allow a few minutes for members to write their responses to select questions before opening them up to discussion. This will enrich the conversation and enhance the likelihood that all will participate. Some questions will intrigue you more than others. Feel free to pick and choose.

"The Death of Fred Astaire"

To what extent does your life—its shape? its texture?—feel as if it's following an inherited script? To what extent does it feel chosen? Improvised?

To what extent have your romantic decisions been linked to your parenting decisions?

What are your early experiences of feeling different or encountering differences in others? How have these experiences affected your choices and values?

Does this essay give you any insight into how people make difficult decisions—the relative importance of research, logic, and emotion. What is your own style of decision-making and are you satisfied with it?

How do you interpret the tone of the essay's ending? Is Lawrence at peace with her decision? Do you as a reader have enough evidence to know whether you support her decision?

"Becoming Jennie"

To what extent were your parents and grandparents restricted by the gender roles of their times? How did they react to those restrictions and were they able to nevertheless lead lives that seemed rich and meaningful?

What does Lawrence intend with her final phrase—"unbecoming heart"?

We live in an age—in the United States, at least—when many children are encouraged to express their deepest feelings. Do you approve of this trend or do you think it has gone too far?

If you were granted permission to "pour out your heart" to a particular person or perhaps to some hidden part of yourself, what would you say? (I'd suggest you write this one out—with no obligation to share it with anyone.)

"King for A Day"

The Drag King workshop held in the early 90's taught its participants how to behave like stereotypical males of that time. To what extent do those stereotypes seem accurate today?

Why is Lawrence sickened to realize that she never left a rest room without checking her smile?

Which aspects of your own gendered behavior are innate? Which are socially constructed? And what evidence do you have for your answers?

"Fits and Starts: Notes on (Yet) Another Writer's Beginning"

To what extent did you identify with Lawrence's early alliance with her father? How has your life been shaped by role models or lack therof?

Consider a painting, a book, a piece of music, or some other work of art that made a strong impression on you as a youth, and discuss why it spoke to you.

This essay is more associative than chronological. Why do you think the author chose this approach here? In the end, did you feel the parts formed a satisfying whole? How would you summarize what Lawrence wants to convey here?

While watching her young son, Lawrence is reminded that much of "adult behavior is an elaborately disguised, cleaned-up version of fears, rages, and longings" we had as children (46). Discuss whether you agree.

Lawrence questions her pleasure in her son's stoicism while getting stitches. Discuss your own comfort or discomfort when you see people of all ages step out of the prescribed behavior for their gender.

"Karl Will Bring a Picnic"

Make a list of associations you have with a beloved (or despised) relative. Do they cluster around certain themes as Uncle Karl does for Lawrence?

On p. 60 Lawrence says that "like many of the once bedazzled, I became devoted to searching for the hidden smudges and nicks in the shiny gifts bestowed upon me. I began to consider their costs." Do you identify? Is this process pathological? Healthy? Inevitable?

Examine the messages inherent in the folklore of your family. What stories are left out?

Have you ever found yourself considering the darker side of your devotion to people or causes?

Lawrence conveys Karl's character through both his typical traits as well as his inconsistencies. Create a true or fictional character sketch by highlighting someone's inconsistencies.

"Fun is what you make yourself; otherwise it's entertainment" (65). Are you content with the balance of fun and entertainment in your life?

"Dogs and Children"

Why do you think Lawrence was disdainful of Corky's desire to please?

If you're a parent, to what extent does your parenting match the fantasies you had?

How much of your life feels "propelled by love?""

"Andee's Fiftieth and The Way We Live Now"

Is the "typical American family" alive and well in your circles?

Do you buy that Lawrence's generation is any more "caught in the middle" than other generations? To what extent does everyone struggle with "what gets passed on" and "what's left behind" (66)?

Does Lawrence's assessment of her cohort at the brunch seem fair-minded, or are you more inclined to see the people assembled as she imagines her father would— as "sad sacks and weirdos"?

"Yard Sale"

In light of the current trend toward decluttering, Lawrence's celebration of "other people's junk" is surely controversial. Look around your house. Which things are gifts? Do they create a feeling bond? Which help with your "soul work" by connecting you to "ancestors and to living brothers and sisters in all the many communities that claim our hearts" (97)?

In this essay we find a big dose of Lawrence's characteristic mix of humor and seriousness. Do you think it works? Why or why not?

"Always Someone!"

Endings are always a crucial spot for understanding an author's intentions. What ideas or feelings does Lawrence convey by her ending to "Always Someone"?

"Swinging"

Reflect on your most and least courageous behavior. Can courage be cultivated? Is it transferrable as Lawrence hopes?

What activities do you engage in that create a sense of pleasurable single-mindedness? That make time stop still?

"The Third Hottest Pepper in Honduras"

Take an honest look at your circle of friends. Are you satisfied with the extent to which you've moved out of your comfort zone?

What insights does this essay provide into how to improve public education?

Why did Lawrence title this essay as she did? What idea does the title emphasize?

What is the tone of this essay's ending? What is Lawrence's attitude toward her current position?

"On the Mowing"

One critic called this essay the collection's spiritual center. Why might this be so?

Lawrence says we return to familiar places to "measure our fickle selves against their steadfastness" (142). What else might we gain (or lose) by returning to familiar places?

The relatively new genre of "creative nonfiction" uses the tools of the poet or fiction writer to convey facts and tell true stories. In this essay, more than most here, Lawrence includes factual information. Does her melding of autobiographical material with geographic and historical material form a satisfying whole? Do you have a preference for one or the other?

Is "grief anger's more difficult sister" for you? Or is it the other way around?

"Enough Tupperware"

To what extent do you agree with Lawrence's claim that "few of us are immune to the premium our culture puts on self-sufficiency, and yet, when we open ourselves up to being helped, the rewards are many" (159). Do you find it easier to give or receive? To what extent does accepting help oblige you to reciprocate?

How do you interpret the essay's last line, "Or so I'd like to believe." What experiences in your life have really changed you?

"Provincetown Breakfast"

What exactly is Lawrence satirizing in this essay? What exactly is she celebrating?

"My June Wedding"

While Lawrence considers herself privileged in numerous ways, when she experiences "not merely approval, but celebration" of her love and commitment, she is deeply moved. She thought of it as so delicious and so unlikely that she hadn't "even allowed [herself] to want" it (169). Lawrence wrote this piece in 2004.

Tolerance toward the LGBT community has increased dramatically. Has acceptance and celebration increased as much? Do people have an obligation to celebrate diverse cultures? How do you decide how far you want to extend your celebratory rituals?

"What Can You Do?"

As mentioned above, Lawrence experiences very little if any overt hostility or discrimination because of her unusual family; however, in this essay she alludes to a painful invisibility (181). Do you understand why such invisibility would be painful? What other populations might suffer from the same pain?

What insights into the grieving process does this essay provide?

Which version of that firefly dance do you buy? Is Sandy talking to Leslie—or are the fireflies merely talking to each other?

"Wonderlust"

This is the book's most demanding essay. Each section's connection to the previous one is not always initially apparent. It's an essay that benefits from repeated readings as you discover the threads connecting the parts and the logic of Lawrence's structure. Are you able to articulate the questions Lawrence is most interested in addressing here? If you looked back on the pivotal moments in your own education and development, what moments come to mind?

How have your own tastes in art and music changed over time?

How has your conception of the divine changed?

How important is it for you to feel creative?

This lengthy essay raises endless questions. Articulate one that grabs you by the neck.

"At the Donkey Hotel"

In what ways is this essay a fitting ending for the collection? Which of the book's main themes does it echo? How might it be said to bring the book full circle?